NORTHWEST
Readers

Other Titles in the Northwest Readers Series

Series Editor: Robert J. Frank

Badger & Coyote Were Neighbors: Melville Jacobs on Northwest Indian Myths and Tales, edited by William R. Seaburg and Pamela T. Amoss

The Collected Poems of Hazel Hall, edited by John Witte

Fishing the Northwest: An Angler's Reader, edited by Glen Love

A Richer Harvest: The Literature of Work in the Pacific Northwest, edited by Craig Wollner and W. Tracy Dillon

Wood Works: The Life and Writings of Charles Erskine Scott Wood, edited by Edwin Bingham and Tim Barnes

Nature's Justice

Writings of William O. Douglas

edited by James O'Fallon

Oregon State University Press
Corvallis

Publication of this book was made possible in part
by a contribution from

The Delmer Goode Fund

The Oregon State University Press is grateful for this support

The paper in this book meets the guidelines for permanence and durability of
the Committee on Production Guidelines for Book Longevity of the Council
on Library Resources and the minimum requirements of the American National
Standard for Permanence of Paper for Printed Library Materials Z39.48-1984.

Library of Congress Cataloging-in-Publication Data
Douglas, William O. (William Orville), 1898-
  Nature's justice : writings of William O. Douglas / edited by James
O'Fallon.— 1st ed.
    p. cm. — (Northwest readers)
Includes bibliographical references and index.
  ISBN 0-87071-482-1
  1. Douglas, William O. (William Orville), 1898- 2. United States
Supreme Court—Biography.   3. Judges—United States—Biography.
4. Natural areas—Northwestern States—History. I. O'Fallon, James.
II.Title. III. Series.
  KF8745.D6 A43 2000
  347.73'2634—dc21
                                        00-009322

**OREGON STATE
UNIVERSITY**

Oregon State University Press
101 Waldo Hall
Corvallis OR 97331-6407
541-737-3166 • fax 541-737-3170
http://osu.orst.edu/dept/press

Dedication

Dedicated to the memory of

Colin Ruagh Thomas O'Fallon

Contents

Acknowledgements

The writings of Justice Douglas are published with the permission of the William O. Douglas Estate. I thank Cathleen Douglas Stone, executor of the estate, for her kind cooperation in this venture.

As always, I am greatly appreciative of the support for my work provided by the Frank Nash Professorship. The association with Frank Nash, one of Oregon's most distinguished lawyers, is a signal honor.

Dennis Hyatt, Law Librarian at the University of Oregon School of Law, prepared a bibliography of Justice Douglas's writings which guided my reading in making the selections for this volume, and which provided the basis for the selected bibliography. It is but one of many examples of the support that Dennis and his staff provide for the scholarly efforts of their faculty colleagues.

I want to thank Robert J. Frank, editor of the Northwest Readers Series and a long-time colleague in a very different context, for approaching me with the idea of preparing this volume. He has been a most patient and encouraging editor. Jo Alexander, Managing Editor of the Oregon State University Press, has been a pleasure to work with in bringing the volume to press. Warren Slesinger and Tom Booth have also made significant contributions for which I am appreciative.

I owe the most to my family: Ellen, Dylan and Cheyney, Ken and Dorothy, Kerry and Mary Jo, Quyen and Sahalie. They are the northwest readers most likely to read the pages of this book that were not written by Justice Douglas.

Introduction

Cause and effect in the formation of human personality is an elusive matter. Nonetheless, one can say with confidence that the marks of his youth in the Northwest stayed with Justice William O. Douglas for life. His love of the mountains and the outdoors were only the most obvious of those marks. His fierce independence, his concern for outsiders, his suspicion of concentrated power, all have roots in childhood experience.

Douglas was born in the tiny town of Maine, Minnesota, on October 16, 1898, to Julia Fisk Douglas and the Reverend William Douglas, a Presbyterian minister. The family moved from Minnesota to Estrella in southern California when Douglas was three, hoping to find relief from physical problems that afflicted Reverend Douglas, and then moved again, to Cleveland, Washington, less than two years later. The moves did not resolve the health problems, and Reverend Douglas died after an ulcer operation in 1904.

After her husband's death, Julia Douglas moved her family— William, his older sister Martha, and his younger brother Arthur—a few miles north to Yakima, where her sister lived. Yakima would be Douglas's home until he went away, though not too far, to Whitman College in Walla Walla when he was eighteen.

Julia Douglas used some of the proceeds of her husband's life insurance policy to build a modest house for her family across the alley from the Columbia Grade School. She invested the rest in an irrigation project, promoted by a local lawyer, which failed, leaving the family in a state of poverty that would have important consequences for Douglas's childhood. Most significantly, it dictated that the children would work, at whatever jobs or tasks they could find, to help support the family. From the age of seven, when he would prowl the byways of Yakima looking for scrap iron or burlap sacks that he could sell for a few pennies, Douglas was gainfully engaged. He washed windows and swept out stores, picked fruit and harvested wheat. He worked his way through college at Whitman, and through Columbia Law School.

The experience of growing up poor left Douglas with an acute sense of class distinctions in American society, though he denied their significance on himself. In a telling passage in his autobiography, he said, "We never felt sorry for ourselves; we never felt underprivileged. Class distinctions were nonexistent in our eyes: we went to the same schools as the elite; we competed for grades with them and usually won."[1] Yet in the next paragraph he wrote "Because of our poverty, we did occasionally feel that we were born 'on the wrong side of the railroad tracks.' "[2]

Douglas wrote with feeling of the circumstances of junk collectors in Washington, D. C., migrant workers and "Wobblies," hoboes and prostitutes. He rode the rails to get from job to job around Eastern Washington, and even to get to New York for law school. He recalled having been hired by one of the pillars of Yakima society to act as a "stool pigeon" in the red light district, attempting to buy liquor and inviting solicitation, in order to facilitate prosecutions. The experience left him with an abiding sense of the hypocrisy of the elite, who would hire him to do a job that they would not set their own children to do. Douglas would spend most of his adult life among the elite, but in important ways he would always remain an outsider.

As an infant, Douglas contracted polio. The attending physician told Julia that William might not walk again, and would probably be dead by forty. The only therapy he could recommend was regular massage of the boy's legs with salt water. For weeks, Douglas's mother followed a regimen of soaking and rubbing his legs every two hours. Eventually, he did regain the use of his legs, and learned again to walk, but his legs were spindly, and became the object of jibes from his schoolmates when he was older. Douglas was never a gregarious person, and he attributed his preference for being alone to a sense of physical inferiority that had separated him from others of his age as a young teen.[3]

Attempting to overcome the lingering physical effects of the polio, Douglas eventually turned to walking the foothills around Yakima to build strength and stamina in his legs. It worked, and started him on a lifetime of hiking that included treks through the Himalayas and a famous walk down the C&O Canal in 1954, to protest plans to turn the canal path into a parkway.

What began as a discipline for building strength soon was transformed into an abiding love for the outdoors. A powerful sense of that attachment is conveyed by a passage from his autobiography.

> *Another trip into those hills marked a turning point in my life. It was April and the valley below was in bloom, lush and content with fruit blossoms. Then came a sudden storm, splattering rain in the lower valley and shooting tongues of lightening along the ridges across from me. As the weather cleared, Adams and Rainier stood forth in power and beauty, monarchs to every peak in their range.*
>
> *Away from the town, in the opposite direction from its comforts, the backbone of the Cascades was clear against the western sky, the slopes and ravines dark blue in the afternoon sun. The distant ridges and canyons seemed soft and friendly. They appeared to hold untold mysteries and to contain solitude many times more profound than that of the barren ridge on which I stood. They offered streams and valleys and peaks to explore, snow fields and glaciers to conquer, wild animals to know. That afternoon I felt that the high mountains in the distance were extending to me an invitation to get acquainted with them, to tramp their trails and sleep in their high basins.*
>
> *My heart filled with joy, for I knew I could accept the invitation. I would have legs and lungs equal to it.*[4]

Julia Douglas adhered to the familiar notion that education was the way to success. She inculcated that view in her children, who had both the natural talent and the persistence to make it come true. Martha became a successful businesswoman. Arthur followed Bill to Columbia Law School, and went on to a Wall Street law firm, to the General Counsel's office for the Statler Corporation, and eventually to the presidency of the Statler Hotel Chain. But even in the context of this accomplished set of siblings, Bill Douglas stood out. His biographer recounts an incident when a teacher remarked to Julia "Both Martha and Orville are good students, but Orville has the

The young man who was to become Justice Douglas. Photographer unknown. Collection of the Supreme Court of the United States.

more unusual mind."[5] Douglas would gather his share of detractors, perhaps more than his share, but none seemed to doubt the special quality of his mind. Indeed, his brilliance may have been the source of some of his problems, as well as the font of his success. The pace of his life suggests someone who was easily bored, and he had little patience for those who had to struggle to understand what came to him almost intuitively.

Douglas thrived in the competitive forum of high school debate when physical limits precluded athletic achievement—though he did play on the basketball team. He completed his preparatory work as class valedictorian, which earned him a full tuition scholarship to Whitman College in Walla Walla. He paid his way (including twenty dollars a month sent home) by working two or three jobs at a time, while sustaining a record of academic excellence.

He joined the army early in World War I, when he was still a student, but after basic training was sent back to the ROTC unit at Whitman, where he remained for the duration. He joined Beta Theta Pi and clearly enjoyed the camaraderie of that association, though in later life he would conclude that the clannishness of college fraternities was a handicap.[6] It was not a handicap when it saved him from a night on the street after he arrived in New York dirty and broke to begin law school. Douglas was about to be turned away from the Beta club in New York by a skeptical clerk; an old Whitman friend fortuitously intervened and vouched for him, and provided a loan to get him through his first days in the big city.[7]

Douglas spent the first two years after graduation from Whitman as a high school teacher and debate coach at Yakima High School. He hoped to go to graduate school, either in English literature or in law, but did not have the financial means. He finally decided on law school, and was led to Columbia by James Donald, a Yakima attorney and Columbia graduate, who informed him that it would be possible to find work to support him through his course of studies.

The journey to New York was an adventure in itself. He signed on to escort a shipment of two thousand sheep by rail from Yakima to Minneapolis. He rode the caboose for nearly two weeks, enduring a rail strike, rain and dust storms, hunger, and lack of sleep. After delivering his wooly charges to a broker in Minneapolis, he hopped a freight for New York, but was tossed from the train in Chicago. Different versions of the story disagree on whether he completed his trip to New York on another freight, or in a coach paid for by money wired from his brother.[8] In any event, Douglas arrived in New York dirty and broke, but undaunted.

Douglas spent his first day at the Columbia Law School in a desperate effort to come up with the money to pay his tuition. Dean Harlan Fiske Stone, who would later be Douglas's colleague on the Supreme Court, suggested that he should find a job and reapply to the school when he had saved the tuition. In a last-ditch attempt to solve the problem, Douglas responded to an ad for a third-year student to assist in drafting a correspondence course in commercial law. He talked his way into the job—he did not mention to the employer that he was a beginning student—and received an advance that allowed him to enter the law school.

He continued to work during his three years at Columbia, primarily as a tutor for students trying to gain admission to Ivy League colleges. Douglas cited the two criteria for his services—that the student be rich and stupid. He was well compensated for his work. By the summer of his second year, he had saved enough to return to the West, where he married Mildred Riddle at her parents' home in La Grande, Oregon. They had met while both were teaching at Yakima High School. They spent their honeymoon camping, fishing, and riding in the Wallowa mountains of eastern Oregon. Douglas was broke by the time they got back to New York for his last year at Columbia, but he continued tutoring and Mildred got a teaching job.

High academic achievement was the norm for Douglas, and he continued in that pattern at Columbia, and he was selected to the law review staff at the end of his first year, indicating that he stood near the top of his class. During his last two years, he worked as a student assistant for Professor Underhill Moore. He helped Moore revise his casebook on commercial law, and in his final year worked with Moore on a study of the marketing practices of the portland cement industry, in anticipation of a possible antitrust investigation.

Douglas described Moore as having a mind with "a cutting edge, sharper than any other."[9] Underhill Moore was one of the most important figures of a movement in legal thought that came to be identified as "American Legal Realism." The Realists criticized traditional legal thought as overly formal, and out of touch with the real world. They were inclined toward empirical study rather than looking to legal precedents, and many of them promoted work in other disciplines, such as psychology, sociology, and economics, as essential to an adequate understanding of how law functions in society. Moore was probably the most committed and successful of the empiricists among the Realists, conducting studies that examined the influence of local banking practices on legal outcomes, and sitting for hours on a sidewalk in New Haven, observing the parking behavior of the residents. It is not difficult to find the influence of this commitment to fact in Douglas's later work as a judge.

Among Douglas's instructors at Columbia were other men of noted achievement, including, of course, Harlan Fiske Stone, later Douglas's Chief Justice on the Supreme Court. Herman Oliphant was another of the major figures in the Legal Realist movement. Thomas Reed Powell was for years the most prominent academic critic of the Supreme Court; he gave Douglas a C in constitutional law. Richard Powell became the country's leading scholar on the law of property. Harold Medina, who taught Douglas the intricacies of New York practice, would later sit as the trial judge in *Dennis v. United States*. In this case, eleven leaders of the Communist Party of America were convicted of violations of the Smith Act, which made it a crime to advocate the violent overthrow of the government, even if no further steps were taken. Douglas would write one of his more famous dissents, insisting that the defendants be judged on the basis of what they had done—the facts—rather than on speculation about what they might do.[10]

Douglas graduated second in his class. That minor slip cost him a cherished opportunity. Harlan Stone had left the deanship in 1923. After a brief period in private practice, Stone was appointed Attorney General of the United States, and shortly thereafter was appointed to the Supreme Court. Douglas was passed over for an appointment as Stone's law clerk in favor of Albert McCormack, who had finished first in the class.

Douglas had a position with Grant Bond in Walla Walla to go to, but he could not go without first testing himself against the demands of a big city law practice. He secured a position with the prominent Wall Street firm of Cravath, deGersdorff, Swaine, and Wood. At the same time, the Columbia faculty offered him the opportunity to teach three courses as an adjunct member of the faculty. The work schedule at his firm was notoriously demanding. Sixteen hour days were not uncommon. Douglas added to that the demands of preparing for and teaching a class each morning at 8:00.

Douglas's work at the firm was the legal equivalent of latrine duty in the army. He and one other junior associate, John McCloy, were assigned to work with Donald C. Swatland, a demanding senior associate who was coordinating work on the reorganization of the Chicago, Milwaukee & St. Paul Railroad. The reorganization became a major target of critics bemoaning the role of law firms and corporate banks in taking advantage of the problems of struggling railroads. The Cravath firm made $450,000 on the St. Paul case. A sense of the significance of that figure can be gained by comparing it to Douglas's annual salary of $1,800.

Less than a year after starting with Cravath, Douglas was having health problems and was not enjoying himself; he decided to return to the West and his beloved mountains. He took up practice in Yakima, in the office of James Cull—the lawyer who had talked Douglas's mother into the ill-fated investment that had cost her the family nest egg. But the reality of small town practice, both financially and intellectually, soon set in. After only a few months, he was back at Cravath and teaching his Columbia courses. In the spring of 1927 he was offered a full-time teaching position at Columbia, which he accepted.

The next decade of William O. Douglas's life can fairly be characterized as meteoric. He began his full-time teaching career on the eve of his twenty-ninth birthday. He would celebrate his forty-first birthday as an Associate Justice of the United States Supreme Court. In the interim, he would serve on the faculties of Columbia and Yale, turn down appointment at the University of Chicago, teach courses at the Harvard Business School, and serve as a member and then Chairman of the Securities and Exchange Commission. His scholarly production between 1929 and 1934 included five casebooks and more than a dozen articles. It was a record that reflected both his great intellectual talents and his capacity for prolonged hard work.

Douglas began his tenure at Columbia at a time of ferment in legal education and turmoil within the Columbia faculty. The Legal Realists were making waves, and those waves were breaking hard in upper Manhattan. Douglas joined forces with Underhill Moore and other colleagues to push for a complete and systematic restructuring of the curriculum. There was broad agreement across the faculty that reform was in order, but there was a basic schismy. One group wished to transform the basic mission of the law school, subordinating the training of prospective lawyers to a primarily research mission. The others, perhaps with a more realistic appreciation of how their salaries were paid, wanted to bring change within the traditional context of a school devoted to the education of future lawyers.

Douglas aligned himself with the first group, though perhaps not as forcefully as his retrospective account in his autobiography suggests.[11] The ensuing battle focussed on the question of who would be appointed Dean. Oliphant was the Realists' candidate, while Young B. Smith was the choice of the more traditional faculty. According to Douglas's autobiography, the appointment of Smith, whom he characterized as "the antithesis of what we wanted" and "utterly opposed to what we were trying to do," precipitated his resignation from the faculty.[12] Another account suggests that Douglas did not formally resign from Columbia, though he accepted a position at Yale. In the fall of 1928 Douglas moved to New Haven and began his tenure at Yale.

Here Douglas found compatible associates in Thurman Arnold, Wesley Sturges, and Dean Robert Hutchins. Arnold, too, had come from the West, having grown up in Wyoming, though as the son of a prosperous Laramie lawyer, he had not shared the financial hardship that was Douglas's lot. Douglas described Arnold as "an unorthodox, nonconformist, unpredictable man with an extremely sharp mind and an unusual wit. He was a brilliant lawyer and a wild and wonderful companion."[13] The stories of their companionship include an evening of driving on the sidewalks of New Haven, after Arnold's wife threw him out for showing up late and intoxicated for a dinner party she was hosting. Arnold recounted a story of a prank that Douglas played on him. Arnold received a note from a woman named Yvonne, claiming to have met him at a party, and lavishing flattery on him. When he called the number given on the note and asked for Yvonne, he was informed that he had called the morgue.

Douglas and Arnold worked together on a report for the National Commission on Law Observance and Enforcement, for which they collected and correllated massive amounts of information about the functioning of courts. On Arnold's account, "We ... proceeded to count everything that happened in courts in Connecticut ... we counted everything ... that we or anyone else could think of ... the result was the most fascinating body of legal statistics that has been collected in this century. They had only one flaw. Nobody then and nobody yet has ever been able to think of what to do with them."[14] Some years later, Douglas reminded Arnold that he still had ninety-nine of the one hundred copies of the report that he had ordered for himself. Arnold responded that he still had his full one hundred.[15]

Douglas's academic career was as far removed intellectually from his future fame as a civil libertarian as New Haven was from Yakima. He made his scholarly mark studying business organizations, corporate finance, and bankruptcy. True to the empiricist roots of legal realist thought, Douglas undertook extensive field studies of business failures, hoping to gain information upon which legislators could base more enlightened bankruptcy regulation.

Douglas and his former Columbia classmate, Carrol Shanks, produced casebooks on the law of corporate reorganization, business finance, and business management. They sought to bring the insights of other disciplines, including economics and sociology, to bear in the law school classroom—an innovation at a time when the standard casebook was little more than its name implied, a collection of highly edited appellate court case reports. His scholarship earned him the designation, by his former dean, Robert M. Hutchins, now at Chicago and hoping to presuade Douglas to join him there, as the nation's outstanding professor of law. To keep him, Yale jumped him ahead of his colleagues in salary, and awarded him its most prestigious chair, as Sterling Professor of Law.

It was, of course, a propitious time to be studying business failures. Following the stock market crash in 1929, the economic fortunes of the country sank into the Great Depression. With the election of Franklin Delano Roosevelt to the presidency in 1933, it soon became apparent that government would become much more aggressively involved in seeking solutions to economic problems. Bright young men began migrating from the faculties of elite universities to the administrative agencies of Washington, D.C. Congress passed an act in 1933 giving regulatory authority over the sale of securities to the Federal Trade Commission. The Securities Exchange Act of 1934 required the registration of all securities traded on an exchange, such as the New York Stock Exchange, and created the Securities Exchange Commission (SEC) to oversee the operation of the law.

Douglas had been actively pursuing an opportunity to join the parade to Washington for two years, when he was offered the opportunity to direct a study for the SEC. While it was not all that he wanted—he would continue to teach at Yale while directing the study, thus becoming a regular on the train between New Haven and Washington—it was a step in the right direction. Little more than a year after the SEC got underway, Joseph P. Kennedy stepped down from its chairmanship. During that year, Douglas had established a strong relationship with Kennedy, which would continue and would eventually encompass Kennedy's sons John and Robert. James Landis, a member of the Commission, was promoted to the chairmanship, and Douglas was appointed to fill Landis's position in January 1936.

Douglas quickly became an outspoken critic of the Wall Street establishment, and a defender of New Deal economic policies. When Landis resigned to accept the deanship of Harvard Law School in September 1937, Douglas was appointed to chair the SEC. He had by then become a nationally prominent figure, profiled in *Newsweek* as a brilliant scholar and a remarkable man. His appointment to the chairmanship was strongly opposed by the leaders of the securities

Douglas posing for photographers the day after President Roosevelt nominated him to the Supreme Court, on March 20, 1939. Photographer: Harris and Ewing. Collection of the Supreme Court of the United States.

industry, but that very opposition worked in his favor in the president's consideration. Douglas's tenure was dominated by a struggle with the leadership of the New York Stock Exchange. He insisted that the "insider's club" method of management which had controlled the exchange since its establishment should give way to a paid professional president, not a member of the exchange, and a board of directors including representatives of the public interest. The battle was intense, but Douglas finally won out in the aftermath of public exposure of the frauds and embezzlements of Richard Whitney, long the leading force in the management of the exchange.

In March 1939, Douglas was nominated to replace retiring Justice Louis Brandeis on the Supreme Court. Brandeis had been a highly visible advocate of the public interest, particularly with regard to business regulation, prior to his appointment to the Court, and Douglas had long been an admirer. Douglas's nomination was confirmed by the Senate with only token opposition; upon taking the oath of office he became the second youngest Justice in the history of the Court. He would retire in 1975, the longest serving Justice in history.

Douglas joined a Court that was in rapid transition. In 1935 and 1936, the Court had handed down a number of decisions invalidating President Roosevelt's economic initiatives, generally on the ground that the programs exceeded the constitutional powers of the federal government. The Court was bound to a view that limited federal power in the interest of preserving the independent authority of the states, notwithstanding the fact that the states were incapable of addressing the nationwide distress of a highly integrated economy.

After his landslide reelection in 1936, Roosevelt proposed a plan for reorganization of the Court that, not incidentally, would provide him with the opportunity to make a number of appointments; obviously, he would select justices whose views of federal authority would accommodate his New Deal programs. The plan, quickly dubbed the "court packing" plan, would have provided that if a justice reached the age of seventy and did not retire, the president could appoint an additional justice to the Court. At the time of the proposal, six justices were over seventy.

The plan met with immediate disapproval from a variety of quarters, including some staunch supporters of the New Deal, but Roosevelt persisted in pushing it. Whether in response to the political attack represented by the plan, or because of a rethinking of basic constitutional principles, the Supreme Court began to shift towards a view of constitutional power that permitted federal regulation of activities that had previously been held to be of exclusive state concern. Most significantly, the Court sustained the National Labor Relations Act and the Social Security Act, two cornerstones of the New Deal.

Though the court packing plan failed legislatively, a number of the most conservative justices retired. Roosevelt's first appointment was Hugo Black, Senator from Alabama and stalwart champion of the New Deal. Stanley Reed, who as Solicitor General had argued for the government in a number of the early New Deal cases, was appointed to replace George Sutherland, one of the most conservative members of the Court. Benjamin Cardozo, a relatively moderate justice, died in office and was replaced by Felix Frankfurter, who, as a Harvard professor and close associate of Justice Brandeis, had been deeply involved in the politics of the Roosevelt presidency from the outset. Shortly after Douglas's appointment, Pierce Butler, another conservative, retired, to be replaced by the very liberal Frank Murphy.

Thus by 1940 Roosevelt had appointed a majority of the sitting justices of the Supreme Court. He had, in his own words, lost the battle, but won the war.

Frankfurter had a hard time leaving his professorial ways behind him. In fact, he did not even try. He assumed that a lifetime of teaching and writing about the Constitution would give him a leadership position among the recent appointees; only Douglas was a scholar, and his work had had little to do with the Constitution. However, the combination of a rankling personal style—the accomplished men of the Court did not take kindly to being lectured—and differences of opinion soon led to a breakdown of relations between Frankfurter and his fellow Roosevelt appointees. Douglas's biographer traces the breakdown to two cases involving a requirement that schoolchildren begin the day with the pledge of allegiance to the flag.[16]

In the case of *Minersville School District v. Gobitis*[17] Frankfurter wrote for eight members of the Court, sustaining the pledge requirement against a challenge by Jehovah's Witnesses, who claimed that the compelled recitation violated their religious scruples and thus the First Amendment guarantee of free exercise of religion. While acknowledging the gravity of the issue, Frankfurter wrote that the state's legitimate interest in inculcating patriotism outweighed the infringement of the Witnesses' religious freedom. Only Douglas's old dean, Justice Harlan F. Stone, dissented from the ruling.

In the months following *Gobitis*, Witnesses were subjected to repeated violent attacks. Douglas, Black, Murphy, and Reed began to rethink the question. In *Jones v. Opelika*,[18] another case involving Witness claims of invaded religious freedom, Douglas, Murphy, and Black announced that they now believed *Gobitis* to have been wrongly decided. The flag salute issue returned to the Court in 1943, and a majority consisting of recently appointed Robert Jackson, with Douglas, Murphy, Black, and Stone held the pledge requirement unconstitutional.[19] Frankfurter wrote an extremely personal dissent, beginning with the sentence "One who belongs to the most vilified and persecuted minority in history is not likely to be insensible to the freedoms guaranteed by our Constitution."[20]

Frankfurter had joined the Court with the reputation of a champion of civil liberties. However, during most of their common tenure, it was Douglas and Black who took the strong civil libertarian position, while Frankfurter showed persistent deference to elected authority in clashes over individual rights. Nowhere was the difference more clearly displayed than in the prosecutions of members of the Communist Party. Douglas and Black insisted that the convictions violated the First Amendment, while Frankfurter called for judicial subservience to the decisions of the legislature regarding the danger posed by the Party.[21] While Douglas denied it in his autobiography, there is ample evidence to support the widely held view that the Douglas-Frankfurter relationship was exceedingly difficult for most of their shared time on the bench.[22] Douglas was the only member of the Court not to attend Frankfurter's funeral.[23]

Douglas and Black were close both personally and in their constitutional views. They shared antipathy for the practices of the justices who had, in their view, inserted their own political predelictions as barriers to the legislative innovations of the New Deal. With regard to federal authority to regulate the economy, they believed that any activity that substantially affected interstate commerce was within the national government's reach. They both voted to sustain the 1964 Civil Rights Act, which prohibited racial discrimination in public accommodations, such as restaurants and hotels, on the ground that the discrimination itself was a burden on interstate commerce. While Douglas preferred to support the act under the federal government's power to enforce the equal protection provisions of the Fourteenth Amendment, he had no doubts regarding the adequacy of the commerce power.

As the Court drew back from imposing limits on government power over economic matters, it began to pay closer attention to individual rights claims in matters such as criminal procedure and racial discrimination. In a 1938 case, *United States v. Carolene Products Co.*,[24] Justice Stone said, in a footnote that would become famous, that the Court owed less deference to the other political branches in cases involving Bill of Rights claims, or when the situation involved "discrete and insular minorities" who could not rely on the political process for protection.

The Fourteenth Amendment provides a federal guarantee against state action that deprives people of life, liberty, or property without due process of law, or that denies them equal protection of the laws. The old Court had used the Due Process Clause to impose constraints on state economic regulation, in the name of preserving property rights—constraints that had drawn the fire of the New Deal appointees. Black, particularly, was loath to use the Due Process Clause in this way, because he viewed it as so open-ended as to invite judges simply to substitute their own views for those of the elected representatives of the people. He insisted that the purpose of the Due Process Clause was to impose the specific restraints of the Bill of Rights, originally applicable only to federal actions, on the states. Douglas initially joined him in this view.

Other members of the Court, led by Frankfurter, insisted that the test of due process was what "shocked the conscience" or violated a "concept of ordered liberty." Because not every practice that violated a provision of the Bill of Rights also shocked the conscience or offended the justices' sense of ordered liberty, there were times when Black and Douglas were in vocal dissent.

In similar fashion, Black adopted an "absolutist" approach to the First Amendment's prohibition of laws infringing the freedom of speech and press. For Black, the amendment's opening words said it all: "Congress shall make no law"—and this meant "no law." This often put him in sharp dissent from a majority that employed the "clear and present danger test" to weigh the harm likely to follow from the speech against the harm done by suppressing it. In Black's view, the balancing had already been done by the authors of the constitutional provision, and the Court's only task was to enforce their work.

Throughout the '40s, '50s and early '60s, Black and Douglas could usually be found together on civil liberties issues, sometimes prevailing but often in dissent. In later years they sometimes parted company. Black held to the view that due process included only the guarantees of the Bill of Rights; Douglas eventually adopted the position that it could also include some practices that were offensive to liberty even though not mentioned in the first ten amendments. In order to make sense of his absolutist view of the First Amendment, Black had to draw a clear line between speech and other activities that, while communicative, were not speech—such as carrying picket signs. This led him to deny constitutional protection to some activities that Douglas thought were legitimately included.

Douglas was less worried than Black about the coherence and consistency of legal doctrine. He tolerated the disruption of the civil rights protesters of the '60s and '70s, while Black warned that courts and the law were the appropriate path to vindication of civil wrongs. In 1965, Black vigorously dissented from Douglas's opinion in *Griswold v. Connecticut*,[25] which laid the groundwork for the right to privacy that would provide the foundation for *Roe v. Wade*,[26] limiting the power of states to regulate abortion. While the two men's friendship endured, their ideological partnership had come to an end.

For much of his career on the bench, Douglas was the object of controversy. Early on, his friendship with President Roosevelt led to speculation that he had political ambitions. That was considered inappropriate by some of his colleagues on the bench, particularly Frankfurter. There is irony in this, considering Frankfurter's own penchant for behind-the-scenes maneuvering in political affairs. But, despite Douglas's own denial of political ambition,[27] it is clear that he was given serious consideration for the Democratic nomination for vice-president in both 1944 and 1948, and he did little to squelch efforts to advance his candidacy. He declined Truman's offer of the position in 1948, perhaps because he shared the widespread feeling that Truman was unlikely to be re-elected.[28]

Douglas's personal life was also a source of controversy. He divorced his first wife, Mildred Riddle, in 1953, after twenty-nine years of marriage. Divorce was still an anomaly in American culture. Douglas understood that it would mark the end of any hopes he might harbor for political office. His second marriage, to Mercedes Davidson, lasted for ten years. Upon divorcing her in 1963, he married Joan Martin, who was twenty-three years old—forty-two years his junior and eleven years younger than his daughter Millie. Three years later Martin and Douglas were divorced, and a few months later he was married to another much younger woman, Cathy Heffernan. That marriage lasted until his death.

More significantly, Douglas was an articulate public voice for political views that, near the end of his career, were becoming increasingly unpopular. His opposition to Communism was always accompanied by attention to the ways in which anti-communist regimes fell short of their own ideals, particularly with regard to their dealings with former colonies. He insisted that the best response to the communist threat was more democracy for the emerging countries, when United States foreign policy seemed to favor manipulation and military control. As his writings on Vietnam suggest, his understanding of the situation on the ground in various parts of the world, informed by his own travels and talks with local people, often put him out of line with the prevailing official position of the U.S. government. Throughout the Vietnam war, he was the one member of the Court willing to entertain claims that the war was unconstitutional because it had not been declared by Congress pursuant to Article I, § 8 of the Constitution.

Much of this came together in a series of threats to impeach Douglas, the most serious of which was led by Congressman Gerald Ford in early 1970. Republican congressmen were upset with the refusal of the Democratically controlled Senate to confirm two successive Supreme Court nominations by President Nixon: Clement Haynsworth, Jr., and G. Harrold Carswell. Douglas's connection with Albert Parvin, a major investor in Las Vegas hotels and casinos, whose charitable foundation Douglas chaired at an annual salary of $12,000, had been under scrutiny and attack for a number of years. In early 1970, Douglas published *Points of Rebellion*, a short but vigorous attack on the "establishment" which appeared to align him with student anti-war activists. Ford's charges against Douglas included his work for Parvin, characterized as "moonlighting," and referred to a variety of unsavory characters who were associated with Las Vegas, if not directly with either Parvin or Douglas. The charges also referred to *Points of Rebellion*, described as an "inflammatory volume" in the spirit of "the militant hippie-yippie movement."[29] The impeachment effort ultimately foundered; it was clear that none of the charges against Douglas met the constitutionally prescribed standard of "high crimes or misdemeanors." Democratic control of the Judiciary Committee led to delay of the report of the committee until after the fall election, taking the political pressure off the situation. An exhaustive report by the committee, while not laying to rest all questions about the propriety of some of Douglas's activities, made clear that no impeachable offense had occurred. Douglas understood the attack as entirely political: rather than retire, as he had been considering, and perhaps suggest that there was something to the charges against him, he resolved to stay "until the last hound dog had stopped snapping at my heels."[30]

Douglas suffered a stroke while on vacation in Nassau at the end of 1974. He attempted to return to active service on the Court in the spring of 1975, but the stroke had taken too great a toll, both physically and intellectually. He submitted his resignation in

November 1975, having served longer than any other justice in the
history of the Court. He died on January 19, 1980.

The writings collected here exhibit the range and power of this
most extraordinary man. Lawyer, administrator, judge, civil
libertarian, conservationist, student of international affairs, but
perhaps most persistently, son of the mountains, prairies, and streams
of the Pacific Northwest. From the top of those mountains, one can
see a very long way. Douglas saw farther, and deeper, than most.

The identification of William O. Douglas as "Nature's Justice" may
seem ironic, since he rejected the perspective of "natural justice" that
tended to associate the right with the familiar. But it powerfully
underscores the extent to which Douglas was the unique product of
the environment in which he grew, with talents and virtues that were
fostered in that rugged, stark, and beautiful setting.

The legacy of a Supreme Court justice is problematic. Court
opinions often reflect compromises made to secure other votes, and
the work of the Court is constantly subject to change. Douglas is
probably most clearly identified with the Court led by Chief Justice
Earl Warren and, for better or worse, little of this Court's work has
escaped revision by later justices. However, Douglas's legacy need not
rest on the shifting sands of judicial fashion.

Exploiting the special visibility that comes with a seat on the
nation's highest court, Douglas "spoke truth to power," both on and
off the bench. His passion was to secure the conditions necessary to
human flourishing. In the realm of organized society, that meant the
preservation of liberty. He warned that government efficiency is often
achieved at a cost to individual liberty. He understood and protested
against the moral price that colonizers pay to maintain control of
their colonies. When it came to the threats supposedly posed by
domestic dissenters, including the Communist Party, civil rights
protesters, and anti-war activists, Douglas lived by the adage of his
friend F.D.R.—"we have nothing to fear but fear itself."

Douglas also maintained a commitment to preserving wilderness,
both for its own sake and because it was vital to the human spirit.
Part of his legacy is quite visible. The National Historic Park that
protects the C&O Canal along the Potomac River is a product of
Douglas's leadership, before environmentalism had a name. An
unspoiled stretch of Pacific Ocean coastline in the Olympic National

Park similarly owes its continued wilderness character to agitation led by him.

A less visible part of his legacy is exemplified by one of my colleagues, a rising young star in the field of environmental law, who spends her summers in the Cascades. Each year while there, she reads Douglas' *My Wilderness*, drawing inspiration for her work. In Douglas's writings there is inspiration aplenty, not only for environmentalists, but for all concerned to see a world in which liberty, equality, and justice prevail. That is the legacy that Justice Douglas—Nature's Justice—would cherish most.

Notes

1. *Go East, Young Man: The Early Years.* New York: Random House, 1974 (herafter *Go East*). P. 19.
2. Id.
3. *Go East*, p. 32.
4. *Go East*, pp. 37-38.
5. James F. Simon, *Independent Journey: The Life of William O. Douglas.* New York: Harper and Row, 1980 (hereafter *Independent Journey*). P.35.
6. *Go East*, p. 97.
7. Id., p. 130.
8. *Independent Journey*, p. 63.
9. *Go East*, p.142.
10. Douglas's dissent can be found on page 201.
11. Compare *Go East*, pp. 156-159 with *Independent Journey*, pp. 93-99.
12. *Go East*, p.158.
13. *Go East*, p. 164.
14. Thurman Arnold, *Fair Fights and Foul*, pp. 62-63.
15. *Go East*, pp. 169-70.
16. *Independent Journey*, pp. 197-215.
17. 310 U.S. 586 (1940)
18. 316 U.S. 584 (1942)
19. *West Virginia State Board of Education v. Barnette*, 319 U.S. 624 (1943).
20. Id. at p. 646.
21. Douglas's opinion in *Dennis v. United States* can be found on page 201.
22. William O. Douglas, *The Court Years, 1939-1975: The Autobiography of William O. Douglas.* New York: Random House, 1980 (hereafter *Court Years*). P. 22.
23. *Independent Journey*, p. 217.

24. 304 U.S. 144
25. 381 U.S. 479 (1965). Douglas' *Griswold* opinion can be found on page 216.
26. 410 U.S. 113 (1973)
27. "[T]he truth is, I never had the Potomac Fever and could not be excited about catching it." *Court Years,* p. 283.
28. *Independent Journey,* pp. 257-275
29. *Independent Journey,* p. 405.
30. *Court Years,* p.377.

Editor's Note

Some of the selections have been edited for length and a few typographical errors in the original texts have been corrected.

PART ONE

At Home in the Mountains

Of Men and Mountains was Douglas's first foray into autobiography. Many of the stories that he told there were later incorporated into the first volume of his official autobiography, *Go East, Young Man.* Selections from both books have been chosen for this first section, which shows how Douglas's early love of the wilderness remained a vital part of his life.

In the Foreword to *Of Men and Mountains*, Douglas lays claim to the formative influence of his youthful experiences in the mountains, and recounts the story of the riding accident that nearly cost him his life. He had been putting the finishing touches on the manuscript at the time of the accident, and the book was published as he was completing his recovery.

The first chapter, "The Cascades," sets up Douglas's theme of the mountains as a place of retreat and renewal, of spiritual sustenance, against a background of workday drudgery and bleak cities. The central section tells how he made his way east to go to law school, hopping a freight for part of the journey, and talked to an old man in Chicago whose homesickness for the mountains was leading him back to the West.

"Sagebrush and Lava Rock," also from *Of Men and Mountains*, tells of the hills surrounding Yakima, where Douglas walked as a teenager, intent on overcoming the lingering effects of his childhood polio. He weaves together the geological history of the place, accounts of its flora and fauna, stories told by native inhabitants, and personal experience to produce a vivid and attractive portrait of a place that, to the passing eye, might seem little more than rock and brush.

"Coming of Age in Yakima," from the first volume of *Go East, Young Man*, is Douglas's account of the formative influence of his youth in that small Washington town. Three themes stand out in this brief narrative: the corruption of the "establishment," as represented by the man who employed him as a "stool pigeon," sympathy for the poor, and veneration of the heroic individual who stands with the people, and against corruption.

The last two selections in this part are both from *Of Men and Mountains*. In "Fly v. Bait," Douglas's pleasure in that most solitary of tasks, the stalking of the wild trout, shines through. One may suspect that he exaggerates the dimensions of his catch, but the circumstances were very different in the time of which he is writing and fewer people and more difficult travel helped to preserve wild fish populations for those who were hearty enough to seek them out.

"Roy Schaeffer" introduces us to a man who, in Douglas's estimation, belonged among the legendary mountain men. Massive in size and steeped in knowledge of the outdoor world in which he lived and worked, for years Schaeffer was Douglas's companion and guide on his summer retreats to Oregon's Wallowa mountains. For Douglas, the mountains harbor simple virtue. Roy Schaeffer is their human epitome.

Foreword

The mountains of the Pacific Northwest are tangled, wild, remote, and high. They have the roar of torrents and avalanches in their throats.

Rock cliffs such as Kloochman rise as straight in the air as the Washington Monument and two or three times as high. Snow-capped peaks with aprons of eternal glaciers command the skyline—giant sentinels 11,000, 12,000, 14,000 feet high, such as Hood, Adams, and Rainier.

There are no slow-moving, sluggish rivers in these mountains. The streams run clear, cold, and fast.

There are remote valleys and canyons where man has never been. The meadows and lakes are not placid, idyllic spots. The sternness of the mountains has been imparted to them.

There are cougar to scout the camp at night. Deer and elk bed down in stands of mountain ash, snowbrush, and mountain-mahogany. Bears patrol streams looking for salmon. Mountain goat work their way along cliffs at dizzy heights, searching for moss and lichens.

Trails may climb 4,000 feet or more in two miles. In twenty miles of travel one may gain, then lose, then gain and lose once more, several thousand feet of elevation.

The blights of forest fires, overgrazing, avalanches, and excessive lumbering have touched parts of this vast domain. But civilization has left the total scene in strange degree alone.

These tangled masses of thickets, ridges, cliffs, and peaks are a vast wilderness area. Here man can find deep solitude, and under conditions of grandeur that are startling he can come to know both himself and God.

This book is about such discoveries. In this case they are discoveries that I made; so in a limited sense the book is autobiographical.

I learned early that the richness of life is found in adventure. Adventure calls on all the faculties of mind and spirit. It develops self-reliance and independence. Life then teems with excitement. But man is not ready for adventure unless he is rid of fear. For fear confines him and limits his scope. He stays tethered by strings of doubt and indecision and has only a small and narrow world to explore.

This book may help others to use the mountains to prepare for adventure.

They—if they are among the uninitiated—may be inspired to search out the high alpine basins and fragile flowers that flourish there. They may come to know the exhilaration of wind blowing through them on rocky pinnacles. They may recognize the music of the conifers when it comes both in whispered melodies and in the fullness of the wind instruments. They may discover the glory of a blade of grass and find their own relationship to the universe in the song of the willow thrush at dusk. They may learn to worship God where pointed spires of balsam fir turn a mountain meadow into a cathedral.

Discovery is adventure. There is an eagerness, touched at times with tenseness, as man moves ahead into the unknown. Walking the wilderness is indeed like living. The horizon drops away, bringing new sights, sounds, and smells from the earth. When one moves through the forests, his sense of discovery is quickened. Man is back in the environment from which he emerged to build factories, churches, and schools. He is primitive again, matching his wits against the earth and sky. He is free of the restraints of society and free of its safeguards too.

Boys, perhaps more deeply than men, know this experience. Eleanor Chaffee has expressed that concept poignantly:

> *Who but a boy would wander into the night*
> *Against the sensible advice of those much older,*
> *Where silent shadows cut the moon's thin light*
> *And only maples lean to touch his shoulder?*
> *What does he hope to find, what fever stirs*
> *His blood and guides his feet to walk alone?*
> *He will return, his sweater stuck with burrs*
> *And in his hand a useless, shapeless stone,*
> *But something in his face, secret, withdrawn*
> *Will go with him upstairs, and to his sleep.*
> *He is as furtive now as a young wild fawn:*
> *His eyes are darker now, and large and deep.*
> *Who but a boy can find such subtle magic*
> *In the world his elders find so grave, so tragic?*

These pages contain what I, as a boy, saw, felt, smelled, tasted, and heard in the mountains of the Pacific Northwest. At least the record I have written is as accurate as memory permits. Those who walked the trails with me as a boy—Bradley Emery, Douglas Corpron, Elon Gilbert, Arthur F. Douglas—are happily all alive. So they have let me draw upon their memories too and make many demands on their time and energies in the preparation of these chronicles.

The boy makes a deep imprint on the man. My young experiences in the high Cascades have placed the heavy mark of the mountains on me. And so the excitement that alpine meadows and high peaks created in me comes flooding back to make each adult trip an adventure. As the years have passed I have found in these experiences a spiritual significance that I could not fully sense before. That is why the book, though about a boy, is in total effect an adult version.

Many have assisted me in this task. I must add a special word about two of the characters. Elon Gilbert almost gave his life for the book. When field studies were being made in 1948, he was in a truck loaded with horses that rolled into a canyon on the eastern slopes of Darling Mountain. It was he who scaled the cliffs on Goat Rocks to drop a rope to me that I might climb in safety. He also carried much of the burden of the field research that went into this work. We shared together, as boys and men, the adventure of this story.

Doug Corpron was one of the doctors who attended me after the horseback accident in October 1949 that almost proved fatal. During the first few days in the hospital it seemed that whenever I opened my eyes—night or day—Doug was by my bedside. Then one day he stood over me with a grin on his face. There was a note of bravado in his voice as he said, "That was another tough climb we had together. But we made it, just as we once conquered Kloochman."

That was a freakish accident in which Elon Gilbert and Billy McGuffie were also involved.

Billy McGuffie was at Tipsoo Lake on the morning of October 2, 1949, as Elon Gilbert and I started on horseback up Crystal Mountain on the expedition that almost proved fatal to me. He hailed me, and I stopped briefly to talk with him before I took to the trail. Rainier stood naked in all its grandeur across from us. Billy was lighthearted as he pointed out all of the meadows and basins on its slopes where he had once herded sheep. How Billy happened to be at Tipsoo this morning I do not know. "Providence sent him," Jack Nelson whispered to me a few days later in a Yakima hospital.

I had recently been into that country on skis and snowshoes when it was under thirty feet of snow. But there was much of it I had not seen in summer or fall for over thirty years.

This would be the ideal day to see it. There was not a cloud as far as the eye could see. The Oregon grape had turned to a deep port, the huckleberry to blood red, the mountain ash to a rich cranberry. The willow, maple, and tamarack were golden splashes across dark slopes of evergreens and basalt. As we skirted a steep and rugged shoulder of rock, I sensed a quiet air of waiting. It was as if the mountain were gathering itself together for the winter's assault.

Then the accident happened. I had ridden my horse Kendall hundreds of miles in the mountains and found him trustworthy on any terrain. But this morning he almost refused, as Elon led the way up a steep 60-degree grade. Knowing my saddle was loose, I dismounted and tightened the cinch. Then I chose a more conservative path up the mountain. Keeping it on my left, I followed an old deer run that circled the hillside at an easy 10-degree grade. We had gone only a hundred yards or so when Kendall (for a reason which will never be known) reared and whirled, his front feet pawing the steep slope. I dismounted by slipping off his tail. I landed in shale rock, lost my footing and rolled some thirty yards. I ended on a narrow ledge lying on my stomach, uninjured. I started to rise. I glanced up. I looked into the face of an avalanche. Kendall had slipped, and fallen, too. He had come rolling down over the same thirty precipitous yards I had traversed. There was no possibility of escape. Kendall was right on me. I had only time to duck my head. The great horse hit me. Sixteen hundred pounds of solid horseflesh rolled me flat. I could hear my own bones break in a sickening crescendo. Then Kendall dropped over the ledge and rolled heavily down the mountain to end up without a scratch. I lay paralyzed with pain—twenty-three of twenty-four ribs broken.

I could not move or shout. Would Elon ever find me in the brush where I lay concealed? He did—in twenty minutes that seemed like a century. Then, marking the spot where I lay, he raced down the mountain to see if he could find help. Again it seemed an endless wait but in less than an hour there were sounds of men thrashing through brush—the rescue party that Billy McGuffie had organized. Soon there were strong arms lifting me gently onto a litter. Then a warm, rough hand slipped into mine, as I heard these whispered words: "This is Wullie McGuffie, my laddie; noo everthing will be a'richt."

The Cascades

≈)

Most lawsuits, when viewed from the bench, are fundamentally fascinating. But there are dull moments even for a judge. There are interludes when the advocate is fumbling among his papers or having a whispered consultation with his associate. There is the occasional lawyer who drones on with accumulating monotony. I particularly recall one such time when, for a few minutes, I left the courtroom.

It was a day in late spring, when I stepped into the Big Klickitat.

The water was high, so I pulled my waders snug to the armpits. They were stocking-foot waders. The shoes I wore had felt soles, fair footing for the black, lava rock bottom of the Klickitat. The chill of the water at once struck through waders and wool underwear.

"I must keep moving," I thought, "or I'll freeze."

I waded to midstream. The water of the Klickitat was around my waist. The whole weight of the river rushed against me. While it was a friendly push, it warned me to be careful of my footing. I leaned against it slightly, felt firm gravel under my feet, and started the slow ascent of the stream.

I was fishing a dry fly. I found some long floats with a May fly in the flat water below a spot of riffles. But I had no strike. I changed to a caddis bucktail and then to a coachman bucktail. Still no strike. I pushed on upstream. There on the left bank was a stretch of fast, flat water under overhanging branches of willow. The only way I could get a float beneath the willows was to cast across the stream at an angle. I crossed to the righthand bank, and was able to quarter it as I cast up to the base of the riffle.

I opened a fly box to make a new selection. After a moment of indecision I chose a Hallock killer. My first cast reached the base of the riffle. The current carried the fly a foot from the bank and down it drifted sitting high on the water like some new hybrid form of caddis that had dropped from a willow tree. Down it came—ten feet, twelve feet, fifteen feet, twenty feet. There was a swirl under the fly. I lifted the tip of my rod to set the hook. My timing was poor. The fish turned over but I had not touched him. So he might come again.

I waited a few minutes. Once more I quartered the river, casting upstream to the base of the riffle. Again the Hallock killer swung toward the bank and came drifting down under the willows. It had moved about as far as before, when the trout—the same, I believe—struck again. This time I had him. I knew he was a rainbow because he broke water at once. All told, he jumped eight times. He stood on his tail, shaking his head to get rid of the hook. He rushed toward me, leaving the water in a graceful arc, eager for slack line so as to shake the hook loose. Downstream we went until we came to a small pool. There I held him until, in a few minutes, I brought him gently to the net. He was sleek and fat—fourteen inches long and a pound and three-quarters in weight.

I went back upstream and fished a few pools above the willow bank. I took one more trout—a twelve-inch rainbow. But that was the only strike I had in thirty minutes on the Hallock killer.

"Time for a change," I thought, selecting a gray hackle, a No. 17 with a yellow body and red wings. "Maybe that's what they want." I tied it on and continued upstream to a big pool I had seen. This was at least fifty feet long. It was filled with white water at its head. The lower part was calm, and at least six or eight feet deep. I puzzled over the best way to fish it. If I cast upstream to the base of the white water at the head of the pool, the line would stretch across the calm water and disturb the trout. So I decided the best spot for the first cast was the lower end. Here the water picked up speed as it rushed for the exit, which was between two logs lying close and forming a sort of sluice gate. I dropped my gray hackle twenty feet above the sluice gate of the pool. It had gone scarcely a foot when it was sucked under in a swirl. I set my hook and knew by the feel that I had the champion.

Just then I heard the marshal's gavel. I came to. The court was rising. It was 4:30 p.m. The argument was over and another session of court at an end.

When I got to my chambers, I found my old friend Saul Haas waiting to see me. He had been in the courtroom during the latter part of the case. "Were you asleep in court this afternoon?" he accused.

I told him I had not been asleep; that when I became a judge I swore I would never doze on the bench, and my record so far was unsullied. Then I asked why he thought I had been sleeping.

"Well," he said, "you were off gathering wool."

I confessed I had been fishing.

"Fishing?" he queried. "For trout?"

I told him I had been after trout in the Big Klickitat of the Cascade Mountains in eastern Washington.

"Any luck?" he asked. I assured him I had had wonderful luck.

"You know," he said, "I'll bet you had better luck fishing this afternoon than you usually have." I inquired why.

"Well," he said, "I'll tell you. The loveliest, most beautiful women are those we meet in our dreams. And I figure that fishing is the same."

It was March, and there was only a touch of spring along the banks of the Potomac. The sun had not yet awakened the Japanese cherry trees. Neither the violets nor the dogwood had blossomed. The trees, though expectant, were still naked. Summer pressed harder each day. But winter hung on and kept its chill in the air.

There were robins everywhere. A meadow lark sang from a field by the river. A cloud of redwings swept across the sky, headed downstream for marshlands. A heron flapped lazily along the Virginia side of the river. And I saw on the edge of the path the year's first lily of the valley.

I stooped to pick it; and as I rose, I noticed a burst of yellow against a stand of dry and brittle weeds a hundred yards or so into the barren woods. After a long absence, the forsythia had returned overnight. The brilliance of its color against the drab shrubs and trees made it seem that the woods had been filled with the great rush of spring. The endless cycle persisted. There had been apparent atrophy and death. Now the floodtime of life was near. There would soon be a mysterious awakening of grass and trees. Melodious invaders from the Caribbean would drop from the sky. A reviving south wind would touch the land with wet wings.

Since the previous fall, I had hardly had time to look for a cardinal in Rock Creek Park or for a flight of geese or redheads over the Potomac. Indeed, I had been in the woods only a few times all winter. Like others in the nation's capital I had been caught fast in official and social duties.

The events of the winter had made me wonder at times, "Whither man?" I recalled an evening's conversation with a group of young folks. They deplored the fact that man was being more and more regarded only as a biological or economic being. He was put into tables and polls and considered as fungible as wheat or corn. One of them made the point that there was a diminishing recognition of the spiritual qualities— of the importance of quickening man's conscience and asking him to search his soul as well as his mind for answers to the perplexing problems of the day.

Perhaps man was losing his freedom in a subtle manner. He was becoming more and more dependent on other men. Part of that dependency was necessary, since man had to look to others for his food and fuel and essential services. But he had also become dependent on others for his entertainment and for his ideas. He looked to people rather than to himself and to the earth for his salvation. He fixed his expectations on the frowns or smiles or words of men, not on the strength of his own soul, or the sunrise, or the warming south wind, or the song of the warbler.

Once man leaned that heavily on people he was not wholly free to live. Then he became moody rather than self-reliant. He was filled with tensions and doubts. He walked in an unreal world, for he did not know the earth from which he came and to which he would return. He became a captive of civilization rather than an adventurer who topped each hill ahead for the thrill of discovering a new world. He lost the feel of his own strength, the power of his own soul to master any adversity.

The forsythia and its brilliant color stirred in me the memory of this after-dinner conversation. As I stood there with those ideas swirling in my head, I felt refreshed. My heart was relieved. I was excited by the very thought of being alive. The golden gleam of forsythia in bleak woods had given me a new hold on freedom.

I felt an almost irresistible urge to go West. It was the call of the Cascade Mountains. The sight of the forsythia this March day along the Potomac tripped the mechanism that flooded my mind with memories of the challenge of those mountains. The same has happened again and again in other circumstances.

Packed tight in a New York City subway, I have closed my eyes and imagined I was walking the ridge high above Cougar Lake. That ridge has the majesty of a cathedral. The Pacific Crest Trail winds along it under great cliffs that suggest walls and spires yet unfinished. At points along the trail are meadows no bigger than a city lot, from whose edge the mountain drops off a thousand feet or more. Here one stands on a dais looking directly down on the tips of pine and hemlock. At other points there are small pockets or basins set like alcoves off the trail and lined with balsam (alpine) fir in colonnade effect. Sharp, jagged shafts of basalt rock often tower over these alcoves. And at various angles they give impressions of roughly hewn church steeples.

When I am on that ridge at daybreak on an August or September day I feel like holding my breath so as not to break the solitude. The heartbeat sounds like a muffled drum. There is dew on the bunchgrass and the low-bush huckleberries. The air is crisp and cool. There is not a breath of wind. I find myself walking softly, almost on tiptoe, careful to avoid twigs and to keep my feet on the grass or the soft pine needles. For it pays to be noiseless when one moves along the ridge at that hour. It is the time of day when deer and elk are on the move.

There is no one within miles. A squirrel sounds an alarm from the top of a western hemlock. A chipmunk scuttles across the trail and, before disappearing into his hole, peers around the trunk of a white fir. There is an impish way about him. This is the first man he has ever seen, and he is full of indecision whether or not to explore the possibilities of friendship. Then he is gone with a flick of his tail. Overhead a hawk circles round and round, catching some current of air that even the tips of the fir and hemlock and cedar do not feel, as it glides gracefully along the contours of the ridge.

There is always a quick excitement, a tingling sensation up the spine, as I turn a bend in the trail and see a doe feeding. Her sensitive antennae detect my presence before I can inhale a breath. She turns her head to face me, her ears spread wide, her nostrils distended, her eyes fixed. In a split second her radar transforms the image into the symbol for an ancient enemy. She clears a patch of hellebore in a bound and disappears with nervous jumps into a stand of mountain ash. Within fifty or a hundred feet even the white tail is blended in the woods and lost to sight.

In life the scene is almost as unreal as the memory of it is on a crowded subway. For the escape of the doe above Cougar Lake is as silent as her exit from a dream. She seldom cracks a twig as she goes bounding through brush and trees.

Long stretches of hard work often rob the night of sleep. There was one period when night after night I would be held at the office until two or three or four o'clock in the morning and then be back at my desk at nine. I would be dog-weary when I reached home, but wide-awake when I got to bed. And so I would roll and toss, unable to sleep. Some people count sheep; others play their golf courses hole by hole.

I would revisit in memory the Cascades and push up the Ahtanum over Darling Mountain and down into the Klickitat Meadows. I would catch cutthroat trout in the Little Klickitat and roast them on a stick over a willow fire.

I would push on to Conrad Meadows; lie on the bank of the South Fork of the Tieton; and watch white clouds in the west build patterns in the sky behind Gilbert Peak of the magnificent Goat Rocks.

I would go up to Goat Rocks on the Conrad Creek Trail; skirt the base of Devils Horns and Tieton Peak; come to the basin below Meade Glacier; cross the glacier and snow fields above it; and finally sit in the rocky crow's-nest at the top of Gilbert Peak, with the vast panorama of the Cascades spread out below me.

Or I would climb Hogback Mountain; drop to Shoe Lake; take the up-and-down washboard trail to McCall Basin; climb Old Snowy of the Goat Rocks, stand atop it, and feel the wind blowing through me.

I never got farther along those old trails before I was asleep. So the memories of my early trips were relaxing influences better than any chemical sedative.

Mount Adams has always had a special lure for me. Its memory has been the most haunting of all. Adams is more intimate than Rainier. Its lines are softer; it is more accessible. It has always been my favorite snow-capped mountain. My long ambition was to climb it. It was a mountain of mystery. It had been at one time, as I shall relate, a brave Indian chief named Klickitat. It had exhibited recent volcanic activity. High on its shoulders are crevasses that spout sulfur fumes. The Indians would not go up to its glaciers. There in the fastness of the mountain lived the Tomanows, the spirit chiefs of the Indians.

This mountain was so legendary I might not have believed it existed had I not lived in its shadow and seen it in sun and storm for twenty years. The vision of it would come back to me in dusty law libraries as I searched for the elusive thing called the law. High in an office building on New York's Wall Street I would be lost in the maze of a legal problem, forgetful of my bearings, and then suddenly look from the window to the west, thinking for a second that I might see Mount Adams, somber in its purplish snow at sunset. I have done the same thing while sitting deep in meditation in a canoe on a Maine lake or in a boat in Florida's Everglades.

After a long absence from my old home town of Yakima, Washington, I have fairly raced by car down from Ellensburg or up from Pasco to see Mount Adams before night dropped the curtain around it. At such a time my heart has leaped at the first sight of it. Getting out of the car I have stood in a field, thrilled at the sight as if it were my first. At those moments my spine has always tingled. There is a feeling of respect and admiration and pride. One has the sensation of being part of something much bigger than himself, something great and majestic and wholesome.

The Cascades have been particularly undeniable when I have lain in sickbed. In days of fever and sickness I have climbed Mount Adams, retraced every step from Cold Springs to the top, recrossed its snow fields, stood in a fifty-mile icy wind at its highest point, and there recaptured the feel of adventure and conquest and the sensation of being back millions of years at the time of the Creation.

During hospital days I have explored many streams of the Cascades, looking for the delicate periwinkle. I have cast a fly on dozens of their lakes, and searched the pools of the Big Klickitat, the South Fork of the Tieton, Bumping River, and the Naches for rainbow trout. I have sat on the crags of Goat Rocks, five hundred or a thousand feet below the summit, waiting for a mountain goat to appear in silhouette against the skyline. I have seen lively bug hatches on Fish and Swamp lakes. I have heard the noise of elk in the thickets along Petross Sidehill.

These have been haunting memories that in illness returned me to the world of reality even when it seemed I might be close to the other side of the river.

But the most vivid recollections have reached me in environments that have been bleak and dreary and oppressive. I remember a room in New York City on West 120th Street that overlooked an air well.

The sun reached that room but a scant two hours a day. There was no other outlook. The whole view was a dull brick wall, pierced by dingy panes of glass. In one of these windows some poor soul had set a tiny, scrawny geranium. There were lively zoological specimens around— such as cockroaches. But the only botanical specimen in sight was the geranium. I would see it in the morning when I arose and on rainy Sundays when I stayed indoors. In the poverty of that view the memories of the Cascades would come flooding back.

Lush bottom lands along the upper Naches, where grass grows stirrup high—succulent grass that will hold a horse all night.

A deer orchid deep in the brush off the American River Trail.

A common rock wren singing its heart out on a rock slide above Bumping Lake.

Clusters of the spring beauty in the damp creek beds along the eastern slopes of Hogback Mountain.

The smell of wood smoke, bacon, and onions at a camp below Meade Glacier.

Indian paintbrush and phlox on the high shoulders of Goat Rocks.

The roar of the northwesters in the treetops in Tieton Basin.

Clumps of balsam fir pointed like spires to the sky in Blankenship Meadows.

The cry of a loon through the mist of Bumping Lake.

A clump of whitebark pine atop Darling Mountain—gnarled and tough, beaten by a thousand gales.

A black, red-crested woodpecker attacking in machine-gun style a tree at Goose Prairie.

The scrawny geranium across the rooming house court in New York City brought back these nostalgic memories and many more. The glories of the Cascades grew and grew in the desolation of the bleak view from my window. New York City became almost unbearable. I was suffocated and depressed. I wanted to flee the great city with its scrawny geraniums and bleak courtyards. The longing for the silences of the Cascades, the smell of fir boughs at night, the touch of the chinook as it blew over the ridges—these longings were almost irresistible in the oppressiveness of my New York City rooming house.

I had had a similar experience on my way east to law school. I had left on a freight train from Wenatchee, Washington, with two thousand sheep. That was in September 1922. We had only reached Idaho when a railroad strike stopped the wheels. We had the sheep to feed and to water. Regular feeding points had been scheduled, but we did not reach them because of the strike. So we took the sheep out of the cars and herded them while we waited for an engine. In this way we spent eleven days moving by slow stages across Montana and North Dakota. Then came a wire from the owner to turn the sheep over to a buyer in western Minnesota. This we did. My companion returned to Yakima, and I caught the first freight to Chicago.

I knew the freight trains well. Hitchhikers of the period prior to the First World War chose them as a matter of necessity, because the great flow of highway traffic had not yet started. Like many others, I had ridden the rods up and down the Yakima Valley and to points east, to work in the hay- and wheatfields and in the orchards.

A literal riding of the rods is seldom done. This ordinarily means to ride under boxcars or passenger cars on a small platform of boards laid across rods that run lengthwise beneath some cars. It is a cramped space at best. It is frightfully dusty down there, the motion of the train whirling dirt and cinders its whole length. You lie on your stomach with your eyes closed, grimy and miserable. I hated that place. The open boxcars were more comfortable. But in them you might meet a fellow traveler who would not hesitate to toss you off the moving train after taking your money. Yet if you rode on top of cars you were subject to two other risks.

The first was the freight yard police, whom we called yard bulls. They were armed; and I was in mortal fear of them. They were not men of discretion or manners. Their technique was to beat you up first and then arrest you. The other risk was the train crew. More often than not they were friendly, but occasionally a brakeman would try to collect fares from the hitchhikers. A dollar or perhaps fifty cents would be enough; but unless payments were made, the passenger might be handed over to the yard bulls at the next station. This was the shakedown, but the immunity it purchased often seemed worth the price.

On this trip through Minnesota I paid toll to the crew of the freight train—fifty cents apiece, as I recall. When we came to a new division point, I discovered that the new crew was also collecting fares. I was easy prey, for I was on a flatcar—the only available space, except the rods and the top of the boxcars. This was a loaded and sealed train, carrying for the most part fruit in refrigerator cars. When the new brakeman came along he asked for a dollar and I paid him. Nothing more happened for a long time. Then along came the conductor. We were on the outskirts of Chicago. It was three or four o'clock in the morning on a clear, cold night. The conductor asked for a dollar; he said there were yard bulls ahead, he did not want me to get into trouble, and he would see that the yard bulls did not arrest me. It was the same old story.

I was silent for a while, trying to figure how I could afford to part with another dollar. I had only a few left. I had not had a hot meal for seven days; I had not been to bed for thirteen nights; I was filthy and without a change of clothes. I needed a bath and a shave and food; above all else I needed sleep. Even flophouses cost money. And the oatmeal, hot cakes, ham and eggs and coffee—which I wanted desperately—would cost fifty or seventy-five cents.

"Why should I pay this guy and become a panhandler in Chicago?" I asked myself.

He shook me by the shoulder and said, "Come on, buddy. Do you want to get tossed off the train?"

"I'm broke," I said.

"Broke?" he retorted. "You paid the brakeman and you can pay me."

"Have a heart," I said. "I bet you were broke some time. Give a guy a break."

He roared at me to get off or he would turn me over to the bulls. I was silent.

'Well, jump off or I'll run you in."

I watched the lights of Chicago come nearer. We were entering a maze of tracks. There were switches and sidetracks, boxcars on sidings, occasional loading platforms. And once in a while we roared over a short highway bridge. It was dark and the train was going about thirty miles an hour. The terrain looked treacherous. A jump might be disastrous. But I decided to husband my two or three remaining dollars. I stood poised on the edge of the flatcar, searching the area immediately ahead for a place to jump.

Suddenly in my ear came the command, "Jump!" I jumped.

Something brushed my left sleeve. It was the arm of a switch. Then I fell clear, hitting a cinder bank. I lost my footing, slid on my hands and knees for a dozen feet down the bank, and rolled to the bottom.

I got slowly to my feet as the last cars of the freight roared by and disappeared with a twinkling of lights into the east. My palms were bleeding and full of cinders. My knees were skinned. I was dirty and hungry and aching. I sat on a pile of ties by the track, nursing my wounds.

A form came out of the darkness. It proved to be an old man who also rode the rods. He put his hand on my shoulder and said, "I saw you jump, buddy. Are you hurt?"

"No, thank you," I replied. "Not much. Just scratched."

"Ever been to Chicago?"

"No."

"Well," he said, "don't stay here. It's a city that's hard on fellows like us."

"You mean the bulls?"

"Yes, they are tough," he said. "Maybe they have to be. But it's not only that. Do you smell the stockyards?"

I had not identified the odor, but I had smelled it even before I jumped.

"So that's it?"

"Yeah. I've worked there. The pay ain't so bad. But you go home at night to a room on an alley. There's not a tree. There's no grass. No birds. No mountains."

"What do you know of mountains?" I ventured.

It led to his story. He had come, to begin with, from northern California. He had worked in the harvests, and as he worked he could look up and see the mountains. Before him was Mount Shasta. He could put his bedroll on the ground and fall asleep under the pines. There was dust in the fields of northern California, but it was good clean dirt. People were not packed together like sardines. They had elbow room. A man need not sit on a Sunday looking out on a bleak alley. He could have a piece of ground, plant a garden, and work it. He might even catch a trout, or shoot a grouse or pheasant, or perhaps kill a deer.

I listened for about an hour as he praised the glories of the mountains of the West and related his experiences in them. Dawn was coming, and as it came I could see the smoke and some of the squalor of which my friend spoke.

I asked what brought him to the freight yards at this hour of the morning. He said he came to catch a west-bound freight—back to God's own land, back to the mountains. Lonesomeness swept over me. I never had loved the Cascades as much as I did that early morning in the stockyards of Chicago. Never had I missed a snowcapped peak as much. Never had I longed more to see a mountain meadow filled with heather and lupine and paintbrush. As dawn broke I could see smokestacks everywhere, and in the distance to the east the vague outlines of tall buildings. But there lay before me nothing higher, no ridge or hill or meadow—only a great monotony of cinders, smoke, and dingy factories with chimneys pouring out a thick haze over the landscape.

The old man and I sat in silence a few moments. He said, "Do you know your Bible, son?"

"Pretty well."

"Then you will remember what the psalmist said about the mountains."

I racked my brain. "No, I don't recall."

Then the old man said with intonations worthy of the clergy, "I will lift up mine eyes unto the hills from whence cometh my help. My help cometh from the Lord who made heaven and earth."

There was a whistle in the east. A quarter-mile down the track a freight was pulling onto the main line.

"That's my train," he said. "That train takes me to the mountains." He took my hand. "Good luck, son. Better come back with me. Chicago's not for us."

I shook my head and said good-by with sadness. He smiled. "Stay clear of the flophouses. They'll roll you when you're asleep. Go to the Y.M.C.A. It's cheap and clean and they're on the level."

The engine went by. The passing train was picking up speed. The old man was more agile than he looked. He trotted easily along the track, grabbed a handhold, and stepped lightly aboard on the bottom rung of the ladder. Climbing to the top of the boxcar, he took off his hat, and waved until he was out of sight.

I watched the freight disappear into the West. That old man had moved me deeply. I recognized his type from the hobo jungles I had visited between Yakima and Chicago. In Yakima the jungles were usually under or near one of the Northern Pacific bridges across the Yakima River. There hoboes met, contributed food to the pot, and cooked their meals. Not once was I allowed to go hungry in a jungle. I was always invited to share in whatever meal was cooking. Sometimes I could contribute to the pot, other times I could not; but that made no difference. There was companionship and friendship in the jungle.

I felt the jungle companionship in this old man of the stockyards. He was only a vagabond. But he was not a bum. I later realized that he had been a greater credit to his country than many of the more elite. He had made me see, in the dreary stockyards of America, some of the country's greatness—kindness, sympathy, selflessness, understanding.

I sat in the stockyards, watching the sun rise through the smoke and haze. There was a smell in the air that even the touch of the sun would not cleanse. There was not a tree or shrub or blade of grass in view. The Chicago I saw that morning was not the gracious, warmhearted city I later came to know. Nor was it the Chicago that Carl Sandburg painted:

> Hog butcher for the world, Toolmaker, stacker of wheat,
> Player with railroads and the nation's freight handler;
> Stormy, husky, brawling,
> City of big shoulders.

That morning I had only a distorted and jaundiced view. I was hungry, dead tired, homesick, broke, and bruised. And my welcome had not been cordial.

It seemed that man had built a place of desolation and had corrupted the earth in so doing. In corrupting the earth he had corrupted himself also, and built out of soot and dirt a malodorous place of foul air and grimy landscape in which to live and work and die. Here there were no green meadows wet with morning dew to examine for tracks of deer; no forest that a boy could explore to discover for himself the various species of wild flowers, shrubs, and trees; no shoulder of granite pushing against fleecy clouds and standing as a reminder to man of his puny character, of his inadequacies; no trace of the odor of pine or fir in the air.

I had a great impulse to follow my vagabond friend to the West, to settle down in the valley below Mount Adams and to live under its influence. Most of my friends and all the roots I had in life were in the Yakima Valley. There would be a job and a home awaiting me, and fishing trips and mountain climbs and nights on the high shoulders of Goat Rocks. It was a friendly place, not hard and cruel like these freight yards. People in the West were warmhearted and open-faced like my hobo friend. I would be content and happy there.

Then why this compulsion to leave the valley? Why this drive, this impulse, to leave the scenes I loved? To reach for unknown stars, to seek adventure, to abandon the convenience of home? And what of pride? What would I say if I returned? That I didn't have the guts to work my way east, to work my way through law school, to live the hard way?

These were my thoughts as the freight carried my vagabond friend into the West. Law school would open in a week. There was challenge ahead. New horizons would be opened, offering still untested opportunities.

My decision was spiritual. It was too late to go back. I would sleep the clock around and then return to the freight yards to catch a ride to New York City and Columbia Law School. I turned my face to the East— to my convictions—and walked along the railroad track, headed for the Y.M.C.A. as my friend had recommended.

Since that time I have often wondered whatever happened to the agile old man who befriended me in Chicago. I knew nothing much about him. But at least I have known that the mountains were important in shaping his kindness when he came to me through the night.

Mountains have a decent influence on men. I have never met along the trails of the high mountains a mean man, a man who would cheat and steal. Certainly most men who are raised there or who work there are as wholesome as the mountains themselves. Those who explore them on foot or horseback usually are open, friendly men. At least that has been my experience.

I saw the CCC camps in the early thirties work miracles with men. I remember a chap from Brooklyn whom I picked up out of La Grande, Oregon. We drove to Portland together. During the six or seven hours with him I learned something of his transformation. By his own admission he had been a pretty tough, mean character when he arrived in Oregon for work in the woods. He carried a chip on his shoulder. He was itching to punch "any bird" that pushed him around. And he did. One of them was the supervisor—an army officer, I believe—of the camp. He had found the world hard and cruel. There was always some guy to trim you, to do you in. You had to take care of yourself with your fists. He had learned the art on the streets of Brooklyn. When he punched the supervisor, he was given punishment—what, I do not recall. That did not soften him. It was the two years in the woods that changed his character.

He poured out his story on this long automobile ride. Things were different in the woods: "No use getting sore at a tree." There was nothing in the woods to hurt you—"but the mountains can give you quite a beating if you're careless." The air up there is "sure pure. Can't smell no garbage." It was kind of lonesome back in the woods: "No dames. And say, mister, I sure miss those Dodgers." But it was nice to have it quiet. "No radio blaring at you across the alley." The nights in the woods got to be pretty nice: "There's a kind of music in the pine trees at night when the wind blows."

This chap was mellow. Now he had no chip on his shoulder. He was considerate. He was a tough guy transformed into a philosopher. He had found how great and good his country was. He was going to try to repay it for what it had done for him.

The CCC had paid great dividends in citizenship of that character. His was not an isolated case. I heard the same story repeated again and again by supervisors of CCC camps. Jack Nelson, woodsman and philosopher (whose story I will later tell), bears witness to the miracles that happened.

I had puzzled many times over the reason for such a transformation of man by the mountains. A few summers ago an old friend, Dr. George Draper of New York City—father of psychosomatic medicine in this country—was spending a month with me at my cabin in the high Wallowas of Oregon. One night before the fire I put the question to him.

He thought a while and then said, "Man is at his worst when he is pitted against his fellow man. He is at his best when pitted against nature."

He was silent for a few moments. The tamarack log in the fireplace popped and threw sparks and coals against the screen as the fire roared up the chimney. The memory of my vagabond friend in the stockyards of Chicago came back to me as the doctor spoke. For the doctor too recited the words of the psalmist: "I will lift up mine eyes unto the hills from whence cometh my help. My help cometh from the Lord who made heaven and earth."

The doctor paused and then went on to say, "By 'help' the psalmist meant strength. By strength he meant spiritual vitality that comes from faith—faith in a universe of which he is a part, faith in a universe in which he has a place."

We sat for half an hour or so in silence. Mountains can transform men, I thought. Their lofty peaks, soft shoulders, and deep ravines have some special value to man, even though he does no more than view them from a distance. Those operating underground in the French Resistance during Nazi occupation often took a mountain as their code name. For mountains symbolize the indomitable will, an unbending resolution, a loyalty that is eternal, and character that is unimpeachable.

There are other ways too in which mountains have spiritual values. When man ventures into the wilderness, climbs the ridges, and sleeps in the forest, he comes in close communion with his Creator. When man pits himself against the mountain, he taps inner springs of his strength. He comes to know himself. He becomes meek and humble before the Lord that made heaven and earth. For he realizes how small a part of the universe he actually is, how great are the forces that oppose him.

Maybe all this is meant by West Virginia's motto, *Montani Semper Liberi*: mountaineers are always free men.

Those were the thoughts that went through my mind after the doctor gave his answer to my question. Finally he turned to me and said, "You should write a book some day about the influence of mountains on men. If man could only get to know the mountains better, and let them become a part of him, he would lose much of his aggression. The struggle of man against man produces jealousy, deceit, frustration, bitterness, hate. The struggle of man against the mountains is different. Man then bows before Something that is bigger than he. When he does that, he finds serenity and humility, and dignity too."

Sagebrush and Lava Rock

These early hikes put me on intimate terms with the hills. I learned something of their geology and botany. I came to know the Indian legends associated with them. I discovered many of their secrets. I learned that they were always clothed in garments of delicate hues, though they seemed to be barren. I discovered that though they looked dead and monotonous, they teemed with life and had many moods.

There is a Russian saying that every devil praises the marshes where he was born. Early associations control the nostalgic urges of every person. For Holmes it was granite rocks and barberry bushes. For others it may be lilacs, sycamores, willows, the checkerboard of wheat lands, or rolling hills. My love is for what many would put down as the dreariest aspects of the dry foothills of the West—sagebrush and lava rock.

This sagebrush (*Artemisia tridentata* Nutt.) is found throughout the West. It is as American as the New England twang, the Southern drawl, the "You bet" of the West, or "Youse guys" from Brooklyn. It covers the foothills around Yakima. It grows at 8,000 feet on Hart Mountain in southern Oregon. It holds the soil in place throughout the western belt from Canada to Mexico. It is the bush that Lewis and Clark called "southern wood." It commonly grows only a foot and a half or two feet high. But in gullies and ravines and other spots that collect water for part of the year, it may grow as high as a man's head. John Scharff, superintendent of the Malheur Bird Refuge in southern Oregon, bragged of the Steens Mountain sagebrush, "It's real timber, boys. This fall my first job is to run some lines and cruise and scale it."

It's tough and wiry; and it makes a quick, hot, pungent fire. In the springtime its tender new leaves make browse for antelope and sheep. Bunchgrass that cures on the stalk, and provides year-round food for stock, grows in its shade. It also furnishes protection and moisture for the myriad of wild flowers that in springtime briefly paint light streaks of blue and yellow and white on desert slopes. And it is in its full glory when spring rains fall.

That's the way I first remember it on the foothills of Yakima at night. A light, warm rain was falling. The air was permeated with the smell of freshly dampened dust and with the pungent but delicate odor of sage.

The lava rock is part of the great Columbia lava or basalt, which includes some andesite. Layer upon layer of it underlies eastern Washington and Oregon. During the Tertiary period it boiled up from the bowels of the earth. The period of its greatest activity was the Miocene, some thirty million years ago. There were at times centuries between the various flows. This molten rock poured largely out of great fissures, not from volcanoes. It flooded the entire Yakima country, which then was largely a lowland, and covered most of what is now the Cascades. There were at least twenty-eight layers of the hot, liquid rock poured over this country. Their aggregate thickness is over 5,000 feet. The magnitude of the Columbia lava as a geological phenomenon has never been surpassed and has been equaled only by the great Deccan basalts in India. The Deccan trap covers about 200,000 square miles on the west side of the peninsula of India. In the vicinity of Bombay it is about 6,000 feet thick. The Deccan trap is older than the Columbia lava for it belongs to the Cretaceous rather than the Tertiary period. It is largely horizontal and has suffered greater decay than ours.

In the late Miocene there was great volcanic activity in the Cascades. Streams flowing eastward deposited light-colored sandstones and gravels (known as the Ellensburg Formation) on top of the basalt. Near Yakima are clay deposits covered by a lava flow a hundred feet thick. So it must be that a huge wave of molten rock once overran a large lake, obliterating it with a hissing of steam and filling the sky with clouds of smoke from the trees and shrubs that were ignited in the process. We know that this was long before the glacial period. The lava surfaces have been polished by thick tongues of ice that moved down from the north in the Pleistocene age, a million and a half years or more ago. A glacier indeed moved to the edge of the Yakima Valley and lay there on the lava for tens of thousands of years.

The Columbia River, eating its way through the Cascades as it pours its water toward the Pacific, has revealed many of these layers. The Snake River, when it carved Hell's Canyon between Oregon and Idaho and dug down 7,900 feet to make the deepest hole on the continent, disclosed even more. That canyon reveals dozens of layers of the black lava, each twenty or thirty feet thick. They look at a distance like layers of rich chocolate in a Paul Bunyan cake.

A whole hillside 3,000 to 4,000 feet high is carved into a series of plateaus shaped like huge steps. Vast fields of bunchgrass run down hill between these outcroppings. Each field ends at the edge of a cliff of rimrock. Thus in this region it is not unusual during slippery weather to have cattle literally fall out of pasture and be killed.

Out of Yakima, along the Naches and especially the Tieton, the lava takes bizarre and startling forms. It may lie in sheets that appear as thin as flakes of chocolate candy. It often stands like cordwood on end, or rises like giant pillars against a hillside. Huge corners of it will form the shoulder of a ridge or a spire above the crest. And the discoloration caused by the lichens and moss that often grow on its exposed surfaces suggests the unfinished work of unseen artists.

This rock retains the heat of the sun throughout the night. For that reason the orchards of Yakima that are surrounded by outcroppings of it are quite free from frosts that kill fruit less favorably located. For that reason also, rattlesnakes are sometimes found curled on lava rock, warming their bellies.

Once a rattler, so positioned, struck at me. I was standing on a steep hillside, shoulder high to a ledge of rimrock. I heard the rattle, and from the comer of my eye I saw him coiled and ready to strike, not more than two feet from my cheek. As he struck I jumped, lost my footing, and rolled forty or fifty feet down the ravine. Remembering, I still seem to feel his hissing breath near my ear.

That was carelessness. For we who were raised in the environment of the Columbia lava know the risks of the rattler. All up and down the Ahtanum, Tieton, and Naches were stories of fishermen who were bitten on the fingers or face when they grasped lava ledges above them without first exploring the top. One moves warily through this lava rock country.

The rattlesnake—Wak-puch—is not entirely evil. Unlike other poisonous snakes, he is sufficiently friendly to speak before he strikes, to give notice of his plans. And he much prefers to escape man than to attack him. His attack is only to repel a trespass. This is his domain, his ancestral home. He was here long before man. Hence there is reason why he can speak with authority. Moreover, according to the lore of the Yakimas, he has magical powers. He hears what people say and can avenge insults. To this day the Yakimas are superstitious about killing him. Thus on these earlier explorations of the foothills the rattler added mystery, suspense, and magic to the land of lava rock and sagebrush.

When I walked the foothills of Yakima on wintry nights I would often build a bonfire of sagebrush at the base of an outcropping of rimrock. There I would sit, my back to the rock, protected from the wind, hoping the warmth of the fire would not awaken a den of rattlers with the false message that an early spring had arrived.

I discovered on my early hikes that the moods of the foothills are as variable as the seasons of the year or the hours of the day. In the spring they have a light green tinge. Later they turn to yellows and browns when the cheatgrass (Bromus tectorum) becomes a dry husk and when the bunchgrass cures on the stalk. One who sees them casually from a Pullman car would rate them dreary and dull. Theodore Winthrop, the first white man to cross over the Washington Cascades from the west described these foothills in Canoe and Saddle in 1853 as a "large monotony." But they have great charm for those who come to know them.

In the afternoon sun they can appear as soft and smooth as a lady's velvet gown. In the gathering haze of a storm they can be a bluish-green in the distance, somber and threatening. At sunrise after a storm they often glisten like a hillside of ripe grain. In the fall they take on a mustardy yellow hue.

Clouds can transform them from a drab to a warm, colorful backdrop for the valley. And the transformation can come as fast as the conception of life itself. A setting sun can turn their dull brown to red, orange, or blue. Those who were raised under the spell of the Green Mountains, the Berkshires, or the White Mountains would have difficulty in accommodating themselves to the poverty of our barren foothills. But one who watches them closely for an hour on a summer evening will see as many different moods as man himself has in a day.

It was a real ordeal for me to walk them in the dead of summer. Then they were parched and dry. They offered no shade from the hot sun and no springs or creeks where thirst could be quenched. Then the rattlesnake seemed to thrive. But in the spring, fall, and winter the foothills were interesting places to explore; my exercises on their slopes were then more fun than ordeal.

In the spring the tender leaves of the sage appeared. Blossoms of the bitterbrush painted streaks of yellow through the sage. In the draws and ravines the western ryegrass sent up new shoots. The earliest of the wild flowers was the pepper-and-salt, the diminutive member of the *Lomatiums*. It often flowered under the snow as the trailing arbutus does in New England. A soft carpet of violets, buttercups, yellow bells, and eye grasses would appear. But these were fragile flowers that hardly had a chance to taste the sweetness of life before they died. Then came the dwarf phlox and the delicate shooting stars. The lupine, dwarf sunflowers, sage pinks, and blue bells were hardier specimens and lingered longer. But they too were usually gone by June, leaving some relics behind. The relics were the pods of lupine that were poisonous to stock, and the dry leaves of the sunflower plant that rustled and rattled when I walked through them. That sound always startled me with the thought that I had disturbed a snake.

Yet the disappearance of these flowers did not mark the passage of all color that transformed this parched land into a colorful garden. Later came the purple and white asters; the ever-present yarrow; the sedum with its starry flowers of bright yellow; the wild onion, one of the loveliest of all the filigrees of nature, its six petals of deep purple set off by anthers of pale yellow; and the exquisite bitterroot. In some ravines, especially those out Cowiche way, came scatterings of wild rose, elderberry, chokecherry, and mockorange.

I do not envy those whose introduction to nature was lush meadows, lakes, and swamps where life abounds. The desert hills of Yakima had a poverty that sharpened perception. Even a minute violet quickens the heart when one has walked far or climbed high to find it. Where nature is more bountiful, even the tender bitterroot might go unnoticed. Yet when a lone plant is seen in bloom on scabland between batches of bunchgrass and sage, it can transform the spot as completely as only a whole bank of flowers could do in a more lush environment. It is the old relationship between scarcity and value.

These are botanical lessons of the desert which the foothills of Yakima taught me.

In the early spring, when the soft chinooks came up from the southwest, I especially loved to leave the city and take to the foothills. Chinook is the name of Indians who lived on the west side of the Cascades. Early settlers on the reaches of the Columbia called warm, damp winds by the name chinook because such winds ordinarily came from the direction where these Indians lived. Gradually the name was attached to the equatorial trade winds that sweep the north Pacific coast from the southwest. It was the wind I first felt on my cheeks the night Father brought us to Yakima. It was a beneficent wind. And because it sang softly on the ridges and stirred the whole valley to life, it seemed full of romance and enchantment.

The Yakimas have a legend about this wind that centers around the coyote. Coyote (Speel-yi) had a unique symbolic significance among the Yakimas and other tribes that inhabited the Columbia River Valley and the eastern slopes of the Cascades. He was the agent through which the Spirit Chief worked his will. Coyote had supernatural powers. He had only to give the command and a salmon would jump out of the river into his arms. He could change himself into a man, a dish, a board, or any other object. He could also transform others by his magic. Thus the water snipe and the kildee had been women who had rejected his overtures and scorned him, and whom he therefore had decreed should always live near the river and eat fish.

Coyote could be killed and yet return to life in his old form or in a new one. He was wily and smart, with keen insight into human motivations. Compared to him the fox was slow-witted. And though Coyote was crafty and selfish, his main concern was for the welfare of the people.

In each tribe there were a few elderly Indians who could understand the meaning of the howls of the coyote. In this manner the death of some important man in a far-off community was predicted by listening to the changing howls of the coyote. In addition to forecasting future events, these coyote howls were a method of communication between tribes. Thus Alba Showaway, son of Alex, chief of the Yakimas, told me that the death of a leading Indian in Warm Springs, Oregon, hundreds of miles away, was relayed by coyotes the very next day to the medicine men of the Yakimas.

Even today some of the Yakimas will not kill a coyote. Though many of them have discarded their old superstitions because of the bounty and the value of the pelts, a residue of the old attitude persists. Only recently Alba Showaway accidentally killed a coyote. He directed that the hide be removed and the carcass buried deep down in the ground. The next morning he discovered that his dog had dug up the body and was eating it. Shortly thereafter the dog had four puppies, which, according to Alba, died one after the other because the mother had partaken of the flesh of the coyote.

It has been thought that the deification of Coyote was due to the fact that Tyhee, the Spirit Chief of the Indians of the Pacific Northwest, was a revengeful not a beneficent deity. He had no kindness or compassion in his heart. The Indians observed that in the woods the weaker animals survived only by cunning. That was therefore the only route by which they could escape the vengeance of their god. So they deified the weakest and craftiest of all major animals, the coyote, to help them in their struggle for survival.

The legend of the chinook wind runs as follows: The Chinook brothers caused the warm wind to blow from the southwest. The Walla Walla brothers caused a cold wind to blow from the northeast. These two groups were always fighting. The Walla Walla brothers would freeze rivers; the Chinook brothers would thaw them. There would be floods and the people would suffer.

Coyote finally refereed between these warring factors. Every time a contestant fell down, Coyote would cut off his head. At last there were only two left, and Coyote let each live. But Coyote told the Walla Walla that he must blow lightly and never again freeze the people. Coyote told the Chinook that he was the warm breath to melt the winter's snow but that he should blow hardest only at night and that he should always warn the people by blowing first on the ridges of the mountains. Thus Coyote brought a mild climate to the people.

The chinook wind did in fact seem to blow hardest at night. Then it was exhilarating to be abroad. That was one reason why I liked to start for the near-by foothills at dusk, have a light supper at the top of a ridge before a sagebrush fire, and take off into the west.

The outdoors always seemed to come to life at night. These barren windswept ridges, which seemed so dead and dull and listless under the high sun, would fairly murmur in the darkness. When I stood still and listened I could hear the chinook wind rustle the sage and set up in the cheatgrass a faint vibration.

If I stretched out on the ground and listened, I could indeed hear the cheatgrass singing softly in the wind. The sage, too, would join the symphony. It was Peattie who said that the sage lets the wind go softly and tirelessly through its fingers (*The Road of a Naturalist*). But the legend is that, as it does so, it sings in memory of the Idaho Indians whose plains it covered as far as the eye could see and whose mountains it decorated far above the deep-snow line. And the verse of its song is always the same, "Shoshone, Shoshone."

A startled jack rabbit would stomp and give the alarm and make off through the sage. A mouse would scurry for his hole. An owl, interrupted in his prowl, would screech his disapproval of the intrusion and, flapping coarsely, make off into the night. In the early evening I would often see silhouetted against the skyline a coyote standing on some ledge or point of rock. Almost invariably, if I were out for a few hours, his plaintive cry would come floating down to me on the wind from a distant rimrock. And when I disturbed the desert life by putting a dog out in front, the noise was for a place of desolation a veritable commotion.

The air was fragrant with the delicate odor of sage. The chinook always carried, as it swept across this desert area, the distinctively refreshing smell of dusty earth freshly dampened. The chinook was soft and balmy and brought rain to the dry interior of Washington which had become parched when the Cascades rose to such heights that they cut off the moisture from the ocean.

When I tramped the foothills in dead of winter, the pulse of life on the ridges was slow. The wind swept down from Mount Adams and Mount Rainier, cold and piercing. When I bent forward walking into it, I soon would be looking for some black rimrock where I could find protection from the wind and where I could build a sagebrush fire. When I turned around and started home, the strong wind at my back made me feel as if the strength of giants was in me. I strode along the barren ridge in ease, commanding the city that lay at my feet.

Once the valleys hemmed in by these foothills were lakes. Beyond the gap to the north in the Kittitas Valley, there had been a lake. There had also been one in the Selah Valley to the northwest, in the Naches to the northwest, in the Ahtanum to the west, in the Moxee to the east, and in the Lower Valley south of Union Gap. The Indians had first arrived in the valley by boat. They came in the fashion of Noah, bringing with them various types of animals. That was the legend, and A. J. Splawn, early settler and noted authority on the Yakimas, marked the spot where they landed. It was north of the Yakima River on the side of the foothills where there is an oval-shaped spur resembling an inverted canoe.

The Indians lived on the ridges surrounding those lakes. They had difficulty with their food supply. Wishpoosh, a giant beaver, was abroad in the land. He took possession of the lakes north of Yakima. He was a vicious monster. He molested and devoured every living thing that passed his way. He was so dangerous that the people could not fish the lakes.

When Coyote came to this region he found the people in the midst of plenty of uncaught fish and on the verge of famine. So he decided to help them by destroying Wishpoosh. He took a strong spear and lashed it on his arm. He then went hunting for Wishpoosh. He found him asleep by the shore of the lake north of Yakima and at once drove the spear deep into his body. Wishpoosh, enraged, dived into the lake and went to the bottom, taking Coyote with him. There began a struggle for life or death between these powerful gods.

They plunged through the lake, tearing a gap in the foothills to the south. They went from lake to lake, crashing against ridge after ridge. Through the gaps they created, the whole region was drained of water.

There are geologic facts that may be the roots from which some of these legends have stemmed. The first land of the Far West was the Blue Mountains of eastern Oregon and the Siskiyous of southern Oregon and northern California. They started to emerge during the long Cretaceous period, from about sixty million to seventy million years ago, when most of Europe was still under the sea. Then came the Rockies and the Cascades. Before the end of the Cretaceous period the Cascades had become a dike, shutting out the ocean and creating a great inland sea that washed the western slopes of the Rockies and later was divided into a series of vast lakes. By the beginning of the Tertiary period, the Cascades had not reached an elevation sufficient to exclude the warm, moist air from the Pacific. The Gulf of Mexico reached far to the north. Moreover, much of Alaska was probably then under water, making it possible for the Japanese current to flow northeast to Greenland and eliminate all snow and ice between the Pacific Northwest and the Arctic Ocean. These great inland areas were thus subtropical. There the palm tree and sequoia flourished; there the rhinoceros and saber-toothed tiger roamed.

But the Cascades did not remain a dike. They continued to emerge from the sea, casting off the sand and mud of the ocean bed, and reached an elevation that cut off the moisture of the ocean from the interior. The Alaska range pushed its backbone above the waters and shut off the Japanese current from the northern reaches of the continent. The interior country changed in climate, fauna, and flora. As folds of the earth rose and tilted, lakes were tipped like huge saucepans and emptied of their waters. Hot, molten lava overran others and destroyed them. Then came a new series of lakes. This was in Pleistocene time, about a million and a half years ago. For some reason not fully understood, water backed up along the Columbia and its tributaries and formed large fresh-water lakes. Water rose to about 1,250 feet above sea level.

Probably the greatest of these was Lewis Lake, which lay in the Yakima Valley and reached far to the south and west. Icebergs that floated on it carried a cargo of boulders of granite, gneiss, and basalt and dropped them hither and yon across the valley. The herds of horses and camels that had inhabited the area were driven south by the cold. The mastodon, mammoth, mylodon, and broad-faced ox appeared. When the glaciers receded, great floods occurred. These floods followed the channels that had been dug in preglacial days and accelerated the creation of the drainage system of the Columbia. The vast region drained by the Columbia was spotted with a whole series of lakes, rimmed by foothills and ridges like those surrounding Yakima. These lakes became connected by drainage links from one to another, until they all finally linked up into one continuous stream that wore its way to the ocean through all barriers, including the Cascades. Thus was the mighty Columbia River created.

The Yakima had the same kind of origin, though it grew on a lesser scale. It, too, wore through ridges separating various lakes and linked them into one drainage system. Most rivers run around mountains or follow the contours of their base. But the Yakima was unorthodox— like the Columbia, it went cross-country, cutting through at least seven ridges or foothills as it reached out serpentine fashion to join the Columbia at Pasco.

The reason for this, geologists say, is that the surface movements of the hills, beginning in Pliocene time, and the erosive action of the water apparently were closely synchronized. The uplift of the ridges was so slow that the water was able to keep its spillways open and wear away the rock as fast as it rose in the channels.

When the region was drained, the hot, dry breath of the desert touched the land and parched it. The sagebrush appeared, perhaps from some airway of the world, and covered the land in a gray-green blanket. Wind and water and frost began a process of erosion that exposed the dark lava. It broke through the garment of topsoil that had covered it and disclosed patches of its black body throughout the farthest reaches of this desert land.

There are two early trips to the foothills that stand out specially in my memory. One was in early spring. I had left town before dusk and climbed the barren ridge west of Selah Gap. On the way up I had crossed a draw and caught the sweet odor of the mockorange. The species around Yakima is *Philadelphus lewisii*, discovered in 1806 by Lewis and Clark and named in honor of Lewis. It is the state flower of Idaho. It has four or five cream-white petals with a golden center of bright yellow stamens. Elk and deer browse it. The Indians used its slender shoots for arrow shafts, hence its other name, Indian arrow-wood. In the darkness I could vaguely see the lone shrub that filled this draw with the fragrance of orange blossoms. It stood six feet high and in this barren ravine seemed strangely out of place because of the delicacy of its fragrance.

The night was clear and the moon had just reached the horizon. Mount Adams loomed in the west, "high-humped," as Lewis and Clark aptly described it when they saw it on April 2, 1806. Along the ridge of the Cascades to the north was Mount Rainier, cold, aloof, and forbidding. Below at my feet the lights of the town had come on, blinking like stars of a minor firmament. A faint streak of light, sparkling in the moonlight, marked the course of the Yakima as it wound its way across the valley, through dark splotches of sumac, cottonwood, and willow.

Above the dark rim of the foothills were the stars of the universe. They were the same stars that saw these valleys and hills and mountains rise from the murk of the ocean, reaching for the sun. They saw the Columbia lava, hot and steaming, pour in molten form across this land again and again, scorching to cinders everything it touched, burying great ponderosa pine four and five feet thick under its deep folds, and filling the sky with smoke that finally drew a curtain over the sun. They saw a subtropical land touched by the chill of the Arctic and rimmed with ice and snow. They saw the mighty Columbia and the Yakima grow from driblets to minor drainage canals to great rivers. They saw the glaciers recede and floods come. After the floods they saw the emergence of a desert that some unseen hand had sown with fragrant sage and populated with coyotes, rabbits, kangaroo rats, sage hens, sage sparrows, desert sparrows, bluebirds, and doves. They saw the Indians first appear on the horizon to the north, spreading out to all parts of the continent in their long trek from Asia. And thousands of years later they saw some newcomers arrive, the ones that fought, quarreled, and loved, the ones that built houses and roads and planted orchards, the ones that erected spires and lifted their eyes to the sky in prayer.

On the foothills that night I think I got my first sense of Time. I began to appreciate some of the lessons that geology taught. In the great parade of events that this region unfolded, man was indeed insignificant. He appeared under this firmament only briefly and then disappeared. His transit was indeed too short for geological time to measure.

As I walked the ridge that evening, I could hear the chinook on distant ridges before it reached me. Then it touched the sage at my feet and made it sing. It brushed my cheeks, warm and soft. It ran its fingers through my hair and rippled away in the darkness. It was a friendly wind, friendly to man throughout time. It was beneficent, carrying rain to the desert. It was soft, bringing warmth to the body. It had almost magical qualities, for it need only lightly touch the snow to melt it.

It became for me that night a measure of the kindliness of the universe to man, a token of the hospitality that awaits man when he puts foot on this earth. It became for me a promise of the fullness of life to him who, instead of shaking his fist at the sky, looks to it for health and strength and courage.

That night I felt at peace. I felt that I was a part of the universe, a companion to the friendly chinook that brought the promise of life and adventure. That night, I think, there first came to me the germ of a philosophy of life: that man's best measure of the universe is in his hopes and his dreams, not his fears; that man is a part of a plan, only a fraction of which he, perhaps, can ever comprehend.

The other trip was in April when I walked the ridge north of Yakima on a Sunday afternoon. Below me the Yakima Valley was a vast garden in bloom. The peach and cherry blossoms were out in all their glory. The valley resembled a giant bowl of short-stemmed flowers. The pink and white blossoms covered the bottom and sent traces of their fragrance even to the ridges. It was a delicately perfumed scene. Nature had brought a whole valley to life in a rush, changing its color, filling it with the hope of things to come, making it pregnant with the bloom of a new crop.

I looked down, and there in the sage at my feet was a scattering of the bitterroot or rockrose. It is a gentle membrane that the Creator has fashioned out of dust and made to decorate even places of desolation. It is a low plant with waxy flowers, delicate pink with a rib of darker hue. It has a translucent quality that makes it look fragile to the touch, as fragile as the gossamer wings of some tropical butterfly. It is the state flower of Montana. It was collected by Lewis at the mouth of the Lou Lou Fork of the Bitterroot River in Montana. Its roots are the spatlum known to Indians, explorers, and early settlers as valued food. They do indeed contain a rich supply of starch, and when eaten (dried and raw) have that taste. But it is a taste that is slightly bitter; hence its name. Its leaves dry up and vanish when the flowers appear. And the blossoms open with the sun and close with darkness. I never see the bitterroot blooming among the sage without feeling that I should take off my hat and stand in adoration at the wondrous skill of the Creator. I'll always remember the words of the artist who said, "I have grown to feel that there is nothing more amazing about a personal God than there is about the blossoming of the gorgeous little bitterroot."

A strong wind suddenly came up from the south. It brought the dust of Pasco and Prosser on its wings, and produced small flurries of petals from the fruit blossoms as it swept across the orchards. Behind the wind came dark clouds splattering rain on the Lower Valley. With the rain there were forked tongues of lightning that played along the ridges across the valley from me; then there was thunder that rolled endlessly as it echoed off the hills of the Ahtanum and Naches. In a little while the storm veered, turned east over Moxee, and slowly melted away on the eastern horizon. The sun appeared and the flowering basin of the valley once more lay in splendor below me.

To the west Adams and Rainier stood forth in power and beauty—monarchs of every peak in their range. The backbone of the Cascades was clear against the western sky, its slopes and ravines dark blue in the afternoon sun. The distant ridges and canyons seemed soft and friendly. They appeared to hold untold mysteries and to contain solitude many times more profound than that of the barren ridge on which I stood. They offered streams and valleys and peaks to explore, snow fields and glaciers to conquer, wild animals to know. That afternoon I felt that they extended me an invitation—an invitation to get acquainted with them, an invitation to tramp their trails and sleep in their high basins.

My heart filled with joy, for I knew I could accept the invitation. I would have legs and lungs equal to it.

Coming of Age in Yakima

My love of the mountains, my interest in conservation, my longing for the wilderness—all these were lifetime concerns that were established in my boyhood in the hills around Yakima and in the mountains to the west of it.

Of course, it was not only the natural surroundings of Yakima which influenced me, although my fellow townsmen sometimes denied responsibility for me. When I was named to the Supreme Court by President Franklin D. Roosevelt in 1939, the Yakima *Daily Republic* wrote an editorial entitled "Yakima Not to Blame." The editorial first praised the local schools and their superintendent, A. C. Davis, a very superior man. Next it listed the roll of teachers one by one under whom I had studied, and said good things about each. Finally it stated that if I were judged solely by the education I had received in Yakima, I would have in me nothing but pure strains of Americanism. But alas, noted the writer, I had developed symptoms of strange *isms* that were not compatible with Americanism. Where I got infected with these *isms* was not known; perhaps in Washington, D.C. The conclusion was, "We want to go on record as saying that Yakima is not to blame."

The *Daily Republic* was owned by W. W. Robertson, a most reactionary man. The editorial was written by N. K Buck, one-time police judge and later mayor. Buck wrote editorials and small news items for Robertson, and their styles were remarkably similar. But this column about me was written with particular verve and feeling, for Buck disagreed violently with what he thought were my political and constitutional views. The piece delighted me no end, and I foolishly carried it in my wallet for so long that it finally crumbled away. Unfortunately, someone destroyed that entire edition of the paper after a few hundred copies were run off, and apparently no copies are extant.

The conclusion of the editorial was humorous, but wrong. The Yakima system was in large measure responsible for the kind of person that I became, in the sense that its teachers were quickening influences that helped me see the dimensions of the world of that day. In the

Columbia Grade School, under Grace Shrader and Pearl Hibarger, I first became aware of the beauty and power of words. They read poetry and made it musical. They read prose and brought to it magical qualities. We were much too young then to learn how to put prose or poetry to effective use ourselves, but life acquired new dimensions when the dictionary became an instrument of conquest and we discovered how to appreciate the words of others.

Louise DeGraff, in my eighth grade, taught American history with emphasis on the economic system. We did not learn much about depreciation or depletion or the relation of wages to profits. But we got some glimmering of the problems of costs and profits and the historic place of business in the American scheme. Miss DeGraff neither made business a graven image to worship nor did she make us think it was suspect. Rather, she taught what business was and some basic things about its anatomy and how it had helped shape the American destiny. I was to learn about the robber barons later. Under Louise DeGraff, I made my first distillation of facts; and from her I received, I think, my first lesson in the nice distinction between the relevant and the irrelevant in any analysis.

Yakima High School, which I entered in the fall of 1912, was a joy. A. C. Davis was then principal; Susan Anthon (later a columnist for the Yakima *Daily Republic)* taught botany; C. A. Palmer, physics; Lucille James and Elizabeth Pryor, English; Lillian Wheeler, Latin; and Rose M. Boening, history. As a newspaperwoman, Susan Anthon came to represent a conventional point of view, yet she pleasantly tolerated me in later years. As a teacher, she introduced me to a new world of flora, where I discovered that many flowers, trees, and shrubs of the Pacific Northwest had marched all the way from Asia to become established here. From Mr. Palmer we learned about some of the phenomena of physics in our daily lives. From Lucille James, I acquired a love of Latin and gained such proficiency that I could converse or orate in that tongue by the time I was a senior. From her also, and from Elizabeth Pryor, I discovered great tides of history in our literature and learned something of their meaning.

Miss Pryor also taught public speaking and debate; in retrospect, I marvel at her ability to take a slightly crippled, nervous, frightened young man and give him poise and stage presence. I became such an excellent orator under her tutelage that I was selected for the school finals in my sophomore year. I had a beautiful oration and I practiced it to perfection.

When the big night arrived, I walked onto the platform with the two other contestants, sure of victory. The others spoke first, increasing my confidence. But as I was being introduced, my mind went blank. I could remember only the first sentence of my speech. I stood in the spotlight, saying it over and over again, each time with more emphasis. The rest was utterly gone. I had learned to speak only from memory, not yet knowing how to extemporize. After what seemed an eternity, I gave up, tears welling to my eyes. I left the platform in utter humiliation, disappeared into the darkness of the night and did not return home for hours. By the end of another year, however, Elizabeth Pryor had not only restored my confidence but also introduced me to the rough and tumble of debate—a contest that I greatly enjoyed.

Lillian Wheeler and Rose M. Boening were also inspirations. Miss Wheeler made Latin a thing of beauty, and she tidied up our minds, making perfectionists of us. Miss Boening, in history, emphasized not what happened but *why* it happened. She made the question *why?* ring in our ears. America now turned on a different axis for me, as ambition, greed, self-sacrifice, lust for power, face-saving, all these and many more motives gave new dimensions to the history in our texts. Years later I was to discover Thorstein Veblen and John Dewey, Underhill Moore and Karl Llewellyn at Columbia, Robert M. Hutchins, Thurman Arnold, and Charles E. Clark at Yale, asking the same questions about law. I have always thought that Miss Boening of Yakima started my bent toward what was later dubbed "sociological jurisprudence."

Mr. Palmer, the physics teacher, coached track as well. By the time I was a junior, my slightly impaired physical condition had pretty well gone, so I went out for track. I chose the mile run as my specialty. I never came in better than third and I never quite broke five minutes. Years later Paavo Nurmi of Finland became my hero when he set the world's mark at 4:10.4. Once when I was in Helsinki, I walked the city over trying to locate him to express my admiration, but I never did meet up with him. When Roger Bannister of England broke the four-minute barrier in 1954, I was amazed. When in 1962 Peter Snell of New Zealand ran it in 3:54.4, I was dumbfounded. And when in 1967 Jim Ryun lowered the outdoor mile to 3:51.1, I gave up wondering. My own five-minute time was to me the outer limit of endurance.

Another powerful force in my high school days was Tony Savage— football and basketball coach. I was too skinny for the former sport, but I had fair success as a basketball center. Tony, who was a hero just out of the University of Washington, became a god to us. He was kind but outspoken, quick to criticize and slow to praise. His tap on the back that meant "well done" was a tremendous reward. His quick, soft reprimand could be crushing. I never felt the full force of it, though my pal Elon Gilbert did. Elon was a quarterback, and try as he did, he never could satisfy Tony. In desperation Tony took Elon aside so that no one else could hear, and said, "Elon, if anyone ever says you played quarterback for the Yakima High School, deny it." Nothing worse ever happened to Elon.

There was a beautiful, wholesome girl in my class whose name was Fern Graham. I was much too busy ever to date her, but she stayed in my thoughts for years. On a debating trip to Ellensburg, I met another lovely young girl, Mildred Barton, with whom I was deeply enamored. Ellensburg was nearly forty miles to the north, however, and I did not see Mildred Barton again until thirty-five years later, when I was autographing my book *Of Men and Mountains* in Seattle. Much to my regret, I went through high school without the benefit of women.

I won many honors in high school, and when our class graduated, the prophecy about me in the yearbook was that I would be President of the United States. Grace Rhine, who made the prophecy, recorded this "vision":

> *Scene IX—Presidential Parade*
> *President: Orville Douglas, in small automobile*
> *Secret Service Men: Russell Nagler and Elmer Carlsen*
> *Senators: Kenneth Coonse, Warren Chase*
> *Representative: Henry Hughes*
> *Reporters: Conrad Alexander and Agnes Scott. Show great*
> *excitement and take down items on shorthand pad.*
> *Directly following: George Butler leading great crowd and*
> *carrying an I.W.W. banner.*
>
> *Secret Service Men come back to arrest George, accusing him*
> *of attempting a riot.*
> *George denies the charge, saying that they intend to be*
> *peaceable.*
> *Reporters rush back madly to get all the news.*
>
> **Curtain**

I graduated first in my class, and while being valedictorian brought me a scholarship to Whitman College, there was another honor that pleased me even more. During my last three years I was in charge of the alarm that brought students to classes, that adjourned classes, and that was used when fire drills were held. The alarm was a huge iron triangle that hung from a rope, and I wielded the iron rod that sounded the alarm and played the tunes. It was a coveted position, for it excused the gong-ringer from the end of every class a few minutes early, and allowed him to arrive a few minutes late. I enjoyed it immensely.

Not all my days in Yakima were quite so glorious. When I was thirteen I became a carrier for the local newspapers—the *Morning Herald* and *Daily Republic.* On Sunday, I handled the Seattle *Post Intelligencer,* too. My employment as carrier for the *Herald* and *P. I.* was somewhat irregular, but I stayed with the *Republic* for some years, delivering it on a scheduled route six afternoons a week for $1.75 a week. When I was in the fruit harvest, I left the orchards to meet the paper's deadline; and in due time, when I went to college, Arthur inherited the same route.

Part of that route was a business section on the east side of town, north of Yakima Avenue between Second Street and the railroad track; the other part was residential, extending from North First east to North Tenth, and north about nine blocks: an area of about eighty-one square blocks. The carrier in those days was a newspaper employee. Should his rolled paper hit a puddle or should he miss the porch, leaving the paper concealed in bushes, the irate householder would call the paper, in which event the company would send a paper out by Western Union at a charge of ten cents, which was deducted from the carrier's weekly check. It did not take many deductions to leave little of $1.75. A severe man—a Mr. Guthrie—supervised us, and we all thought he enjoyed docking our weekly pay check, though we doubtless did him a disservice.

One of my jobs was being pin boy in a bowling alley. This was a job for Friday and Saturday nights. The game was tenpins; and the mechanical pin-setter had not been invented. As I remember it, my fee was ten cents a game. The trick was to get one's feet and legs up quickly, on a ledge above the backboard, for the balls came hard and the pins flew. I watched how skilled bowlers knocked one or more pins down by bouncing another pin off the backboard, but in spite of my early experience, I never amounted to much as a tenpin bowler.

One summer I worked in an ice cream plant, and forever after did not care for ice cream. The men who ran the vats where the ingredients were mixed chewed tobacco, and when either had collected a mouth full of juice he would let go into the vat, saying, "That should beef it up a bit."

While there were many children's parties in Yakima, we were never invited to a single one, and we were far too poor to have one in our own home. We grew up never seeing the inside of another home. In the after years I thought it was a blessing that I had not. For if I had been united with the elite of Yakima even by so tenuous a cord, I might have been greatly handicapped. To be accepted might then have become a goal in later life, an ambition that is often a leveling influence. To be accepted means living in the right area, wearing the right hat, thinking the right way, saying the right thing. What it means in the law is a Dean Acheson or John Foster Dulles or a reactionary president of the Bar Association. They cause all the beauty to disappear in a pontifical emptiness.

One experience of my adolescence enforced my feeling that I had been born on "the wrong side of the railroad tracks." A prominent churchman in town, the father of one of my friends, was bent on ridding Yakima of prostitutes and bootleggers. The prostitutes were scattered in brothels along South Front Street in establishments that advertised "Rooms" or "Hotel," most of which have now been reclaimed as "Gospel Missions," carrying luminous signs: *Jesus Saves.* The bootleggers were supposed to operate there, too. At that time Yakima, having the benefit of local option, allowed beer to be sold but no hard liquor. The bootleggers, however, brought the whiskey to everyone, including high churchmen and other members of the elite.

This particular reformer had several sons, my age and older, and he and they would have made an admirable vice squad. But as he told me, he would have none of that; he wanted to "save" his sons from being polluted by these evil people. That is why he approached me. Would I, for one dollar an hour, spend Saturday and Sunday nights "working Front Street"? My instructions were, "See if you can get a woman to solicit you. See if you can buy a drink from someone. When the night is done, check in at the office, execute an affidavit, and the police will move in."

And so a teen-age boy became a stool pigeon in a red-light district. Never did I have such a shabby feeling, and in the end, never did I feel sorrier for people than I did for those I was supposed to entrap. I met voluptuous women whose faces were etched in sorrow, suffering and fear. Their tears never seemed very far beneath their coarse laughs and dirty stories. The men who brought "white mule" in gallon glass jars for sale to these brothels were shadows respected neither by the prostitutes nor by themselves. They had hunted looks; they swore softly under their breath; their eyes never met mine. I shamefully bought "one shot" glasses full of the fiery stuff for a dollar each, putting it to my lips and then tossing it into a basket or potted plant or under a sofa when no one was looking.

In time I came to feel a warmth for all these miserable people, something I never felt for the high churchman who hired me. They were scum that society had produced—misfits, maladjusted, disturbed, and really sick. What orphanages had turned them out? What broken homes had produced them? Which of these prostitutes had first been seduced by her father, causing all standards of propriety and decency to be destroyed? Which of them had turned to prostitution and bootlegging as a result of grinding poverty?

As much as my family needed the money, a few weeks of this job were all I could endure. As the evening hours passed along South Front Street, I heard stories about my employer whose sons were too precious to expose to crime and criminals. South Front Street did not know that he was financing stool pigeons; it heard, however, of his other doings. He had put enterprise after enterprise together, including many orchards, in his own lawless way—ruthlessly foreclosing mortgages, ruthlessly forcing competitors to the wall, ruthlessly reducing wages. I went to South Front Street to entrap a low, petty class of criminals; I discovered on South Front Street that on the day of the final reckoning there was one high churchman who would have to make a more severe accounting than they.

From this experience two impressions burned themselves into my memory. First was the only class consciousness I ever had. Most of my own experiences prior to this one, and virtually all of them subsequent to it, spelled equality as the dominant American theme. But South Front Street in Yakima made me realize that there were those even in this free land who thought that some men were more equal than others, that their sons were to be preferred over the sons of other people less worthy. Second was a residue of resentment of which I have never quite got rid—resentment against hypocrites in church clothes who raise their denunciations against the petty criminals, while their own sins mount high. This feeling somehow aligned me emotionally with the miserable people who make up the chaff of society. I never sought their company, nor engaged in their tricks or traffic, nor spent my hours with them. I think, however, that I have always been quicker to defend them than I would have been but for the high churchman of Yakima.

Later I had an ice route that included South Front Street. I drove a one-horse wagon filled with three-hundred-pound blocks of ice that I sawed, then cut with a pick to fit each box. Once, when the tailgate was down and I was inside serving a customer, the horse got frightened and bolted away, strewing ice cakes down the middle of the dirt road for the next two blocks.

Usually the job was simpler—removing food from iceboxes to make room for the ice and then re-packing the icebox. The "girls" in these "rooming houses" along South Front were friendly and garrulous and very unattractive. They had somehow or other missed out on love and security. "Bring on your ice, honey," one would shout, "and I'll throw open my community chest." Yet they "belonged" to their group, and that fact of belonging produced a keen sense of togetherness. There was friendship and compassion in these houses of ill repute. The women were vulgar in one sense, but they were also kind and tolerant and tender. I saw more of those qualities there on South Front Street than I later found on more sedate avenues.

The story goes that one of these Yakima prostitutes finally decided to leave the "house." She had been there twenty years and had made many friends. The prospective parting promised to be sorrowful. So the "girls" decided to give her a farewell sociable. There was much merriment at the party, the cheap booze flowing freely. At the end the heroine was in tears.

"Then why don't you stay?" her associates importuned.

"I love you all. I enjoy the work. Everyone has been very kind to me. But my legs and my arches are getting me. I can't climb those damn stairs any more."

The memories of the brothels of Front Street in Yakima came back to me years later during my travels. On a visit to Casablanca, I saw a lovely Moorish town with white adobe houses where the Establishment, then French, lived; down below were the miserable huts, made out of pieces of tin and packing cases, of the poor majority. The French word for the area was Bidonville, meaning the oil-drum slums. High on the hill overlooking the squalor was what a Frenchman called "the best investment in North Africa." It was a brothel whose tentacles stretched into the elite of Paris and her institutions. I saw the same in Saigon, where French development projects exalted two things: plush gambling casinos and deluxe brothels. These too were owned by the Establishment in Paris. The influence corrupted both Casablanca and Saigon, tying into the underworld, putting petty local officials on its payroll, and corrupting the police.

I learned that this industry was not a French monopoly. The Chinese had similar rich projects in the sector of free enterprise in Southeast Asia, notably Singapore. America had a like bent. In Cuba we built brothels of splendor and American finance reaped huge dividends. We paid off Batista for his cooperation, and we made our Havana brothels "first class" by barring Cuban males from them, though staffing them, of course, with Cuban girls.

On my later world travels I learned that slavery still thrives in the world. In the 1960s there were probably four million slaves, white, brown, black, and yellow. Of these people, the women have usually been kidnapped. They fill the brothels of Turkey and Iraq. In Damascus, I was offered by a broker not only a mistress but a cook, a housemaid, and a chauffeur from the black market for slaves.

What I had seen as a boy in Yakima, I later saw on a vast scale across the country. Our brothels are financed by our banks and protected by real estate lobbies and owners who reap huge profits. That means a close working relationship between the underworld and our Establishment. If anyone doubts it, talk to the mayors and governors who tried to close these places down and found out from what sources the great opposition came.

I was too naive to know these things as a boy in Yakima. But since then I have often wondered who owned and financed the Front Street houses. My crusading friend who hired me did not last long. His campaign fizzled out in a few months. I now suspect, though I do not know, that the financial and real estate Establishment bore down on him.

Charles Darwin wrote that "a man who dares waste one hour of time has not discovered the value of life." It was, I think, the same idea that kept me out of the pool halls of Yakima. After visiting them a few times, and finding only indolent men with empty talk, I put these places behind me forever. The Yakima public library was much more interesting. In this squat, square building, donated by the Eastern philanthropist Andrew Carnegie, I was introduced to all sorts of new books by the lovely Lucille James, my former English teacher, then serving as the librarian. Darwin, Perry, and other great explorers could be read, Shakespeare consumed, and American history absorbed here.

These were the years, too, in which I began to read newspapers regularly, and to take an avid interest in politics. It was the era of the muckrakers, and of such giants as Bryan, Borah, Johnson, and Pinchot. My appetite was whetted by the very real three-way fight over the Presidency in 1912, and I came to regard myself as a Woodrow Wilson progressive, a stand I later regretted when I saw Wilson's repressive policies in the area of civil liberties.

An earlier Democratic standard bearer, William Jennings Bryan, became my hero for a while, although disillusionment eventually set in. Bryan was probably the first national politician I ever saw in person. I remember hearing him speak at a chautauqua in Yakima.

In those days chautauquas were an important summer forum. They had spread from Lake Chautauqua, New York, where they were originally a sort of vacation camp assembly for Bible study and incidental visiting speakers. Chautauquas came to the Far West, where they were very popular. Bryan often toured the circuit, and usually kept his audiences spellbound.

The big brown tent where Bryan spoke was hot that summer I heard him, and the great man perspired profusely. To keep himself going during the two hours he spoke, he relied upon a pitcher of ice water and a huge handkerchief with which he wiped his brow. I do not remember much of what Bryan said; his ideas were largely lost because I became mesmerized by his voice. It was deep and solemn, with a wide range, and he could make it soft and pleading or angry like a torrent. I tried to follow his words for sentence structure, for grammar, for figures of speech, but I remember only his general tirades against rum and whiskey, and the tones in which he extolled the virtues of water.

I found this excerpt from what must have been a typical Bryan speech:

> *Water is the daily need of every living thing. It ascends from the seas, obedient to the summons of the sun, and, descending, showers blessing upon the earth; it gives of its sparkling beauty to the fragrant flower; its alchemy transmutes base clay into golden grain; it is the canvas upon which the finger of the Infinite traces the radiant bow of promise. It is the drink that refreshes and adds no sorrow with it—Jehovah looked upon it at creation's dawn and said, "It is good."*

In later years a man who talked two hours would be deserted by his audience, but in those days Americans were not in such a hurry. Radio and TV had not arrived. The human voice, always entertaining, meant listening to a live speaker. There were no amplifiers; a man had to have lungs and larynx to match. Bryan kept the tentful of people so quiet on that blistering day, one could have heard a pin drop, and the admission price was so low that even we could afford to go. It was only years afterward that I wondered whether his ideas had any relevance to the world I knew.

In the meantime, Bryan was very influential in the choice of Woodrow Wilson as the 1912 Democratic nominee, and Wilson made Bryan his first Secretary of State. Bryan, who was greatly interested in foreign affairs, had always been anti-colonial and anti-tariff; now, in his new position, he tried to negotiate treaties providing cooling-off periods for disputes among nations, and arbitration by international commission. I had admired his earlier speeches for his style, rather than his substance; reading about him in these years left me with a more favorable impression of the man.

Although Bryan resigned from Wilson's Cabinet in protest over the President's second war note to Germany, he did not really fall from grace in my eyes until he prosecuted John Scopes in Tennessee in the 1920s for teaching Darwinian theory. Years later I found Bryan preaching under palm trees in Florida, and at the end of his sermon, selling municipal bonds to hapless investors. These bonds and their committees I investigated while with the Securities and Exchange Commission. Bryan, my idol, turned out to be nothing but a bag of wind, after all.

Hiram Johnson, another one of my heroes, was different. Bryan was once asked who was the greatest speaker, he or Hiram Johnson. Bryan replied, "When I speak, I can draw ten thousand persons and so can your governor. When I speak in an arena, I can fill the arena and so can your governor. But when Governor Johnson speaks, the people believe him."

I never heard Johnson speak, but his ideas had wings. As governor of California, when he issued his famous proclamation summoning the people of that state to enact massive reform measures in 1911, he was a knight in shining armor to a fourteen-year-old boy. He inveighed against the Southern Pacific. He proposed the initiative and referendum, free schoolbooks, a workmen's compensation law, a railroad commission to put an end to oppressive practices, a limitation on hours of work in mines and other industries, a child labor law, and a law restricting the hours of work for women. Hiram Johnson got these laws passed. He also promoted and obtained a law prohibiting employers from putting discharged employees on black lists. I did not understand all the nuances in his proclamations nor did I thoroughly comprehend all his measures, but he was a thundering voice that I admired more than I did the Establishment in Yakima.

Hiram Johnson was a Republican, and in 1912 he ran as Vice-President with Teddy Roosevelt on the Bull Moose ticket, which he had helped to form when his wing of the party split off from the more conservative Taft. This did not diminish my admiration for Johnson, however, and I was pleased when in 1916 he was elected to the United States Senate from California, serving nearly five terms and dying in office in 1945. As a young senator, Johnson opposed conscription for the Armed Forces. He denounced those who "with great enthusiasm" would "send men into battle" and "blow to pieces humanity," while at the same time professing the "most tender regard for individual rights" and "descant upon the fundamental principles of the nation" when it comes to "property rights of the individual." Hiram Johnson also led the fight against the regime of censorship in 1917. I was to meet him years later in Washington, D.C

A boyhood hero who was to play an important role in my life many years later was William E. Borah of Idaho. Borah was elected to the Senate in 1906, and served until his death in 1940. I did not know him

personally while I was growing up in Yakima, of course; I only read about him.

I knew that Borah had championed the cause of an unpopular minority, the Mormons, and that he had led the fight to bring them full suffrage. My first impression of Borah was not entirely favorable, however. Shortly after taking his seat, he was appointed special assistant to the prosecutor in the trial of "Big Bill" Haywood, an early labor organizer accused of the 1905 bomb murder of the governor of Idaho. Darrow defended Haywood.

The trial, held at Boise, Idaho, in 1907, was big news throughout the Northwest, and dominated all the newspapers of the region. I was only nine years old at the time, but I remember the flavor of the stories. The actual assassination had been a tragic episode in the ongoing conflict between the Idaho mine operators and the mine workers, and actually, Haywood was only one of four men allegedly involved in the crime. Haywood, already denounced by President Teddy Roosevelt as an "undesirable citizen," had been secretly indicted in Idaho. With the connivance of Colorado officials, Haywood was arrested in Colorado late at night when the courts of that state were closed. He was denied access to counsel, then rushed to Idaho by a special train that stopped only at isolated spots to take on water and fuel.

The trial was a tense affair. Absentee mine owners, bitterly opposed to unionism, were on one side. On the other side was the Western Federation of Miners, who were fiercely opposed to the management. Haywood was their militant secretary. The clashes between the two groups had been numerous and bloody. Management had often called out the militia on its side, and sometimes the miners had retaliated with violence. Blood had run on both sides. The murdered ex-governor had used the National Guard to break a strike some six years earlier, and when he was killed, people concluded that the miners were "getting even." Haywood however, was probably innocent.

Borah's side lost its case against Haywood; Darrow won. I remembered both men for their stature and courage. I remembered Darrow for his defense, which was unusually eloquent. Darrow, too, became an early hero; my admiration for his skill and courage in taking on unpopular causes grew as the years went by.

At about the same time, as a result of an episode which took place in Nampa, Idaho, Borah acquired in my mind some of Darrow's stature. There were then not many Blacks in the Pacific Northwest. One young

Black was the mascot of a baseball team in Idaho which played a game at Nampa, a railroad town twenty miles from Boise, the state capital. He had shot and seriously wounded a policeman, claiming the officer had kicked him off the sidewalk. The Black was jailed, and word came to Borah in Boise that a lynching was being readied. Although there were no scheduled trains that would get him there, Borah immediately persuaded a train crew to rush him to Nampa, where he raced from the station directly to the jail, and mounting the steps, addressed the crowd. Though repeatedly jeered, Borah was persistent and kept on orating. As he talked, an ally of his obtained the jail keys from the constable. Unlocking the jail, the ally appeared with the young man, and while Borah pleaded with the mob, the Black was marched through the crowd to the train in safety and taken to the security of Boise.

Years later I met Senator Borah in Washington, D.C. When I was being considered for a seat on the United States Supreme Court, it was Borah who claimed me as a Westerner, and thereby smoothed the path to my nomination. My tie to him went deep.

A fourth boyhood hero was Gifford Pinchot. He was Chief of the United States Forest Service when I was young. Pinchot and Teddy Roosevelt were in my eyes romantic woodsmen. I did not then know about Pinchot's "multiple use" philosophy, which, as construed, allowed timber companies, grazing interests, and even miners to destroy much of our forest heritage under the rationalization of "balanced use." I only knew that Pinchot was a driving force behind setting aside wilderness sanctuaries in an effort to save them from immediate destruction by reckless loggers. I was so thrilled by Pinchot's example that I perhaps would have made forestry my career had the choice been made in my high school days. I kept vaguely in touch with Pinchot in later years, admiring him for his role as governor of Pennsylvania in the twenties and again in the thirties.

I was to meet Pinchot in Washington, D.C., and of my boyhood public heroes—Hiram Johnson, William Borah, and Gifford Pinchot—Pinchot was the most enduring influence in my life.

Fly vs. Bait

Fly-fishing for trout has no equal. And of all the fly-fishing, the dry fly is supreme. The dry fly floats lightly on the water, going with the current under overhanging willows or riding like a dainty sail on the ruffled surface of a lake. It bounces saucily, armed for battle but looking as innocent as any winged insect that rises from underneath the surface or drops casually from a willow or sumac into a stream or pond.

There is the split second when the trout rises to the fly—an instant that is flush with tenseness. The trout may rush from the bottom so hard that he leaves the water, as a salmon does when, fresh from the ocean, he jumps over and again to free his body of lice. Or the trout may come up to it gently and take it in his lips softly, as a lady would a cherry. Or he may more discreetly whirl under it, sucking it down to him as he turns in the excitement of the hunt.

However it happens, the heart stands still. There is the tenth of a second when the trout has the fly in his lips and before he rejects it as false. The anxious thought races through the mind, Have I too much slack line on the water to set the hook? If the reflexes of the fisherman are fast, and no slack line is on the water, then he sets the hook in a flash. A trout so hooked is not hurt, for it is usually his lips alone that are involved. Thus he has the full use of his energies and an excellent chance to get away. The game's the thing, with victory going to the one most skilled. One three-pound rainbow caught on a No. 12 or No. 14 dry fly with a 2x or 3x 9-foot leader is worth three or four caught with worms or salmon eggs or on the hardware of spoons or plugs.

It was experience with bug hatches that committed me to fly-fishing. I saw my first one at Fish Lake, headwaters for the Bumping River in the Cascades, on a warm July day when I was a boy. My brother Art and I had walked in from Bumping Lake and tossed off our hot horseshoe packs. We were lying on the shore, dozing. There was not a cloud in the sky and the lake was smooth. In a little while a breeze came up, causing a lapping of water at our feet. It was seductive. But before we had a chance to drop off to sleep, I heard a splash. I bolted upright and saw before me a calm and quiet lake come suddenly to life. A bug hatch was on. The nymphs or naiads of a species of the mayfly had left the bottom of the lake, worked their way to the surface, and spread their wings. Thousands of them were now playing the surface of the lake, rising, then falling and dipping the surface, flitting in pairs, dropping fresh eggs in the water. They seemed to be rushing to sow the seed that would perpetuate their line, lest the brief and hurried minutes of their own lives be expended on less important matters.

An old dugout canoe at Fish Lake went with the prospector's cabin that stood there for years. It was fashioned from a cedar log in the manner in which the Indians of the Pacific Northwest made their boats. It was constructed, I believe, by a prospector, though it looked pretty much like the Indian canoes that Lewis and Clark described in their *Journals*. We carried it to the lake and settled down to fishing. We fished a wet mayfly. We started fishing in the nick of time, for the hatch was over in thirty minutes, ending as abruptly as it had started. But in that time we got a dozen cutthroat, eight to twelve inches.

The bug hatch is as old as insect life. The eggs laid on or above the water sink to the bottom and lie dormant for a period. In the case of mayflies it will be a few days, a few weeks, or a few months, depending largely on the species. The nymph or naiad that emerges from the egg hides in the bottom of the stream or lake, or hangs to rocks in swift currents, or swims in quiet water, or burrows into the mud. During his incubation he lives on other aquatic insects if he has the appetite of a stone fly or a caddis, or on plant tissue, algae, and diatoms if he is a vegetarian like the mayfly. During his incubation he molts repeatedly, each molt bringing him closer to maturity. The period of incubation varies. The mayfly will often remain a nymph or naiad for three years.

Nature is prolific in her supply of this form of fish food. The species of the various flies are great in number; the order of the stone flies and salmon flies has over twelve hundred species, the mayflies about the same, the caddis flies around thirty-six hundred, and buffalo gnats about three hundred. They all are amazingly fertile. Female stone flies may lay five or six thousand eggs apiece. Even so, the margin nature has provided for survival is not great; the eggs, nymphs, and flies are prey for every fish and for other aquatic animals as well.

When the conditions are just right, there is a strange stirring of life down in the bottom of the lake or stream. The period of incubation is over. The nymph slowly swims to the surface, where it crawls onto a rock or branch or spreads its wings and flies. Then the mating starts, and new eggs are dropped in the water. The life of the fly may be as brief as a few hours. That is true of the mayfly. For if the mayfly hatches at sunset, it will probably die by dawn.

Izaak Walton observed that "Those very flies that used to appear about and on the water in one month of the year, may the following year come almost a month sooner or later, as the same year proves colder or hotter." Fish biologists estimate that in the three summer months there will be, on the average, a bug hatch every two or three hours on the inland waters of the Pacific Northwest. There is no dry fly box in any pocket that can match all those flies. That is why a fly-fisherman is always adding to his collection against the day when he will see the hatch of a new fly. And he may carry those flies for years and never see their counterpart on the water.

In July 1940 Jim Donald and I were fishing the Deschutes River above Bend, Oregon, near the point where Fall River pours in. In that stretch the Deschutes is a deep, quietly moving millrace. There was no sign of life on the river, not a rise as far as the eye could see. Suddenly the redsides began to roll on the surface. A bug hatch was on. The flies were so dark and small that we could not see them at first. They were a species of the black gnat. I had no artificial fly as small as those on the water. But Jim had in his kit a collection of Nos. 22. and 24 which are so tiny that it is hard to thread them at any time let alone in the dusk. There was a reward for Jim's foresight. He soon had a pound and a half redside on the tiny No. 24 hook. He played him for a half-hour; and it was dark when Jim finally brought him to the net.

No bug hatches are more exciting than those I have witnessed when wading a stream or the shallow water along the shores of a lake. Silver Creek meanders at 6,000 feet through pasture land about twenty miles below Hailey, Idaho, a town memorialized by Nancy Wilson Ross in *Westward the Women*. It has no white water, but purls along like a millrace. It is as broad as a city street and from three to twelve feet deep. Some of its bottom is covered by small gravel, but most of it has a deep stand of grass, weeds, and moss. This is an ideal rainbow stream. It is, I think, the best dry-fly stream for rainbow in the United States.

Jim and I were fishing Silver Creek in waders on a late evening one July. We had gone to the stream on the heels of a heavy thunderstorm. There was at most an hour of fishing before dark. We took to the stream shortly above the Point of Rocks.

There are two ways to fish Silver Creek with dry flies. One is to use as short a line as possible, dropping the fly on the near side of the stream and letting only the leader touch the water. This is a modified version of dapping, but it can be used successfully only on those portions of Silver Creek where the fisherman is concealed by tall grass or willows. It takes a strong heart to work the stream that way. One often cannot see his fly, which intensifies the shock to the nervous system when a two- or three-pound rainbow strikes. Then the fisherman is apt to set his hook too late.

Blaine Hallock taught me the better way. It is to quarter the creek downstream. Upstream casting is poor, for there is neither white water nor riffles in Silver Creek; hence the shadow of the line will most assuredly be seen. Silver Creek fishing is delicate fishing. One must come down on his trout with great finesse. When one quarters the creek downstream, a flip of the tip of the rod will feed out more line without disturbing the fly. In that way one can get a long, long float, fifty yards in some places, thirty yards in most places, before the fly is pulled under by the weight of the line. It is at the end of those long floats that the trout is apt to take the fly.

One who is slow in setting the hook will not get Silver Creek trout. And any trout hooked at that distance is usually lightly hooked. I have met no dry-fly fisherman with more finesse and skill than Blaine Hallock—to me the old maestro. But I have seen him lose twelve of fifteen Silver Creek trout that he hooked at the end of a long float. Even so he brought three rainbows weighing between two and four pounds to the net that day, which was three times what Jim and I together had.

This evening in question Jim and I were quartering Silver Creek. We each had one trout weighing a pound and a half or less. But the strikes had slacked off and it looked like the trout had left the surface for that day. Suddenly a bug hatch started. We never identified the fly and had none to match it. It was a small species of salmon fly. We were in water well above our waists. We could see the nymphs coming to the surface and emerging full blown from the water. A stream that we had thought to be close to dormant burst into frenzied activity. Rainbow, five pounds or better, were rolling within reach of our fingers. Smaller rainbow were jumping. Millions of flies were bubbling from the water. The river was alive, as far as the eye could see, to the left and right. Hundreds of trout were making the river boil. They began to jump and roll within inches of us.

Both of us acted as if we were in a state of semishock. Jim finally found a second or third cousin of the fly that was hatching. He caught a one-pounder in the midst of the turmoil. And the hatch stopped as suddenly as it had started. The flies melted away in the grass and reeds. The creek became quiet. There was no splash or swirl to break the silence. The creek had thirty minutes of frenzied activity and then, as if exhausted, became dormant.

Izaak Walton listed as his artificial flies the dun, stone, ruddy, yellow or greenish, black, sad-yellow, moorish, tawny, wasp, shell, and drake. "Thus have you a jury of flies likely to betray and condemn all the Trouts in the river." If Izaak were alive today he would, I am sure, add the Hallock killer.

Blaine Hallock for years watched what fell off the willows at the water's edge, and put together a fly unique in the Pacific Northwest. The prospectus on the fly, written by the inventor himself, is worthy of the SEC files. Blaine wrote me as follows:

> *I am sending you under separate cover a few trout flies which are locally known as "Hallock's Killers." They were made*

*especially for you but I am sending these few only because, in
the hands of one not thoroughly familiar with their deadly
qualities, and proper method of use, they are really
dangerous. Should you be fishing from a boat and are out
over the water where trout are known to abide, extreme
caution should be employed in affixing the fly to the leader.
You should hump over the fly, concealing it in the pit of your
stomach and between the folds of your coat, preferably
getting down on your hands and knees to the end that the
fish cannot possibly see the fly during the operation. Perhaps
the better method is to carry a tarpaulin or blanket under
which you can crawl while handling the fly. If you are
angling from the shore, you should be careful to get well back
from the bank, say seventy-five or a hundred feet, and if
possible conceal yourself behind thick brush or a big tree.
Trout have been known to attack these flies with such vigor
and accuracy and to leap such phenomenal distances when
seeing the lure that they usually gulp the fingers, sometimes
even the hands of the angler, inflicting deep cuts and
lacerations with their teeth.*

Izaak Walton wrote that his "jury of flies" was not indispensable, that
"three or four flies neat and rightly made, and not too big, serve a Trout
in most rivers, all summer." Each fly-fisherman would be likely to have
a different list of indispensables. Haig-Brown in *A River Never Sleeps*
says that your favorite fly is "the one you'd fall back on if you were to
have no other, something like the one book you'd take along to a desert
island." Two of his are the Gammarus fly and the brown and white
bi-visible, flies that he has not used for years, since he already knows
they will catch fish under most conditions. For trout, my dry flies include
the Hallock killer (giving full discount to Blaine's prospectus), the
coachman bucktail, the blue upright, and the gray hackle with red body.
And my wet flies are the coachman, black gnat, woolly worm, and caddis.

While it is a great day for the fly-fisherman when the trout are on the
rise, it is often necessary to go down for them. Jim Donald and I put in

our first appearance on the South Fork of the Madison several years ago in late July. We had fished Elk Lake, Montana, which lies not far from the Idaho line. We had seen nineteen-pound rainbow taken on a troll. But the best for us on flies was a seven-pounder plus a miscellaneous collection of smaller rainbow in the neighboring Hidden Lake. It was hard, slow work on the lakes, painfully slow in the hot sun that beat down the whole of the windless days we spent there. We decided to repair to a stream where fishing conditions were less likely to be affected by the weather.

We chose the Madison from the reputation it enjoyed, and the next noon checked in at an auto camp in West Yellowstone, Montana. That afternoon we sought out the South Fork. To our dismay it was almost as much a lake as the waters we had left, for Hebgen Dam had transformed a mountain stream into a long slough. We fished hard, using most of our tricks. We fished dry and wet. We got a few small trout but none worthy of the reputation of the Madison.

The next day we sought local advice. Our guide turned out to be a men's-suit salesman for a mail-order house. Each of us ended up being measured for a suit on the banks of the South Fork. (They were good suits, too.) But before that had happened we had experienced the finest nymph fishing we had ever known.

Our guide put us in deep pools. The water was well up to our armpits, almost at the top of our waders. Our feet were on small gravel. We used the woolly worm in various colors at the end of a nine-foot leader, with only the weight of a swivel attached at the head of the leader to carry it down. We would cast out, wait a minute or two for the woolly worm to sink and then start a slow retrieve. We would take the line in with the left hand, an inch or two at a time, coiling it in the palm as the slack accumulated. By mid-afternoon the two of us took thirty trout. We killed five, returning the rest to the river. The smallest one caught weighed two pounds, the largest two and a quarter pounds.

It was delicate fishing. If we had had our afternoon skill in the morning, we would have had more than the thirty. Jim yelled like an Indian at his first fish. Well he might. It broke water, stood on its tail, and shook its head trying to dislodge the woolly worm. I am stirred from the lethargy of an armchair even at the memory of it. "A rainbow!" I shouted. But I was wrong. It was a German brown acquiring rainbow tactics in the cold waters of the Madison.

There is hardly a fisherman who does not discover something about trout, bass, steelhead, or salmon that those before him did not know. Lads a hundred years hence will find the answers to questions that have stumped all who preceded. For the calculus of water temperature, humidity, the moon and sun, the wind, bug hatches, and the like are too involved for any one man to compute. Izaak Walton about three hundred years ago put the problem in the following way: "Angling may be said to be so like the Mathematicks, that it can never be fully learnt; at least not so fully, but that there will still be more experiments left for the trial of other men that succeed us."

I have often seen trout or bass at the bottom of a pool and dangled bait before their noses without results. Yet sometimes, if I were patient, and held the bait right in front of the fish for five minutes or more, I would be successful. I remember such a case when I was bass fishing in Lake Wentworth, New Hampshire. I was anchored in thirty feet of water off Turtle Island in a pool where I seldom failed to take bass. For bait I was using crayfish that are native to the lake and which I caught with my hands. This day the lake was mirror-like. There was no breath of air; and the sunlight fell with the full intensity of July.

For several hours I had been unable to interest any small-mouthed bass in the crayfish. I peered over the edge of the boat and saw a bass poised directly below. I lowered a fresh crayfish until it hung suspended in front of the bass's nose. The crayfish, hooked through the tail, was waving his claws menacingly at the bass. The bass did not move. That went on for five minutes or more. Then the bass lunged at the crayfish. He seized it from the side and slowly turned it in his mouth so as to swallow it tail first. When the tip of the tail was in his mouth, I set the hook. The bass was transformed into a mass of energy. He came straight up from the bottom of the lake as if he had been shot out of a cannon. He came so fast I could not begin to take the line in on the reel. He hit the surface about a foot from the boat and jumped. The force of his jump carried him some three feet in the air; he gave a side twist, shook his head, and landed in the boat—a pound and a half of fighting-mad bass flesh.

One July day I had whipped the shore water of Green Lake in the Wallowas for several hours with a variety of dry flies. I should have had my limit, but only three or four trout were in the creel. I was standing at the meadow's edge on the south side of the lake wondering what to try next. As I stood there perplexed, a fifteen-inch eastern brook slowly swam in to shore. When he was two feet offshore in perhaps eight inches of water, he turned and stopped, perfectly poised and facing the depths. He was not more than three feet from my boots.

I decided to have some fun with him. I reeled in my line, leaving only the nine-foot leader free of the ferrules. I looked in my fly box and spied a McGinty. Playing a hunch, I greased it with mucelin and tied it to my leader. All this time I had not moved my feet, but my arms and hands had been active. Yet my trout was not in the least disturbed.

I risked disturbance, however, when I swung the rod out over the water so as to dangle the McGinty in front of his nose. Even then he was not frightened. When the McGinty touched the water, he had it in a flash. I set the hook and my trout was in deep water fighting for his life. That trout violated all the rules man had made for him.

The bait-fishermen are not only vociferous; they are probably in the majority. The debate between them and the fly-fishermen has been going on for centuries, and will never cease as long as there is a trout pointed upstream in a riffle, waiting to see what the river brings him.

One summer day I came out of the Wallowas with a creel filled with 12- to 14-inch rainbow caught with a dry fly on the Big Minam. I ran into a newspaperman whose curiosity was excited by a glimpse of the catch. I told him of the Big Minam, which rises from the south end of Minam Lake in the heart of the Wallowas. It flows for forty miles through one of the prettiest mountain valleys the Creator ever fashioned. It is fed on its course by several good streams—the Little Minam, Rock Creek, the North Minam, and Elk Creek. Dozens of other smaller creeks flow into it and it is fed by hundreds of springs. The valley is narrow—a quarter- to a half-mile wide. The mountains rise on either side 2,000 to 3,000 feet.

There are great stands of ponderosa pine in the valley. There are huge fir trees, red and white, and towering tamarack on the slopes. Jack pine is scattered here and there in groves so thick no tree can get beyond the spindling stage. There is now and then a touch of spruce and once in a while a yew tree. On the tops of the ridges are scatterings of mountain-mahogany, excellent browse for deer. And in the ravines are alder, willow, and hawthorn. There are whole acres of snowbrush along the mountainsides, filling the valley with its sweet perfume in June and July.

This is excellent elk country—Rocky Mountain elk introduced from Wyoming in 1912. And wise and crafty buck deer watch over the valley from the base of granite cliffs that mark the skyline of the mountains.

In years past the Big Minam has been one of the best trout streams in America. There were streams that had larger rainbow in them, but none harbored lustier ones. Moreover, few streams are more exacting on the fly-fisherman. The water is as clear as water can be. It runs for the most part over sandbars and bright gravel. Detection is easy; delicate fishing is required. One should let a pool on the Minam rest at least five minutes after catching a trout from it.

This is the discourse I was giving my newspaper friend—bragging a bit as I held the trout up one by one. When I had finished he said, "You caught them on bait, I presume."

"Bait?" I snorted. "There ought to be a law against fishing for trout with bait."

My statement was on the wires that afternoon, and Ben Hur Lampman, editorial writer for the Portland *Oregonian*, saw it the next morning. Ben is more than editorial writer. He is a fisherman extraordinary. He is something of a botanist and biologist. He is also a philosopher.

Ben has a plaque entitled "The Angler's Prayer" with a verse inscribed on it that reads:

> *Lord give me grace to catch a fish*
> *So big that even I,*
> *In talking of it afterward*
> *May never need to lie.*

The story of how that prayer on Ben's plaque was answered is told by Ben himself in the greatest fish story ever written. It is entitled "Them Two Guys Is Nuts." It tells how Ben caught a 120-pound sturgeon, 6 feet $10^1/2$ inches long, in Blue Lake, Oregon, after a battle of 2 hours and 15 minutes. I mention the story only to indicate that the primordial man is strong in him—so strong that he tossed out the poet when I endorsed the dry fly. Ben sat down and wrote the following editorial.

> *Tarrying briefly at La Grande on his way to the fine fishing of the Wallowa Mountains, where are lakes with almost incredible trout, Associate Justice William O. Douglas, of the Supreme Court, held that in fishing for trout there can be no sport unless the artificial fly is used, and preferably the dry fly.*
>
> *But the associate justice neglects, we think, to consult a most distinguished precedent which in piscatorial matters has all the weight of the English common law. The authority is one that cannot properly be ignored in the handing down of such a ruling, for surely it is generally conceded to govern these instances, and the name that it bears is warmly luminous in English letters. It may seem tedious to cite Izaak Walton, but none the less there is a duty in the instance, for Walton is Walton, as one might say Blackstone is Blackstone, and not to be altered by individual prejudice or personal inclination. This ethical pillar of what one might term the common law of angling, the veritable father of the code, sets the associate justice, one fears, at naught.*
>
> *We have no intent to reverse an associate justice of the highest tribunal, nor should we know how to come about it with privilege and decorum, but it ought to suffice to refer to the code of the angler as written by Master Walton, wherein a considerable part of the chapter on trout fishing is devoted to the employment of baits, which portion takes precedent over the equally authoritative discussion of using the artificial fly. Izaak Walton was lyric in his praise of the gentle, which is the common maggot, and of the dewworm, the lobworm, the brandling, the marsh worm, the tagtail, the flagworm, the oak worm, the gilttail, the twatchel and many another. He gives explicit and well-nigh affectionate instructions for their culture and care before he turns, with scarcely less of delight, to treating of the grasshopper, the minnow and the caterpillar. All these, and their manipulation, are in the classic corpus juris of the ethics and practice of trout fishing. (People v. Trout, 1 Walton 78)*

> *It seems, clearly enough, that in his ruling on fly-fishing*
> *the associate justice is reversed by a still higher court. The*
> *error is not in individual election of a certain method, which*
> *is as may be, but rather in the implication that trout may be*
> *honestly acquired in no more than the one manner. And*
> *Master Walton is so obviously to the contrary.*

Ben was right in marshaling eminent authority to his side. Izaak Walton endorsed bait for trout. Izaak listed, in addition to those cited by Ben, the beetle, black snail (slit open), and any kind of fly including the lowly housefly. Izaak preferred the grasshopper dangled on the surface of the water. But my son Bill and I bettered the great Izaak one summer day in the Wallowas.

We were camped at Long Lake and had gone over to Steamboat Lake for a day of fishing. Steamboat lies close to 7,000 feet. It has an island that faintly resembles a steamboat; hence its name. It lies surrounded by granite ridges. They rise from 1,000 to 1,500 feet on the east, west, and south; and a few hundred feet on the north. They are steep rock walls, studded with whitebark pine, Engelman's spruce, and alpine (balsam) fir that have managed somehow to extend their roots into tiny crevices, splitting the granite as the roots grow in strength. These are smooth rocks, polished by glaciers.

A lush meadow lies at the south end of the lake where one can find in July and August a purple monkeyflower, the fireweed, daisy, buttercup, larkspur, Scouler St. Johns wort, and pleated gentian. Through this meadow a stream wanders in serpentine fashion and pours clear, cold water into the lake. The waters of the lake wash the other three granite walls. The granite is here and there streaked with marble. The light stone seems to draw out the deep sapphire of the lake.

Bill and I had been fishing with dry flies. We had three or four eastern brook of from ten to thirteen inches and a rainbow or two around twenty inches. But the going was slow. So I started my son on mastery of the roll cast. He was standing on the southern shore at the edge of a rock that is as wide as a paved street and slopes gently into the water. Suddenly a swarm of grasshoppers came over our shoulders from the southwest.

They covered the rock. A high wind blew them out on the water. Then began an extensive, an amazing rise. The only thing comparable to it that I have seen took place in a different medium. At the Malheur Bird Refuge near Burns, Oregon, one July evening I saw hundreds of redwings diving and swooping over swarms of dragonflies that filled the air above the marshes of Malheur Lake. What the redwings did to the dragonflies, the trout did to the grasshoppers at Steamboat Lake. And each scene was equally animated.

The water immediately in front of us became alive with fish. Big trout—two-or three-pounders—rolled under the grasshoppers, sucking them under with a swirl. Smaller trout left the water, jumping again and again for the fresh bait, gorging themselves. There were literally hundreds of swirls and splashes extending farther and farther into the lake as the wind carried the hoppers away from the shore. It would have been impossible to draw a circle three feet in diameter that did not include a rising trout.

The temptation at such a moment is to give the trout what is being offered—to bait hooks with grasshoppers or even to add a grasshopper to a fly hook. But a grasshopper on a hook does not sit as nicely on the water as a grasshopper with his freedom. So we decided on a different course. We decided to try the Hallock killer and to fish it dry. The underbody of the Hallock killer has a yellow-green tinge that is very close to the color of the grasshopper. It was this underbody that the trout would see.

We greased our Hallock killers with mucelin and cast out. Our dry flies rode high and saucily on the surface, bobbing with the riffle that the wind had kicked up. They were surrounded by live grasshoppers, a half-dozen grasshoppers within inches of our flies. In a flash each of us had a strike. The trout chose the Hallock killer over the real thing. We caught trout as fast as we could cast. We caught trout as long as the grasshoppers pulled trout to the surface. The largest was an eighteen-inch eastern brook. My son, fourteen at the time, caught him. In view of the angle of decline of the rock into the water, I decided against the use of a net. So Bill beached it. It was wholly out of water on the rock when the hook became disengaged and it regained its freedom. It was fully eighteen inches long and any fair-minded jury would concede it two pounds.

Blaine Hallock is a purist and the *de facto* head of the Dry Fly League of the Pacific Northwest. He wouldn't use bait on trout if his life depended on it and would expel anyone from the League who was caught doing so. At least that's what I thought. Jim Donald also proclaimed him to be a purist. But he proclaimed it so vociferously that he raised doubts in my mind, like the lady who protested too much. One day my doubts received reinforcement. I was searching Jim's tackle box, with his permission, for a leader. In a box at the bottom of the kit I found several interesting specimens.

One was a grasshopper. I held it up accusingly.

He said, "Must have jumped in and died."

Beside the grasshopper was a shrimp. I held it under his nose and asked, "How do you explain this?"

Jim said, "Brought it along for my lunch."

I looked under the grasshopper and the shrimp and found an artificial mouse. I then had him dead to rights.

On our return from the fishing trip I put the matter to simon-pure purist, the old maestro, for a ruling. I cast into poetry the brief that I filed. It read as follows:

> In days long ago the true dry-fly addict
> Never once cast a covetous look
> At a worm or a frog or a mouse or a hog
> Or at varmints which lived in the brook.
>
> The fly which was dry was a symbol to him
> Of a skill which was noble and fine
> He was careful to note it was always afloat
> All the feathers, hook, leader and line.
>
> He cast in the pool where the granddaddy lay
> He waited and followed the float
> For the surge and the splash, the thrill of the flash
> Of the trout which seemed big as a boat.
>
> But now it appears a decay has set in
> In lieu of a speck of a fly
> A piece of raw meat that a trout likes to eat
> Meets the test if it's greasy and dry.

And all that is spun from the tenuous thread
That a thing which is dry and will float
In fact has a wing though it's only a thing
With four legs and a tail—like a goat.

Alas and alack—and believe it or not
Things have come to a terrible state
Black gnat and gray hackle, and all dry-fly tackle
Are usurped and dethroned by King Bait.

Oh ye who have erred I beseech ye, repent!
Raise your eyes from the earth to the sky!
Leave the mouse to the cat—forsake ye the rat!
Keep your fly like your powder, son, dry!

The old maestro's ruling came in due course. He replied in kind:

If cows can dance the rhumba on an ice pond,
    (And once a cow did jump over the moon)
If listening to the brook a felon's yet fond,
    (Per Gilbert's rhythmic operatic tune).

If men who have a thirst may speak of dryness,
    (And feeling dry is worse than getting wet.)
It may be said with no pretense of slyness
    That lubricated mice may win the bet.

To fly may not imply the use of pinions.
    A flag may fly from any breezy height.
So men may disagree in their opinions,
    And every one of them may still be right.

There are so very many ways of flying.
    There are so very many kinds of flights.
There are so very many sorts of dryness,
    Let's give the oiled mouse his Bill of Rights.

Now you and I may scorn the lowly varmint,
    But scorning cannot rid us of the pest.
So cast aside your black judicial garment,
    Commune with God—and He will do the rest.

Thus did even a purist fall from grace.

My son Bill and I were fishing Silver Creek, Idaho, one September day. On the upper reaches is a large slough, some thirty yards wide and a quarter-mile or more long. There we took our positions, side by side, he up to his armpits, I well over my waist.

It was a squally day, fifteen minutes of gusty wind followed by a half-hour of quiet. When there was no wind the surface of the slough was glassy. Then conditions were too delicate for fly-fishing; for the shadow of the line sounded an alarm to the rainbow. In those periods of quiet we would get out of the water, work our way up the bank that bounds the slough on the south and study it. What we saw at one such time startled us. A school of two dozen or more rainbow swam by us. They were on a lazy cruise. They were not more than twenty-five or thirty feet away. We got a close look. There were eight better than thirty inches long, a half-dozen more were over twenty-four inches and the rest from sixteen to eighteen inches. It was an armada, thrilling to behold.

When the next breeze came, we waded quietly into the water and cast toward the spot where we imagined the cruising rainbow to be. We were fishing dry and had changed from a gray hackle to a bucktail coachman. Within an hour I had three of those big fellows on. There would be a swirl under the fly and the hook would be set. But I was either a trifle slow or a trifle fast. Not once did I set the hook securely. There would be a run, a dorsal fin cutting the water, a jump, a surge and then a slack line.

At last I was discouraged, and decided to forsake the slough for the stream. Bill promised to follow me shortly. Several hours passed and he had not showed up. Slightly concerned, I started upstream where I had seen him last. Pretty soon someone came running and shouted, "Your son needs help. He's got a big one on."

"How big?" I asked.

"About ten pounds I think," was the reply.

Waders are ungainly even for walking. They never were designed for running. But run in them I did. I stopped only once in the half-mile or more, and that was to borrow a net from another fisherman. Neither Bill nor I had one, and a net would come in handy even though the trout should turn out to be but half of ten pounds.

But I arrived too late for the battle. There was Bill, wet to the neck, with a grin on his face, and a rainbow that was slightly over sixteen inches in length hanging on his right thumb.

When I left him he had forsaken the fly. He waded the neck of the slough in water up to his chin, changed to a reel with nylon line, and fished as Sandy Balcom, manufacturer of pipe organs in Seattle, had taught us.

Sandy uses a four- to six-pound clear nylon line, 300 feet long, with a backing of eight- to ten-pound nylon line also 300 feet long. His leader is three feet long, $1^3/4$ to $2^1/4$ pounds strength. His hook is a No. 8 or 10 single-egg type. He puts on two salmon eggs, the lower one having only the faintest part of the hook point showing. There is buckshot on the leader to carry it down. The bait is allowed to settle on the bottom and is then stripped in very slowly. Sandy has delicate fingers. He can make a few passes over the bottom and know at once its character. He can make bait the king under practically any fishing conditions I have known.

Bill played the rainbow he caught with the salmon eggs at least 40 minutes; and when the last ounce of energy was gone from the rainbow's stout heart, he turned on his side. Bill then slipped a finger through the gill and the battle was over.

As we walked through the willows to the road where our car was parked, I saw in my son's eyes an excitement I had not seen before. I knew there had been awakened in him an instinct that has been carried in the blood stream of the race since man first lowered a net in the ocean or first stood by a pool with a spear waiting for the flash that heralded the arrival of a salmon or trout.

Roy Schaeffer

The last words Franklin D. Roosevelt spoke to me were "How are Thunder and Lightning?" This happened at a Sunday luncheon at the White House three weeks before his death. Luncheon was over and he had transferred to his wheel chair. The attendant was wheeling him away when he turned and asked the question.

Thunder and Lightning are horses. Thunder belongs to my son Bill and Lightning to my daughter Millie. We acquired them in a curious way.

Back in northeastern Oregon, my wife and I were building our tamarack log cabin on the Lostine in the Wallowas. Roy Schaeffer, who runs a dude ranch near by, was in charge of the project. Fonzy Wilson, whose work with ax and saw is superb, was head carpenter. The walls and roof were finished, but no windows or doors were in and the floor had not been laid. At the end of a July day we were sitting on nail kegs, listening to Roy tell of the Nez Perce Indians who had the Wallowas for their ancestral home. Roy revered Chief Joseph, whose land had been wrested from him in one of the nation's least honorable undertakings. While Roy talked, a stranger came down the path through the woods. His Levis and his walk showed him to be a cowboy. Roy seemed to know him, for the two spoke. The stranger joined us but sat in silence for the better part of an hour.

Then my son, who was about ten, came up from the river where he had been fishing. At the first break in our conversation the stranger turned to him and said, "Got a horse, sonny?"

Bill shook his head.

"Like to have a horse?"

Bill's eyes lighted. "Sure would."

"I've got a horse for you, sonny."

Perhaps from some Scotch impulse I spoke up, hating at once what I asked: "How much, stranger?"

"How much? I just gave the boy a horse."

We went down to get the horse in a few days. He was a three-year-old chestnut, racing and snorting with tail high, on the range north of Wallowa. The stranger was Dan Oliver, and the horse we named Thunder.

Several weeks after Dan gave Thunder to Bill, Millie came up to the cabin for a few days where Roy, Fonzy, and I were still working. At the end of one day I built a campfire outside and cooked supper for the children. During dinner Roy turned to Millie and asked, "Did Bill tell you about his horse?"

Millie is the horseman of the family. She can ride like an expert and hold up in any competition. She has an understanding of horses given to few. Knowing them, she is unafraid and is their master. The idea that her younger brother had a horse when she had none was preposterous. If there was a horse in the family, it had to be her horse. She turned to me:

"Bill hasn't got a horse, has he, Dad?" And there was a note in her voice that asked me to tell her that Bill certainly did not have a horse.

But I nodded, "Yes, he has a horse."

The effect was worse than if I had slapped her. She burst into tears and sobbed, "Why does he have to have a horse when I want one?"

So I told her of Dan Oliver and Thunder. But the sobs did not stop. A wind came down the canyon and stirred the tips of the jack pines at our backs, a chill wind for early August. I threw a log on the fire and we sat around it. Millie's plate was untouched as she sat with her face in her hands staring into the flame.

Perhaps ten minutes passed when Roy put down his cup, stood up, turned to Millie, and said, "If Dan Oliver can give Bill a horse, I can give you one."

Millie was on her feet, dancing up and down and shouting, "'Where is it, where is it?"

"In the North Minam Meadows."

"Let's go get it! Let's go right now, Daddy."

A few days later we rode the seven miles over the mountain range to the west and down into the North Minam. Roy had a dozen two-year-olds at pasture there, and he rode up the meadows to find them. In a while the horses broke through the woods at the edge of the clearing, stood for a second, and then stampeded across it.

"Take your pick," shouted Roy. And Millie picked a slim-legged, light-footed sorrel—the one with the most fire in his eyes. She named him Lightning.

I told President Roosevelt the story that winter, and he said, "You're doing all right for a Scotchman."

"Not as well as I would like."

"You mean you are looking for a third horse for nothing?" he asked.

"Exactly, Mr. President. And when I thought of people who might give me a horse, I kept thinking of you." He threw back his head and laughed in his hearty way.

Roy Schaeffer is the same kind of warmhearted, generous person Franklin Roosevelt was. With a man in need he'd share his last slab of bacon, his last pound of coffee, and in the mountains he'd care for him and expect no reward. The suggestion of a reward would, I think, hurt. He is indeed one of the few I have known who like to give more than to receive. He will die as he was born, poor in worldly possessions.

Roy Schaeffer is the man I would want with me if I were catapulted into dense woods anywhere from Maine to Oregon. He knows Oregon best, but in any forest he would be king. For he is as much a part of the woods as the snowberry, the mountain ash, or the buck deer. The woods are part of him. Above all men I have known, he would be able to survive in them on his wits alone.

Roy is quiet and unassuming in any crowd. He is tall—six feet two. He is big—240 pounds. His eyes are blue. And his hair, now thinned, was once a wild and unruly shock. Roy's parents were the first white people married in Wallowa Valley. He was born there January 5, 1888. It was 60 degrees below zero that day. The rugged scene into which Roy was born is symbolic of the environment through which he has moved during his life—a life on the plains and in the high mountains of eastern Oregon. He has worked long hours deep in the Snake River canyon in the heat of summer when the lava rock of the canyon walls turned it into an oven night and day; he often has slept in a hollow in the snow at the top of the Wallowas with a blizzard howling overhead.

He married Lucy Downard in 1908 and for the honeymoon took her to Bear Creek Saddle in the high Wallowas. This saddle is a great rolling meadow about 8,000 feet up, at the head of Bear Creek, surrounded by low-lying rims of hills gripped by jagged fingers of granite. They hold Bear Creek Saddle close to the clouds. At the time of his marriage Roy owned a band of sheep. He left them at Bear Creek Saddle while he hurried down to Wallowa to claim his bride. They returned at once on horseback to the sheep camp. From that time Lucy has shared the hardships of Roy's life and also has brought him five children—Charles, Annamay, Ivy, Dorothy, and Arnold—all of whom love the mountains as do Roy and Lucy.

Roy owned this band of about nine hundred sheep for six years. During that time he came to know both the summer and winter ranges of the Wallowas. He sat in snow, rain, and sunshine on their hillsides and saw the life of the mountains at work. The mountains became as familiar to him as a factory is to a man who works there.

After Roy sold his sheep he was a jack-of-all-trades. But most of the jobs took him to the back country. He was the champion of sheepshearers. He sheared by hand two hundred sheep a day and better. He is a strong man; but sheepshearing taxes the strength. Bending over, holding the animal, working the shears through the tough wool—this is killing. Of all jobs, it came close to exhausting Roy's great energy.

Between sheepshearings came a variety of jobs on farms and in lumber camps, with a few winter months in Union Pacific roundhouses repairing locomotives. "That work," Roy once said to me, "was the part of my life that was wasted." He loves the outdoors and it is punishment to assign him to inside work. Most of his days have been spent in t h e mountains taking fishing parties to high lakes and hunting parties to high ridges or deep canyons. In the winters he has done much trapping for marten. In 1934 he bought Lapover, famous dude ranch of the Wallowas.

Roy's strength is prodigious. His hands are like hams. Each of them is so strong it could crush a man. Taking hold of it is similar to grasping a wild steer by the horn. There are many stories of his feats and most of them have a Paul Bunyan touch. One fall he and three others were hunting deer in the Grande Ronde canyon. Roy became separated from the others. He rejoined them late in the afternoon to find that one had shot a buck. The three men had worked out a scheme for division of labor in getting the deer out of the canyon. One would carry the rifles while two would carry the buck. Roy met them as they were resting for a short climb. He tied the four legs of the buck together, slipped his rifle barrel underneath the knot, raised the rifle to his shoulder and started up the canyon wall. It was a good 2,000 feet to the top. The buck weighed 185 pounds dressed. Roy stopped a few times on his way up but he finished ahead of the other members of the party.

Many years ago he figured he was spending $120 a year for chewing tobacco, which was too much for his budget. He decided to short-circuit the retailer and manufacturer and go directly to the producer. He wrote to Hawesville, Kentucky, and found a man who for $10 would send him a good sized box of unprocessed tobacco. It is the leaf and stem of the tobacco plant dried but otherwise just as it comes from the field. It comes in three strengths: mild, strong, and extra strong. Roy orders the extra strong. For $10 he gets a supply that lasts a year. He takes the plant and crushes it into a coarse powder and carries this in a cotton bag that Lucy made for him.

This tobacco is powerful. Though many have tried no one but Roy has been able to chew it. He has bet that no one else can chew it for a half-hour and so far no one has won the bet. One man who chewed Roy's tobacco only ten minutes spent all night behind the chicken coop. Roy's reputation has spread. No one bums a chew off him. He also smokes this tobacco in a pipe, and has yet to find a smoker who can inhale it.

The habit of chewing tobacco has affected his speech, so that he does not move his lips when he talks. He probably could have been another Edgar Bergen if he had tried, for he speaks from the stomach. It is a deep guttural sound, hard for the newcomer to pick up. But it has great carrying power. I have been a hundred yards from him in the woods and heard what he said even though he did not raise his voice. He talks as I imagined, when a boy, that an Indian would talk.

Roy is an expert shot with a pistol and rifle. He can take his six-shooter and hit a horsefly with one shot at a distance of thirty feet. One evening

I saw Roy with his 30.06 hit empty shells that we threw high in the air. He never missed. He can do better than that. I've seen him take a .22 Remington, throw out a shell, load the gun and hit the shell with the second shot before it hit the ground. Roy has seldom missed his buck even at five hundred yards.

Roy has a great respect for the animals that inhabit the forests. Coyote is the exception. Coyote plans his campaign of killing with some of man's thoroughness. Roy has seen coyotes station one or more of their band at the bottom of a draw while one went to the top of the ridge in search of a deer. The deer, once jumped, raced down the ridge with the coyote in full pursuit. When the deer reached the bottom, tired and weary, there would be fresh coyotes lying in wait to take the next leg of the relay.

In hard snow, the coyote takes a heavy toll of deer. He runs on top, while the deer keep breaking through. So the coyote gradually gains on the deer and quickly snaps the tendons in its rear legs. The deer is down, and the coyote is at its throat in a flash. Roy has known one coyote to kill twenty or thirty deer in a winter day in that way, taking a few mouthfuls from each carcass. For the killing is not primarily for food; the coyote kills for the joy of killing. He hamstrings elk as he does deer when he finds them wallowing in deep snow.

Roy is for the extermination of the coyote. "If man wants deer to hunt," says Roy, "he must eliminate the coyote. The deer cannot long stand to be hunted by both."

And so January finds him at Salem, Oregon, talking with legislators in an endeavor to get a bounty placed on coyotes—one sufficiently attractive to make every farmer's boy in the county look for a coyote den when spring rolls around.

Roy and I were hunting in the Snake River country, camped on Lightning Creek several miles above its mouth. Lightning Creek runs into the Imnaha, and the Imnaha runs into the Snake about five miles below the confluence of the Imnaha and Lightning Creek. These waterways flow out of the most deeply scarred and rugged canyons of the continent. Hell's Canyon of the Snake, a dozen miles or so above the mouth of the Imnaha, is indeed the deepest canyon of the continent—2,000 feet deeper than the Grand Canyon. It is 7,900 feet from the lip of the ridge to the surface of the water. Here the Astor overland party foundered. Here Captain Benjamin Bonneville was turned back. Here the Snake is one of the most treacherous of all rivers to run.

The Lightning Creek canyon in which we were camped is no ordinary canyon. The valley at points is a quarter-mile wide, with the canyon walls rising 2,000 to 3,000 feet. Centuries of erosion have exposed on either side layer after layer of dark lava rock, each from a few feet to twenty or thirty feet thick. The north slopes of these canyon walls are carpeted with the famous Idaho fescue (*Festuca idahoensis*), and the south slopes with bluebunch wheatgrass (*Agropyron spicatum*), the bunchgrass that is found on the hills out of Yakima, the most important indigenous grass of the Pacific Northwest. These grasses stand a foot to two feet high in the Snake River country. At a distance of a few miles they look like the nap of a yellow-green velvet that flows softly over the canyon walls.

Here and there thick stands of pine and fir make dark patches on a light green landscape, sometimes sprawling the whole length of a deep draw or lying in a thick mantle over the shoulders of the range. The slopes and hill crests have only straggling evergreens to adorn them. It is as if a forest were sown with an uneven hand.

Sheltered ravines holding springs or a creek cut ugly gashes in the canyon walls. They always have shelter, for even where the pine and fir are absent they are filled with willow, cottonwood, alder, elderberry, sumac, and chaparral. This vegetation forms a spine of high brush that runs the whole length, crawling 2,000 to 3,000 feet up the hillside like a sinewy green serpent. There are rattlesnakes in the draws and on the rimrock.

There are several ways to hunt this country. One is to send a member of the party circuitously to the saddle at the head of one of the draws. He goes a roundabout way so as not to disturb the deer that may be in the draw. After he is at the top, another hunter goes directly up the draw. The deer go out ahead of him at the saddle, where the ambush is laid. That is the way my son and I like to hunt that country. Another method is to work up the mountain along the side of a ravine, rolling rocks into it in order to flush any deer that may be bedded down. That is the way Roy and I hunted on this particular October day.

We usually would be five hundred feet or more above the bottom of the draw, working along its sides under outcroppings of rimrock. The rocks we rolled into the draw bounced in abandon down the slopes, weaving weird patterns in their paths. They would disappear into the brush; and in a few seconds a deep, muffled, crashing sound traveled back to us. Then the silence of the canyon would return, as if its sleep had been only fitfully interrupted. We would stand alert, looking below for the slightest movement in the ravine.

These were tense moments. I knew for the first time the feeling not only of the hunter but of the hunted. The quickened pulse as the rock plunged off the hillside; the tingling suspense as it veered first one way, then another; the pounding heart and the feel of its breath as it went rolling by. I understood the psychology of the deer: to freeze and to hold ground, to stay quiet and still as a statue, until and unless the rock came perilously close. Then and then only would a break for safety be made.

Roy must have made a close hit with one rock. A four-point buck broke into the open, coming out of the draw and onto the slope across from him. The buck first stepped softly and then in two bounds got behind a lone ponderosa pine.

"There is plenty of time," thought Roy. "I'll sit down and take careful aim."

There did, indeed, seem to be plenty of time. For the buck had a thousand feet to travel to the top, with no brush or tree or ledge to offer protection on the way up. Roy sat still for a minute or two. Then he said to himself: "That buck is staying behind the tree. I must run downhill and get my shot before he gets out of range."

Run down he did. He went off at an angle, running fifty yards or more before he stopped. When he prepared to draw a bead on the buck, the tree was still between them. Whichever way he turned the buck kept behind the tree, as a squirrel does in any park in the land when one comes close to him. In a few minutes the buck was gone with the saucy flash of his tail over the saddle. Roy had not even had a single shot at him. Later Roy said, "You know, Bill, that buck was a lot smarter than me."

Roy has a great affection for horses. When this powerful man is near a horse, he is unfailingly gentle. His hand on a horse that is ill or injured has the tenderness of a father's hand at his child's sickbed. His voice is soft. And his gentleness with horses is reciprocated. I have seen a trembling three-year-old, wild and unbroken, become calm as he touched it and talked to it in a low voice.

Roy has never owned a pair of hobbles. His horses never leave him in the hills. This means, of course, that he picks his campgrounds with an eye to the comfort and pleasure of the horse as well as to his own. He looks first for horse feed—not for grass that horses can eat in a pinch, but for sweet and tender grass that is rich in protein, like the alpine bunchgrass that grows as high as 8,000 or 9,000 feet in the Wallowas. As a result, Roy's horses are never far away in the morning. A handful of oats and his soft whistle will bring them to him. From November to May they run wild in the winter range on the lower reaches of the Big Minam; but when Roy goes to get them in the spring they come right to him. Then he puts his arm around their necks and pats them, greeting them as one would a friend long absent.

Once when Roy and I were camped at Cheval Lake in the Wallowas, we took a side trip to New Deal Lake. It is a small lake of ten acres or so, in a treeless basin. It has eastern brook trout up to five pounds. Cliffs shaped somewhat like a horseshoe hem it in. Our approach was from above, which brought us to the lake from the south side. When we first saw it, it was five hundred feet below us. The slope was perhaps 45 degrees or more, but it was not dangerous except for one stretch. That was a flat piece of tilted granite, smooth as a table top, half as wide as a city street, and covered with loose gravel. There was no way around it; it had to be crossed. Roy was in the lead. I watched to see what he would do. His horse stopped and sniffed the rock. Roy spoke to him and touched him lightly with spurs. The horse stepped gingerly on the granite. Then putting his four feet slightly forward, the horse half walked and half slid down the granite with sparks flying from his shoes.

"Might have slipped in these boots if I had tried to walk," said Roy in a matter-of-fact way. And he probably would have, for under his lighter weight the loose gravel would have rolled.

It was then that I thought of Jimmie Conzelman's definition of horsemanship. "Horsemanship," says Jimmie, "is the ability to remain unconcerned, comfortable, and on a horse—all at once."

One November day Roy had his hunting camp set up near the mouth of the North Fork of the Minam. It was a big party, with seven or eight tents. It was so sprawled out that from a distance it looked like an Indian camp. Smoke came from every tent. There was a big center tent where the cooking was done. A few horses stood tied to trees in an outer circle, waiting to be saddled. Three or four elk hung high above the ground from poles laid between two trees.

Roy was preparing breakfast, and as he cooked, Mac, a wise, old mule, age thirty-five, came up and nuzzled him. When I have been at Roy's barn saddling horses, Mac has often come up behind me and given me a push with his head, urging me to the door of the barn where the oats were kept. He seldom stopped until I gave in.

Mac was a favorite of Roy's. He always trusted Mac with the delicate tasks of a pack train. Mac always carried the eggs and the liquids, or any pastry that Lucy might fix for the first night out. Mac was never tied onto a pack string. He followed behind, taking his time and picking his way. I have seen him stop and look closely at the space between two trees, trying to figure whether he could get through without bumping or scraping either side of the pack. Often he would go around rather than take a chance. He never rolled a pack. He often was late in arriving in camp behind a pack string, but he always brought his burden in safe and sound. At breakfast time he was always in camp begging for hot cakes.

This morning Roy turned to Mac and said, "Want a hot cake? Well, go away and come back pretty soon and I'll give you one."

This happened over and again. Finally he fed Mac a few.

"Now don't bother us any more," said Roy. "Go on." And with that he gave Mac a push. Mac stood for a minute and then went over to the trail that ran close by camp and started downstream.

When Roy saw Mac go downstream, he was puzzled. The horses were upstream. Lapover was upstream, up the North Minam and across a high range ruled by the jagged finger of Flagstaff Point. Downstream was the winter range and the town of Minam on the paved highway coming up from La Grande. Roy sometimes went out that way, but only in an emergency; for when he got out, he would be 30 miles by road from Lapover. That was the long way around.

"Let's see where Mac goes," said Roy.

So we followed him down the trail a mile or so. Roy finally stopped and said, "We're breaking camp and following Mac. We're moving down the Big Minam and will go out by the town of Minam. Looks to me like a big snow is coming. Mac usually knows it before I do."

We broke camp and moved downstream. Before morning a heavy snow fell, almost eighteen inches, which meant there were at least four feet on the ridges. And four feet are far too much for any pack train.

The next night beside the campfire Roy chuckled as he said, "Mac knew more than all the rest of us put together, didn't he?"

The high lakes of the Wallowas number one hundred or more and lie at 6,000 to 8,400 feet. Each has a personality. Cheval is hardly more than a pond nestling under granite peaks in a high secluded pocket. It's small and intimate—a one-party camp. Long and Steamboat show wide expanses of water like those in the Maine woods. They show broad acres of deep blue water on calm days, and produce whitecaps in rough weather. Douglas lies in the high lake basin under Eagle Cap. Here there are granite walls mounted with spires like unfinished cathedrals. It is austere or intimate, depending on how one comes upon it. Patsie, Bumble, and Tombstone lie like friendly, open ponds in a pasture. Diamond, Frances, and Lee have the dark cast of wells without bottoms, and water that chills to the marrow a few feet under the surface. Blue, Chimney, and Hobo appear as sterile as slate, showing clayish bottoms with no moss or grass. Green, Minam, and Crescent are lush with algae and moss, rich feeding grounds for trout.

Fish have been planted in fifty or more of these lakes. Roy has packed many thousands of fingerlings in to them, carried in milk cans and kept alive by the sloshing of the water caused by the movement of the horse or mule that transported them. Sometimes Roy while en route to one lake has paused long enough at a smaller one to pour in a dipper of fingerlings. Or having a part of a can left over, he has climbed a ridge or dropped into another canyon and planted a few hundred fingerlings in a remote pond. In that manner dozens of lakes have received their fish. Many are nameless lakes, unmarked on maps, with no trail to designate their locations, tucked away high on ridges or in small basins below granite peaks. They are deep blue sapphires in mountings of gray and green.

One summer Stanley Jewett and I were on a pack trip with Roy. We were studying the problems of the fish, convinced that in many instances the solution was to supply the lakes not with fish but with food, such as fresh-water shrimp or periwinkles. We were camped at Long Lake. One morning Stan suggested we take a look for mountain sheep.

The bighorns were native to the Wallowas, where they once existed in large numbers. Captain Bonneville, who wintered on the Idaho side of the Snake in 1832, reported that the bighorns were the principal diet of his expedition. But none have been seen in the Wallowas for a decade or so, and it seemed incredible. Stan thought the ridge east of Long— the rocky backbone that stands as a thousand--foot granite barrier between it and Steamboat—was where they might be.

We started up the ridge early one morning. We soon had to dismount and leave the horses, for there was a granite wall ahead of us. We were almost to the top when we spotted fresh tracks of sheep-—the unmistakable imprint of the bighorn in fine sand on a ledge. We hurried to the top, thinking he might be going ahead of us. When we peered over the rim, we saw no sign of a bighorn. But there in a meadow of heather was a shallow lake of ten or twenty acres. A breeze swept from the south and touched its surface, ripples dancing like lights in a dazzling chandelier. In the midst of the ripples there was a swirl. An eastern brook, perhaps fifteen inches long, was rising to a fly. This was an eastern brook that Roy four years before had brought here in a milk can tied to a pack saddle of a mule. Now there was life in the once sterile pond. Now there was a new reward at the end of an adventurous climb for those who dared those treacherous cliffs.

The North Minam Meadows lie over the range to the west of Lapover. It is a rich bottom land, a mile or so long and a half-mile wide, coveted by every man who loves the mountains and has seen it. Fortunately it is in a national forest. It has knee-high grass for horses from spring until winter. The North Minam meanders through, spilling over marshy banks lined with tall grass and rushes. Like the Klickitat Meadows of the Cascades, it is ideal for a boy's fishing. Here he can hide himself in the tall grass a few feet from the river's edge and float his fly on the water. It will not go more than a few feet before he has a rainbow or eastern brook. They are little fellows, from six to eight inches, but they are every inch champions and right for the pan.

There are ice-cold springs in the meadow, and groves of trees for camping. In late June the valley is filled with the fragrance of the snowbrush. And from May until August most of the wild flowers of the Wallowas will be found there.

This is where Joseph C. Culbertson came to die. He acquired a lung infection from his chemical researches, and his doctors gave him six months to live. As Joe lay on his bed, trying to think of the place where he would like to spend the last months of his life, he remembered the North Minam Meadows.

"That is the place," said Joe.

His wife put their affairs in order and got in touch with Roy. It was early May 1938, and the snow would be out of the North Minam. Roy made several trips over and set up camp for the Culbertsons—tents and store beds, medicines and provisions, all the accessories of the sickroom. When camp was established, Roy and Mrs. Culbertson went back and got Joe.

Joe was almost too weak for the seven-mile trip from Lapover by the Bowman Trail, but somehow or other he made it. For weeks he lay in a screened tent in a small grove of jack pine and Engelman's spruce at the edge of the North Fork. The Meadows are 5,200 feet high and in sunshine most of the time from May to November. From his tent Joe could see deer and elk at the salt lick, and hear the willow thrush singing. Every morning he watched the sun touch the eastern rim of the canyon, with its great columns of granite rock. One morning as Joe watched he saw the sun touch one rock and transform it into a giant eagle. The breast of this eagle is slightly lighter than its crest. It stands atop the ridge and commands the Meadows.

From his place in the Meadows Joe saw storms make up around Steamboat and Long lakes and swoop down on them, often leaving snow and sleet on the ridges even in August. But they brought only a light rain to the Meadows. There would be the gentle, almost inaudible dripping of the trees during a night of rain. In the morning great fingers of mist would start moving up the canyon. By noon a west wind would have cleared the valley, and the sun would be shining on the rock eagle. Every night there was the soft music of the North Minam as it left the marshlands of the Meadows and picked up momentum for its wild and rugged journey down to the Big Minam, three miles distant.

By the time the Douglas maple, willow, and tamarack had turned, Joe had started fishing in the North Fork. In November when Roy packed him and his wife out, Joe was a new man. The Culbertsons camped in the meadows in 1938, 1939, and 1940, going in when the Bowman Trail was first open and leaving only with the first snow of winter. There I met Joe Culbertson, some six years after he went to the Meadows to die. He and his wife opened their camp to our pack train and gave us lunch. The next summer I came across Joe after I had climbed halfway up the steep trail to Green Lake. Joe had a pick and shovel and was starting to construct a new trail to the lake--one with a more comfortable grade. There was joy in his heart and tenderness in his voice as he spoke of the Meadows.

Others have experienced the same thing. Once Reuben Horwitz, construction engineer, had a long vacation coming to him. He and Janet had Roy pack them into the Meadows for a stay of several months. They camped where the Culbertsons camped. They had not been there long when Reuben was thrown from a horse and seriously injured. He ended with a long convalescence in the Meadows, and like Joe came out well.

Roy took me there in 1939 on our first pack trip together. When we left Lapover, Roy looked to the sky in the south and said, "It's a bit too blue. We're apt to have a storm." The last day or two it had been too hot for August. There had been little breeze and the heat of the valley was in it. The woods were tinder dry and the dust, pounded and churned by many pack trains, lay deep on the Bowman Trail. We rested our horses frequently as we climbed out of the Lostine canyon. The powdery dust rose around us. And when the horses stopped, sweat ran off their bellies and noses and disappeared in the dust.

We were at Brownie Basin, not far from the top of the range, when we heard thunder. The storm came quickly. Clouds moved in from the south. The heat had hung on the mountain as it does in a city long after the sun has set on a humid day. But now it was gone in a flash as a strong cold wind swept in, licking the ridges with a smattering of rain.

The rain turned to snow and sleet. Before we had crossed Wilson Basin, which lies over the top on the western side of the range, the ground was white with snow.

I stopped my horse Dan halfway down to the North Minam Meadows on the zigzag trail that drops out of Wilson Basin. He turned sideways on one of the crooked elbows of the path, as I looked down on the meadows a thousand feet or more below me. They were dimly visible as through a fog, for the snow at this altitude had turned to rain and was falling soft and misty. Suddenly Dan reared and snorted and tried to run. I looked up the trail, and there coming around a bend was what appeared to be a long, dark serpent. It weaved and wiggled as it came down, and once in a while raised its head as if better to mark its course. My first impulse was the same as Dan's. But in a second I understood.

Pulverized dust can be as efficient in shedding water as the feathers on a duck's back. When it is as fine as flour, it contains an air cushion with pores too small to admit water. Thus it can become a roller that carries water off a mountainside. That is what happens when a flash flood rolls off a dry desert hillside of the west, tossing houses and barns as if they were chips. That was what was happening this August day. A great stream of water was running on top of the slick dust of the Bowman Trail. It descended the mountain in a rush. Dan did not stop snorting and rearing until he felt the familiar touch of the water on his hoofs.

By the time we reached the Meadows the rain had settled to a steady drizzle. It had a stubbornness and persistency that indicated it might be with us for days. The trees were dripping; the dampness penetrated everywhere.

Roy found pieces of pitchwood and had a fire going in a jiffy. He piled slabs of dry bark of a red fir on the fire. This is the fuel that produces the hottest fire in the mountains of the West. At once the atmosphere of a home took the place of the wet woods.

The best of all fuels in the Wallowas is mountain-mahogany. Its coals from the night's fire are hot in the morning. But there is no mountain-mahogany in the Meadows, for it grows only on the ridges. So Roy said, "Let's get some cottonwood, willow, or alder. It's a little better if it's on the rotten side. I learned that from the Indian squaws when I was a boy."

We had no tent on that trip, so before dusk Roy said, "Let's see if we can find a dry tree for our sleeping bag." He thought he could find one that would shed water for three or four days, and it was not long before he did. It was a red fir, leaning slightly to one side. It was dry underneath. There we put our bags for two days of rain, and they stayed as dry as they would have in a tent.

The third morning when we wakened the sun was rising in a clear sky. We lolled about camp, hanging out blankets and clothes to rid them of dampness. When we had finished, Roy said, "You know, a man could live in these Meadows just about forever. It's a powerful healthy place."

Then he told me about Joe Culbertson and Reuben Horwitz, and how in the old days he used to come here just to sleep off the fatigue of sheepshearing. "When God made this spot He made the air a little lighter and cleaner. He made the water a little purer and colder. He made the sunshine a little brighter. He made the grass a little more tender for the horses."

As Roy talked, three does and a fawn crossed a clearing above camp. The yapping of a coyote floated down from the ledges high above them. In a little while a bull elk, with at least a six-foot spread of horns, sauntered by, as unconcerned as a window shopper on Fifth Avenue.

"That elk would act different if the hunting season was on," said Roy. "Funny, but they know when it starts. Frighten a herd of elk during hunting season and they may leave the country. I've known them to travel forty or fifty miles without stopping. But deer are different. Each buck has his little domain. Maybe it's a draw or a stretch of woods a mile or so long. Wherever it is, it's home, and he won't leave it. If you're hunting him, he'll circle back to it. He'll stay in the country he knows."

Roy added: "Another nice thing about these Meadows is that they are protected by Uncle Sam. That's the way it should be. It's against the law to graze sheep here. That's right, too. Pretty soon they got to take the sheep out of these mountains. If people are to come here and fish and hunt or take pictures and climb these peaks, they'll need lots of horse feed. Pretty soon people will discover that all the feed in the high Wallowas is needed for horses and deer and elk."

It was snowing when our pack train pulled out of Bear Creek Saddle, headed toward Sturgill Basin and Stanley Ridge. It was a light snow and there was no wind, so the near-zero temperature did not bite. The snow did not melt as it fell; it powdered our hats and shoulders so that we soon were a ghostly looking procession winding among the trees of the silent forest.

An inch of snow had fallen when the pack train reached Sturgill Basin. At this point we were high above the North Minam. On the ridge opposite us was Green Lake, frozen into a great crystal turned milky by the light touch of new snow. And on the far horizon to the south the town of North Powder was only faintly visible as the storm dropped a curtain of dusk over the mountains. When the pack train pulled through the Basin and climbed to the Washboard Trail that leads to Stanley, a cruel wind with a severe bite in its teeth had come up from the southwest. It drove the finely powdered snow into the skin as if it were sand from a blasting machine.

The ridge along the Washboard Trail is cold in any wind. This trail, decorated with prostrate juniper and whitebark pine, winds along the hogback west of Bear Creek. At points the hogback is only a few feet wide, with the ground dropping a thousand feet or more on each side at a dizzy pitch of 60 degrees. In these places the wind howled on this winter day as it picked up speed from the downdraft that sucked it into the Bear Creek canyon, 3,000 to 4,000 feet below the trail on the right. This trail often passes along the base of jagged cliffs that rise as great hackles along the hogback. Here it is often skimpy, carved from the base of the basalt cliffs. At these places this winter wind hurled its weight against the cliffs and whirled clouds of snow into the air. Then it swerved off the cliffs and raced to the north with a whine in its throat.

Below us on the left the land tumbled in disarray into a series of sharp ravines that collect small streams of pure cold water in the spring and summer and carry them to the Big Minam. The slopes leading into them are dangerous. A single horse might pick his way up or across these steep inclines, but neither a pack train nor a horse with a man on him should venture it. One of these draws ends in Chaparral Basin some 3,000 feet below the trail. At that point a sheepherder's train once rolled into the canyon. Five horses were tailed together. The rear one slipped and fell, pulling the other four with him. They rolled for half a mile. When they came to rest, down on the sharp rocks that line the brush on the lower reaches, the five horses were dead and their cargo was scattered over the mountainside. The sheepherder stood briefly with bowed head, as if in reverence at the burial of friends; then sadly he turned his horse around and headed back to get a new outfit.

Roy shouted something when we passed this place, pointing down to Chaparral Basin. Perhaps he was reminding us of the episode I have just told. But the wind was so strong his words were carried away, mere petals of snow in the blizzard.

I have often stopped here on a summer afternoon, enthralled by the view. Off to the west in the valley of the Minam is the great meadow of the Horse Ranch, where Red Higgins welcomes visitors at an airport in the wilderness. The light green of that meadow is the only break in the darkness of the conifers and basalt that line the valley—the only break, that is, except for an occasional glimpse of the blue water of the Minam itself.

This is favorite country of elk and ruffed grouse. Here I have found a vast display of exquisite pink penstemon. Here the wild currant and black-headed cones flourish.

The ridge the trail follows runs north and turns in a great arc to the west. From a distance it seems impassable. The sharp cliffs, the precipitous mountainside, and the ravines that slash its surface in deep and ragged cuts seem indeed to be forbidding obstacles. There are in fact not many places where a trail could traverse this treacherous ridge. But some sheepman years ago picked his way around great rocks, across ledges, and under the cliffs, and found footholds adequate for one-way travel in the six miles it takes to travel the arc of the bowl. I always feel at grips with adventure when I look at this route. Every step must be taken gingerly. It is as though one were walking along a cornice of a building high above the canyons of Wall Street.

Much of the beauty of the scene had been wiped out by the blizzard of this November day. The Horse Ranch and the whole valley of the Minam were lost to view. Even the far points of the ridge we were on had disappeared. Whirling snow made impenetrable clouds in the deep pockets of the canyon below us. The trail traverses a virtual knife-edge above Blow Out Basin. Here it seemed as if the whole pack train would be blown into the void.

The wind soon pierced our heavy mackinaws, slipped under our chaps, and chilled our legs. The six miles along the rim of the basin seemed twelve. Cold reached through to the very marrow. It would have been a relief to walk, but the trail was slippery and no place for half-frozen people who could only stumble. Roy wisely kept to his horse; and the others agreed. We moved in silence, bent forward so as to soften the force of the wind that blew us against the cliffs on our right.

By the time we had cleared the rim and come out on the broad ridge above Stanley, it was mid-afternoon and deep dusk. Low, dark clouds had swept in from the southwest and cut the vision to a few hundred yards. On the open ridge the wind was a gale. Great swirls of snow blotted even the pack train from view. To stay in this place all night with the expectation of being alive in the morning would seem reckless to most people. Yet Roy pulled up by a clump of fir, dismounted, and said, "Guess we better camp here."

He cut two poles about eight feet long, each having a fork at one end. He cut another pole about twelve feet long and, using it as a ridge, lashed it into the fork of each of the other two poles. He then raised these poles and used ropes to anchor each of them to stakes. Then he took longer poles, about fifteen feet long, and laid them as rafters on the windward side of the lean-to, about eighteen inches apart, so that one end rested on the ridge and the other on the ground. These roof poles he lashed to the ridge with twine and rope. Next he took quantities of fir boughs and wove them through these roof poles until he had a snug thatch that was several boughs thick. He closed each end of the lean-to in the same way, weaving fir boughs through cross poles that he had lashed into places in those openings. In front of the lean-to he built a three-walled open fireplace, prying up rocks from the frozen ground and building a horseshoe-shaped wall eighteen inches high with its open side toward the lean-to. A fire was started, and in not much over an hour everyone in the party was snug and warm. The horses were fed oats and baled hay we had packed in. They stood throughout the night with their saddles and blankets on for protection. Before supper was cooked the blacks and bays and sorrels were so heavily powdered with snow they were indistinguishable one from the other. We humans bedded down in Roy's lean-to. The wind howled out the night and in the morning the snow was over a foot thick. But Roy's work had been well done; there were no draughts to disturb our sleep.

Roy knows the Wallowas in winter. He has buried himself in them for a week or more, riding out a blizzard. Sometimes his shelter was a cabin; at other times it was a hole in the snow.

Roy usually ran a trap line for marten from Minam Lake to the head of the Copper Creek Basin, an eight- or ten-mile arc in the high mountains. It had to be at an elevation of 6,000 to 8,000 feet, because that is where the marten are found in winter. He placed each trap on a tree trunk, three to four feet above the ground. He learned about marten bait the hard way. One winter he baited his traps with the trimmings from elk meat, and as a result he lost a winter's catch. Marten do not like fat meat.

Rabbit, pine squirrel, and blue jays are the best marten bait available in the Wallowas. Marten will not touch camp robbers or flying squirrels. They love grouse, which in severe winter weather sometimes bury themselves in snow for warmth.

"We can't see the grouse," said Roy. "But the marten smells him and digs him out."

Roy would leave Lapover on snowshoes every week or so for a five-day inspection of his marten traps.

"About a quarter of the traps caught camp robbers, blue jays, and squirrels," Roy told me.

Roy's pack weighed forty pounds or more. He always took an ax for wood and a shovel to dig a hole in the snow for lodging. He carried a frying pan, kettle, coffee pot, and a cup, plate, and spoon. He took twenty pounds of rabbit meat for bait, and a half-dozen extra traps. For food he had coffee, sugar, bacon, whole wheat cereal, potatoes, and bread. Roy never took blankets or a bedroll on these winter trips, because the weight of the pack did not permit it. At night he slept like a bear in a hole in the snow. He cut off the top of a snag and with that wood built a fire next to the snag.

Those who have built fires in deep snow know, as Gifford Pinchot observed (*Breaking New Ground*), that it promptly melts itself down out of sight, leaving only a hole with a little steam coming out. That's why Roy always carried a shovel on these snowshoe trips. He dug a pit in the snow as he followed the fire down. Since the fire was next to the snag, Roy was able to take his wood supply down with him to the bottom of the pit. In the morning he might be fifteen feet or more beneath the surface. His bed was fir boughs. If it rained or snowed, he would dig an alcove in the side of the pit and crawl into it. There he could ride out a blizzard for several days.

One day, when Roy was reminiscing about these trap-line trips, he said to me, "People think snow is cold, but it isn't. It's a blanket that has a lot of warmth in it. At times birds bury themselves in it to keep warm. I've seen deer do the same thing. They keep their heads out, but they will lie in a snowdrift entirely covered for maybe eighteen or twenty-four hours."

The mountains in the winter are cruel to man and beast. The game leaves the high country and goes down to winter range. There are no berries, roots, or other produce of the woods for food. Travel itself is hazardous. A blizzard in the Wallowas may blow twelve days and drop a swirling cloud through which man cannot see even fifty feet. Or the snow may turn to slush and cling to snowshoes like leaden weights. Then a man may not be able to walk more than two miles in a whole day. In cross-country travel he can readily exhaust himself, and in his fatigue at the end of a day sit down to rest and freeze to death. Roy's first principles of winter travel are: 1) Always take along a shovel and an ax; 2) get under the snow when weather is bad; and 3) go slowly at the beginning of the day, saving energy for the last few hours of the evening, for a blizzard or rainstorm may come up and change the character of the travel. Then a man's life may depend on his reserve of energy.

Throwing a diamond hitch, putting an improvised shoe on a horse, building a lean-to in a storm, carrying a sick or wounded person out of a wilderness, cooking, finding the lair of a buck deer or the den of a bear—these and any of the hundred and one experiences of a pack trip are chores that Roy handles with understanding and high efficiency. It is the competence one respects when one sees the deft fingers of a sculptor at work, or watches the sure eye of an axman, or observes a skilled mechanic at a lathe, or hears the master advocate in court. It is the extraordinary skill that one finds at the top of any profession or trade. There is a finesse and quality about it that distinguishes the skill of any champion.

When I read of the early mountain men I think of Roy. He would have been a credit to Jim Bridger or any of the early scouts. He is the caliber of man I think Captain William Clark of the Lewis and Clark expedition must have been. Clark did not know the outdoors as a botanist or biologist or geologist knew it. He knew it as a country lawyer without benefit of formal legal education may know the law. He knew his way through the wilderness, he could appraise its risks and dangers, and he knew where to find shelter and sustenance. Clark could not spell very well, and his writing shows some vestiges of illiteracy. He was not erudite, but he had wisdom and judgment.

Clark was a simple, uncomplicated man who had the knack of giving every problem in the woods a practical twist. He was the kind of man who could survive though he entered the wilderness empty-handed. He had the competence to deal with the day-to-day tasks, which, though trivial, added up to life or death. Such a man is Roy Schaeffer. He, too, could have done with credit what Clark did.

Roy was a warm admirer of President Roosevelt. Shortly before the 1945 Inauguration he got the idea he wanted to attend. He sat up in a day coach all across the country and arrived in Washington, D.C., late one afternoon. He was dressed in cowboy boots, Pendleton pants, a loud plaid shirt, a mackinaw, and ten-gallon hat. He strode through Union Station with a battered suitcase, stepped into a taxicab, and told the driver, "I want to see Bill Douglas."

Eventually he ended up at our home in Silver Spring, Maryland; and during his two-week visit he captured the town. He went to dinners and luncheons and teas; he stayed in character and wore his cowboy clothes to all of them. He stood on the White House grounds with head bared and saw Roosevelt take the oath. A lady in the crowd said to him, "It's always good to see someone from Texas."

Roy, embarrassed, said, "I'm from Oregon, ma'am."

We walked down Pennsylvania Avenue together, and reserved Easterners looked up at Roy and said with friendliness, "Hello, cowboy."

Roy would touch his hat and, as if speaking to a traveler on a high mountain trail, reply, "Hi."

He pounded the pavements of Washington with his high-heeled boots and said to my wife at night, "Walking the Bowman Trail is easier."

He slept in a bed with white, clean sheets and commented, "Never slept inside but what I caught a cold. Wish I had brought my sleeping bag. Then I'd sleep on the back porch. It's much healthier outdoors."

As a rock fish, famous product of Chesapeake Bay, was being prepared in our kitchen, he said, "If I had a big flat rock, I could build a fire in the yard and cook the fish on the rock. Bet it'd be the best fish you ever tasted."

At a dinner in Georgetown he turned to the hostess who in all her life had probably never been in a kitchen and said, "These are good biscuits you made, ma'am. Some day I wish I could dig a hole in your yard and cook you some sourdough bread. It can be real light and fluffy, too, you know."

One afternoon at a tea I saw Roy surrounded by a group of newspapermen and -women. He towered above them all, as Flagstaff Point towers over his cabin at Lapover. I saw from the expression on his face that he was not wholly at ease. I stepped to the outer circle of the group to discover the reason. He was being plied with questions of politics in Oregon, prices in Oregon, industrial and social conditions in Oregon, and the run of questions a distinguished visitor from the Far West might expect from the press of a friendly metropolitan paper. Roy is not a man of books. His formal education is slight. He seldom reads even in the long winter days when he is snowed in at Lapover. But he listens to the radio; and down in the valley he hears the talk in the poolhalls and on the street corners. He also listens attentively to every traveler who comes up the canyon. His intelligence is of a high order. He has insight and understanding of people and their motives. And so he has a simple understanding of great issues—as sound as the common sense of the common people. But he was too timid to advance his views to the circle of sophisticated correspondents who faced him at the tea. Finally I heard him say, "You folks know all about those things. I know nothing except the mountains. Here in Washington you can write your columns and stories and tell me what is true and what isn't. When you come to Oregon, then it'll be my turn."

"What will you do then?" asked a lady reporter.

"I'll tell you what I'll do," said Roy with great seriousness. "I'll blow up the air mattress of your sleeping bag for you."

In the deep woods Roy would not know how to do anyone a greater favor.

PART TWO

New Deal Judge

Douglas was a New Deal insider. As member, then chairman, of the Securities and Exchange Commission, he played a major role in the reform and regulation of capital markets that was one of the hallmarks of FDR's administration. Douglas played poker with the president, and mixed martinis for him. In "The New Deal," a chapter of his autobiography, *Go East, Young Man,* we are reminded of the circumstances of the Depression and introduced to many of the characters who played leading roles in the establishment of the New Deal administrative state. The picture Douglas paints of Roosevelt is of an essentially conservative leader, very aware that politics is "the art of the possible."

Douglas was appointed to the Supreme Court to fill the seat vacated by Louis D. Brandeis. Brandeis had won fame as "the people's lawyer" for his involvement as a representative of the public interest in railroad rate cases, and for his attack on business cartels. Brandeis had remained involved in policy matters even after going on the bench, through surrogates, including Felix Frankfurter. In "Brandeis and Black," Douglas tells of his relationship with Brandeis during his early years in Washington, as well as his bond to his colleague Hugo Black, all three sharing an aversion to concentrated economic power, and concern for the well-being of the common person.

"Contending Schools of Thought" is a chapter from the second volume of Douglas's autobiography, *The Court Years.* In it, Douglas traces the division in the Court over the appropriate interpretation of the Due Process Clause of the Fourteenth Amendment. One faction, led by Felix Frankfurter, adhered to the view that only practices that "shocked the conscience" or were otherwise outside a conception of "ordered liberty" were prohibited to the states by the clause. Douglas joined Hugo Black in insisting that the clause simply made the provisions of the Bill of Rights, originally applicable only to the federal government, effective against the states. In most instances, at least during the time that Black, Douglas, and Frankfurter were on the Court together, the Black-Douglas view prevailed. While Douglas insists that he and Frankfurter were not enemies, there is ample evidence to suggest that he is here practicing a form of literary diplomacy.

Douglas's service on the Court extended from the middle of FDR's second term through the abrupt end of Richard Nixon's. His successor was appointed, ironically, by Gerald Ford, who had once led an effort to impeach him. "Two Presidents" is taken from a chapter of *The Court Years*, and contains excerpts from his accounts of FDR and LBJ, which are particularly striking. Both presidents led a county at war, but in very different ways, with very different results.

The New Deal

The Big Depression was on us. The banks were closed. I remember walking the streets of New Haven with the great sum of ten dollars in my pocket. I did not feel panicky; personally, it only appeared that the wheel had turned, taking everyone back to the conditions of poverty I had known in Yakima. The common disaster seemed to bring everyone closer together. There was much reexamination in university circles of where we had been and where we were going. The stock market crash had been awesome to watch from the sidelines. Many men committed suicide when they saw their empires crumble. Some men like Joseph P. Kennedy were selling short; some like Cyrus Eaton were buying the blue chips at or near the bottom. Samuel M. Smith—in later years one of my closest friends, but not known to me in 1929—was a CPA working with receiverships on the West Coast; he was shortly to acquire the fabulous Pittock Block, Portland, Oregon, which later became a veritable gold mine.

Receiverships and bankruptcies were rampant. Protective and reorganization committees were formed to represent various classes of security holders of these bankrupt companies. Lincoln automobiles that were brand-new came on the market for a few hundred dollars (and I bought one, which I drove for many years thereafter). The ranks of the unemployed mounted; bread lines increased; soup kitchens multiplied; farm products slumped in price and farmers began dumping their milk in the streets in angry protest; freight cars carried thousands of passengers where once they carried only hundreds; dividend payments stopped and interest payments defaulted, leaving trust accounts dry; the income of colleges and universities plummeted.

President Herbert Hoover's plan to mend the economy was to restore the financial strength of industry so that it could reemploy workers. Federal agencies, such as the Reconstruction Finance Corporation, were formed. Financial loans were poured out to industry, but unemployment mounted.

Opposition to Hoover grew. "The greatest engineer in American history," he was called at one Connecticut meeting I attended.

"He dammed, ditched, and drained the entire country," another platform speaker shouted.

Still another speaker explained Hoover's theory of feeding chickens: "First, feed oats to the horses, and in time there will be enough manure to keep the chickens busy." After a pause he thundered, "I say let's feed the chickens first."

As the 1932 campaign got under way, several of us on the Yale faculty were out on the hustings debating the opposition. I remember one night in Hartford when a fiery professor on the Republican side built his hour-long speech around the theme "You can't make water run uphill." He sat down to thunderous applause.

I arose, to reply briefly: "Come out West and I will show you projects where we send water over mountain ranges, as well as through them and around them. Engineers make water run uphill every day." My thesis was that all we needed were engineering skills, and that we needed a new engineer in the White House.

FDR was storming the country and soon was elected in a landslide.

There was, throughout the days of the New Deal, a good amount of speculation about the political theory and philosophy of FDR's program. The words "liberal," "progressive," "radical," and "conservative," however, are not too meaningful. It is often difficult to fit any one person neatly into one of these categories. A "conservative" in constitutional law would technically be he who stuck closest to the constitutional structure of 1787. But in modern-day parlance, those who do so are called "left-wingers." A "conservative" in constitutional law has come to mean he who construes the Constitution and Bill of Rights the best to serve the Establishment. The "liberal" has come to mean one opposed to existing practices, although still working within the constitutional framework. The "radical" is one who, if necessary, would dispense with the framework in seeking solutions. After the 1940s the word "progressive" disappeared from our vocabulary.

In American politics FDR was not regarded as a conservative, though his roots, his family, his early associations were all with the conservative group. When he used politics to serve causes beyond that group's interests, he was viewed as a traitor, as was anyone who, though an original member of their group, later used politics, education, the pen, the pulpit, or the law to serve ends they considered hostile. My friend

Harry Golden, of North Carolina, who espoused desegregation of the races, was not considered a traitor, since he was not born in the South. The traitor would be the native Southerner who takes a desegregation stance on race. The conservatives of America—members of the Establishment—never forgave FDR for deserting the cause, which they thought was his by reason of birth.

Those of us close to FDR never felt he deserted the conservative cause in principle. Except for the installation of real collective bargaining, he left the social and economic order largely untouched. His energy was spent in cleaning up that order, eliminating its excesses, and making capitalism respectable. FDR was, in American terminology, more a progressive than a liberal. He worked in the La Follette tradition. Probably no politician can survive who moves left from that position, for the United States has usually been conservative in its inclinations.

During the New Deal days the people were prisoners of their own illusions, as Robert M. Hutchins once put it. The major delusions, to use his categories, were: the budget should be balanced annually; currency must be "sound"; the gold standard was untouchable; socialism was a menace; free enterprise could provide a job for everyone, if it were left alone; the states were supreme, the federal government largely impotent. As Hutchins has said, these "received ideas" were alien to the new world that was in the making. These are the reasons why, I think, the New Deal has become largely meaningless to the subsequent generation.

FDR's embrace of capitalism and most of the basic tenets of the Establishment were made evident by his NRA (National Industrial Recovery Act), which was enacted in 1933 and expired in 1935. This was the Blue Eagle scheme whereby industry was given the power to make the rules governing competition and prices. The NRA stemmed from Rex Tugwell's effort to get Roosevelt to give business the authority to fix its own prices and to put such restrictions on production as it chose. Tugwell, an advisor to FDR, was trying to persuade him, even prior to the nomination, as to the merits of "economic self-government." (Tugwell describes that idea in his book *The Brain Trust*.) Tugwell was opposed to the Wilson-Brandeis view that the Sherman Act and Clayton Act, restricting monopolies and restraint of trade, were desirable, that big units should be broken into small components and kept that way. He thought that the antitrust laws prevented "any sort of social management" and kept competition "at a destructive level." He saw that monopoly in electric power was inevitable and competition impractical, but from that example, he argued with FDR that if "power production could not be fractionalized, neither could other similar industries." Tugwell thought that prices could be controlled in ways other than fractionalization and competition, by government responsibility for the planning of production. Tugwell proposed "an orderly mechanism that might enable industry to produce a cooperation now considered illegitimate."

Tugwell did not make much headway in selling the idea to FDR prior to the 1932 election. His plan, as submitted, was in the form of a proposal for a White House Economic Council whose job would be to reorganize industry on the model of the Federal Reserve System in banking. "The antitrust acts can be repealed and each industry can be encouraged to divide itself into suitable regional groups on which will sit representatives of the Economic Council."

In these early years FDR tried to placate business, and he was still in that mood when I reached Washington, D.C., in 1934. I remember his speech to the American Bankers Association that fall, when the audience cheered him to the echo. He proposed an alliance of business, banking, agriculture, labor, and industry to achieve "business recovery." He added, "What an all-American team that would be!" Of all the measures FDR proposed and got enacted in the first year, two were most crucial to business. One was the Agricultural Adjustment Act, which was to make a few farmers rich and make the plight of the sharecroppers more serious. The other was the NRA, which allowed businessmen to control production and fix prices.

Hugo L. Black, then in the Senate, made a prophetic speech:

> *This bill, if it shall pass and become law, will transfer the lawmaking power of this nation, insofar as the control of industry is concerned, from the Congress to the trade associations. There is no escape from that conclusion. That is exactly what has happened in Italy, and as a result, the legislation passed by the parliamentary body of Italy, as expressed by one economist, has reached the vanishing point.*

There are those who still say that NRA was FDR's fling with socialism, but it had no resemblance to any school of socialist thought. NRA was an attempt to grant to industry the power to set production quotas and prices. It was a grant of monopolistic power to private industry, placing the making of the rules governing business in the hands of business itself.

FDR exploited the old liberal clichés, but he never touched the basic problems of the ghettos—the citadels of the bankers, real estate brokers, moneylenders, and the city officials whom they control. He multiplied agencies, but never aimed at permanent control of basic industries. He never reached the race problem. Personally he worried about it, but politically he aligned himself with the powers-that-be in the South so far as Black people were concerned. And during his administrations he never even effected complete integration of the races in the Armed Forces.

In this regard, one day my secretary announced the presence of a Black woman who had come with credentials from my old classmate Paul Robeson. When the woman was escorted in, I offered her a chair, but she remained standing and asked, "Who am I?"

"You are kin to my friend Paul Robeson."

"I know my name. But who am I?"

I shook my head.

She replied, "I am the bastard daughter of the brother of a former Supreme Court Justice."

What she was conveying to me was that she was in the Supreme Court building as a matter of right. Her demand was that I persuade FDR that there should be an immediate desegregation of the races in the Armed Forces.

I talked with FDR about this lady's idea. He did not laugh, scoff, or scorn. He listened intently and with approval and said, "We'll see." After a long pause he added, lighting a cigarette, "You know they call the Missus a nigger-lover. Perfectly dreadful what they say." He reminisced about the strong hold that the South had on the Congress and how his old wheelhorses (meaning people like Jimmie Byrnes and Joe Robinson) had a deep racial bias. And then he passed to other things, and we never did get back to integration in the Armed Forces. When at last integration was achieved under Truman, white officers, who had commanded Black troops, said it was the best thing that had ever happened, for though loyal and a physical part of the Armed Forces, Black troops were understandably sullen and resentful as long as they remained segregated.

Yet in spite of FDR's moderate stance on race and on capitalism, he had a host of bitter enemies. The rancher for whom I had worked in the wheat fields in my early years in the State of Washington was one of them. When I was a field hand, Ralph Snyder was close to bankruptcy. His lands were heavily mortgaged, he was paying at least eight percent interest at the banks, the price of wheat was up and down, making the business extremely hazardous, as the costs were fixed.

Years passed and I did not see Ralph. Finally, in the forties, we met at my log cabin up the Lostine River in the Wallowas Mountains of eastern Oregon. Ralph was then prosperous. His mortgages had been refinanced at an interest rate of about three percent. There was a floor under his wheat. He had tens of thousands of dollars in the bank. Yet for the first half-hour he did nothing but curse FDR.

"How can you be so critical?" I asked. "You are one of the beneficiaries of FDR's farm program. You should be praising him, and all you do is denounce him."

He thought awhile and then gave a most revealing answer. "It is true I am much better off. But let me ask you something—did you ever meet the rancher down the road from me? Well, he's no good—lazy, shiftless, a poor manager. I'd call him worthless. What's happened to him? He's on easy street. He never had it so good. This Roosevelt program makes a no-good guy rich. How can we expect America to be strong if men who couldn't make it on their own are hoisted up by government?"

The power of industry to fix prices was well established. The power of labor to negotiate for wages somewhat restored the balance. The other liberal reform of the New Deal involved the transfer of the financial center of the United States from Wall Street to Washington. Wilson had warned in 1911, "The great monopoly in this country is the money monopoly." The Pujo Committee, dating from 1912, concluded that the great danger was "the control of credit" by private groups.

The Federal Reserve Act of 1913 remedied part of the problem by establishing the Federal Reserve Board in Washington. As FDR said when he dedicated the lovely Federal Reserve Building in 1937, that board, a governmental, not a private, agency exerts "a powerful influence upon the expansion and contraction in the flow of money through the channels of agriculture, trade, and industry."

But the board did not solve the entire problem. Brandeis discussed the matter in his study, *Other People's Money,* published in 1913:

> *The dominant element in our financial oligarchy is the*
> *investment banker. Associated banks, trust companies and*

life insurance companies are his tools. Controlled railroads,
public service and industrial corporations are his subjects.
Though properly but middlemen, these bankers bestride as
masters America's business world, so that practically no large
enterprise can be undertaken successfully without their
participation or approval. These bankers are, of course, able
men possessed of large fortunes; but the most potent factor in
their control of business is not the possession of extraordinary
ability or huge wealth. The key to their power is
Combination—concentration intensive and comprehensive.

It was this citadel that the SEC assaulted. Our basic laws—the Securities Act of 1933, the Securities Exchange Act of 1934, and the Public Utility Holding Company Act of 1935—helped move the power away from the investment bankers.

This transfer of financial power was both painful and exciting. The Federal Reserve Board, with its able chairman, Marriner Eccles, who advocated deficit spending, raised alarming specters in the financial community. I saw another example of this alarm when in 1938 I went to Chicago to address the Chicago Bond Club. After the speech I was followed from the room by an irate investment banker, who kept shouting, "Why are you trying to destroy America?"

My answers did not satisfy him, so as we passed through an ornate room on our way to the elevator, I stopped, and pointing to the paintings on the walls, said, 'We are doing nothing more destructive to America than would be done to this room if we moved the pictures around."

Trembling with anger, my questioner shouted, "Why in hell do you want to move the pictures around?"

This was a time when fear stalked the land. As some brokers and bankers were driven to suicide, so were penniless writers who were deprived of their work cards. Throughout the country there was a haunting fear of the loss of jobs. Never in American history had the total collapse of employment, of confidence, of hope been so complete. Only one who lived close to the edge in those days could ever appreciate the powerful impact in FDR's words spoken at his First Inaugural in 1933: "All we have to fear is fear itself."

Well before the time of FDR's election in 1932, people were suffering badly. Unemployment figures were mounting. In the East there were men and women on street corners selling apples, with the hope of getting enough profit to buy some milk for their children. People were being fed at fire stations and public schools and at any available feeding stations. The cities, largely restricted to property taxes for revenue, were unable to meet the financial need. Begging increased; Salvation Army refuges were full; states were getting into relief work but complaining that they did not have the money to meet the demand. And they certainly did not, in light of their existing tax structure. They clamored for federal assistance. Hoover came out against the "dole"; and dole became an ugly four-letter word. Will Rogers said of FDR during the worst of the Depression, "If he burned down the Capitol we would cheer and say, 'Well, we at least got a fire started, anyhow.' "

The Democrats had carried the House in 1930 and the Senate was evenly split. Robert F. Wagner of New York introduced legislation in 1931 which called for one billion dollars for federal public works and federal employment services. The bill passed Congress, but Hoover vetoed it. Wagner's proposal for unemployment insurance also was voted down by the Senate. Robert La Follette and Edward Costigan in the Senate introduced a bill calling for a federal grant of some millions of dollars to the states for unemployment relief. It, too, was voted down by the Senate. Even Hugo Black, then a senator from Alabama, voted against it, speaking at length before the vote was taken. He was strongly in favor of federal money being used to feed and clothe people but he was opposed to the creation of a new bureaucracy to do so. He was only against the creation of a federal agency to disburse the funds. He thought existing state machinery should be used.

Many other people thought relief was a state, not a federal, matter. FDR, who at that time was the governor of New York, led the way by establishing a state program to supplement local relief funds and by the end of 1932 twenty-four states were providing some money to local agencies for relief.

In 1931 Congress overrode a Hoover veto and passed an Act giving the RFC (Reconstruction Finance Corporation) power to lend three hundred million dollars to the states to supplement local relief funds. But that sum was barely a token: the Senate hearings before its Committee on Manufactures tell the gripping human story. My friend Frank Murphy, then the mayor of Detroit, testified that his city had run out of money, and cut off 1,200 families from welfare. Within a few months three hundred of them could not be found; they apparently had quit the city in desperation. From 1931 to 1932, 150,000 people left

Detroit. The fate of the group which had been deprived of relief was related by Murphy:

> We found 270 of the families were cared for by their
> next-door neighbors in the block; that 170 were cared for by
> relatives; that fifty-six percent of them were in arrears in
> everything—all their bills, groceries, rent, light, and so forth;
> that there were a few suicides; that forty families had
> separated, either sent their children to some home and the
> husband went one way and the wife another, and that the
> average income of the family heads was $1.56 per week per
> person for the family. Having in mind that the standard of
> wages in Detroit, prior to the Depression, was $7 per day, you
> may see what that means.

Relief in those days was only for "survival." A single adult got $2 a week, an adult couple $3.60; a child under sixteen got 75¢ a week, and 3^1/2 quarts of milk; a child sixteen and over got $1.25 a week.

Economic conditions were so bad that by the time of FDR's First Inaugural, many banks in the country had closed, which led him to say "the money changers have fled from their high seats in the temple of our civilization." I heard this particular speech on the radio in New Haven and I felt that I was one with the President on his social program for taking care of the needy.

A host of legislation was hammered through Congress in the first hundred days of the Roosevelt administration to provide at least temporary relief. Most of the funds went not to breadlines, soup kitchens, or food stamps, but was apportioned among projects that were designed to create "work." Of the four billion dollars of "emergency relief" authorized in 1935, the allocation was as follows: highways and grade crossings, eight hundred million dollars; rural relief, water diversion, irrigation and reclamation, five hundred million; rural electrification, eleven hundred million; housing, four hundred and fifty million; assistance for education, professional and clerical persons, three hundred million; Civilian Conservation Corps, six hundred million; loans or grants to local agencies for self-liquidating projects, nine hundred million; sanitation, erosion, flood control, reforestation, three hundred and fifty million.

Overall, the federal government paid about seventy percent of all relief during that three-year period. Harry Hopkins, as the administrator of the Emergency Relief Act, was a good social worker, but was largely ignorant of broader national needs and knew very little about the rest of the world. He made a study of workers on relief in seventy-nine cities, and found that, on the average, they had been unemployed for more than two years. But Hopkins, sensing FDR's opposition to direct payments, parroted the view that only work, not handouts, gave men dignity. He was wont to say that "his" WPA workers looked with disdain on those who received relief.

By the time I reached Washington in 1934, WPA could provide jobs for only about one in four. The situation worsened when federal direct relief was withdrawn and the unemployed were forced back on state and local agencies.

The NRA, as noted, had in it a provision for collective bargaining. Industry tried to capture that clause by forming company unions, and as a result, labor became inflamed. By 1934 ugly strikes were sweeping the nation. Bloody battles ensued—strikers against the police, strikers against the National Guard.

FDR stood behind labor and collective bargaining, and that really spelled the end of his desired alliance with business and finance. The alienation was accentuated by his promotion of the Securities Exchange Act in 1934. Business had tasted its "oats" in NRA and saw in labor relations and the increase in federal regulation the twin forces which it must destroy.

FDR, who always had a keen ear and eye for the grassroots, asked for work relief, rather than direct relief. The unemployed, he said, should be preserved not only from "destitution" but also should work for their "self-respect, their self-reliance and courage and determination." At the same time he opposed a social security measure, which in due course was enacted.

The "work" relief was denounced by the financial world as a menace to private enterprise, which claimed, first, that it invaded fields traditionally reserved for business. Even ditchdigging, some said, was such an invasion, and certainly road and bridge building, and all construction work. Second, it was said, all relief should be local—a revival of the old cry of states' rights.

Those criticisms had an impact on FDR, who had not yet forged the political alliance that was to thrive for a time between the liberals of the North and the Democrats of the South. The 1936 election, however, was a landslide; only Maine and Vermont went Republican. The Social Security Act had been a target of the Republican party, which claimed that it was the end of the workingman's individuality; henceforth, they said, the worker would have not a name but "a New Deal number." During the campaign FDR had said, in a radio speech, that business and finance were "unanimous in their hate for me—and I welcome their hatred. I should like to have it said in my first administration that in it the forces of selfishness and of lust for power met their match. I should like to have it said of my second administration that in it these forces met their master."

Jim Landis and his wife, Estelle, had invited me to their home in Virginia to listen to the broadcast. The room was filled, most everyone sitting on the floor. They all cheered and applauded. I did not cheer, nor did I applaud. I sat in silence, and shortly left. I loved FDR, but I thought his boast that he would be the "master" did not fit America. I thought then—and still think—that America is a complex and diverse pluralistic society and that there is room for everyone, even the brokers and dealers, who, I had discovered, were a species of leeches in the economy. Capitalism, I thought, was better than socialism, a conviction that was strengthened when I started my world travels. For in a socialist state such as Russia there was a suffocating bureaucracy, no First Amendment, no right to protest, no right to strike, no right to denounce the President, the Congress, or the Court. One who was a "master" of business and finance, like one who was a "master" of labor, read the group he "mastered" out of society. Later, I realized that FDR, of course, was using only a figure of speech and did not literally mean what he said. He was "master" in the adroit political way, not "master" in the sense I feared.

Despite FDR's great popularity there were powerful forces of rebellion working in the years preceding the election in November 1936. Father Charles E. Coughlin was one; he would broadcast on the radio from the Shrine of the Little Flower in Detroit. I never met him, but I listened to him regularly. He said the contest for world domination was between

Christ and communism, yet he also denounced capitalism and the international bankers. He thought the government should own the banking system. FDR knew Coughlin, and had Frank Murphy and Joe Kennedy act as intermediaries for him in seeking political friendship. At times they brought Coughlin to the White House. He generally approved FDR's program in 1933 and 1934 and testified before committees of the Congress on some measures, supporting them. Yet while he might support the President one week, he denounced him the next. He was for assistance to business one day, against competition the next day, for government ownership another time. As I listened to him week after week, I decided he was at heart a fascist. What FDR felt, I never quite knew. His tactics were to placate Coughlin, never to antagonize him, and to leave the White House door open to accommodate the man.

A second force of some moment—yet milder and of a completely different character than Coughlin's—was Francis E. Townsend, a doctor in California who became incensed at seeing hungry old people going through garbage cans looking for morsels. He was a tall, thin man without the dynamic force that motivated Coughlin. I knew him only slightly and heard him speak infrequently. His plan was to give every citizen over sixty years old a pension of two hundred dollars a month, provided he or she not be gainfully employed and provided also that he or she spent the money in thirty days. The latter condition was a gimmick of the times, stressing the importance of spreading money around to grocers, clothiers, and other merchants. The first condition was to placate the business group. Townsend Clubs seemed to spring up like mushrooms, and as I read the papers and listened to the radio, the movement seemed to be shaping up as a major political force. But when I talked with FDR about it, he would smile and seem unperturbed which was, from his position, a good political stance.

At about this time a right-wing organization, the American Liberty League, was formed. I was sick at heart because one of my heroes—the great Alfred E. Smith—was a founding member. I admired Smith, who was governor of New York when I was at law school. I would go downtown to hear him speak, and later, when he was running for President, I made campaign speeches for him. Al Smith, a Catholic, was defeated for the Presidency by a bigoted America. I always thought that a man, whether Catholic or Protestant, Jew, or Hindu, should be judged on his merits.

Another force concerned FDR greatly: Huey Long of Louisiana. The Kingfish had been governor of Louisiana and used politics with a vengeance. He built magnificent hospitals and schools; his road-building program was very ambitious. But on my visits to his state I would see a new concrete highway end at a county line, pick up again only at the far side of the county. In between one would bog down in muddy ruts and miserable dirt roads. The reason was that the interim county had voted against the Kingfish in the last election.

Long supported FDR in 1932 and for a part of 1933. Thereafter he was on and off, for and against. Long was law-trained, and according to Senator Frank Maloney, as a senator, was the ablest man on the Hill. I saw Huey Long in action in the Senate, but never knew him. Hugo Black thought Long was a powerful politician, a great debater, and a terrific filibusterer. Late in 1933 Long announced a Share the Wealth program under which every family would be guaranteed an annual income of five thousand dollars. Like the Townsend Plan, the program seemed to spread like a prairie fire, though this seeming popularity was in large part Long's propaganda.

FDR was very concerned about Huey Long but he never denounced the man, even in private conversation with me. He spoke of him gently, praising his political skills. Everyone has always said that Roosevelt was a very astute politician. It seems to me that one of the best bits of evidence is that he never once, in my presence, said anything against his political opponents. About Huey Long he might say, 'Well, the man is certainly fervent,' or, "He is a really forceful speaker." FDR was a clever politician, but he never practiced the politics of destruction.

FDR was consumed with curiosity as to what Long would do next. His counter to the Kingfish Share the Wealth plan was to ask for an increase in inheritance and income taxes, coupled with a program for social security.

When Huey Long was assassinated in Louisiana in the fall of 1935, I sensed that FDR felt relieved. Huey had been planning to run for the Presidency in 1936, and no one knows whether or not he would have made a formidable race. He was, however, the only opponent that FDR saw on the scene. In retrospect it seems obvious that it wasn't the assassin's bullet that eliminated the Kingfish as a real political threat to FDR—it was FDR's cool and calculated moves to counteract Long's proposals.

Harry Hopkins thought the WPA project or programs like it had become a permanent fixture by 1936, that the clock would not be turned back; he expressed that view in his book *Spending to Save: The Complete Story of Relief.* But Harry's book was hardly out before WPA rolls were drastically reduced. The agency picked up again when a new recession hit the nation in 1938, but in 1939 Congress required that anyone who had been on WPA for eighteen consecutive months should be removed. Yet only a small percentage of those laid off—never more than about twelve percent—were able to get private jobs.

WPA did not suit Middle America, nor did direct relief by the federal government. Federal relief would undermine the very low wage structure that existed in some areas, particularly the South. Moreover, as we have discussed, states' rights was a rallying point: if the local agencies lost their control, the Blacks might get on relief. And think how terrible that would be in an area that had a caste system!

This was the kind of infighting that took place in the mid-thirties, and it became a matter of conversation at the White House and on social occasions. Many a time, when I was talking with FDR alone or with others, Eleanor Roosevelt would come in, having just returned from a trip.

"Franklin," she'd say, "I have just returned from [say, North Carolina] and I have discovered something you should know about."

Then she would give him advice. Sometimes it was about racial discrimination. At other times it concerned the inadequacies of local relief and the need for federal standards. Again it might be the use of local relief to keep the Blacks out of the breadlines.

FDR would always listen patiently and with interest, and he would always thank her. Then she would usually say, "Franklin, you must do something about it."

He would smile and say, "We'll see what can be done."

In the thirties, federal funds actually subsidized the operation of sweatshops, which could keep their wages at two dollars or three dollars a week because local agencies refused relief to anyone who would not take such a job. Under FDR's leadership, minimum wage laws eventually raised such salaries, but one inheritance of that system was the practice of deducting from relief clients any money they earned. The hearings before the Subcommittee of the Senate Committee on Manufactures in 1933 unearthed, for instance, the following: A man in Pennsylvania on relief was getting $3.50 a week. His wife got a job in a factory, where she worked fifty-four hours a week, for which she received $1.60. The local board deducted the $1.60 from the husband's relief payment, so the wife quit her job and his check went back to $3.50. That pattern has continued to this day. The welfare system in America in practical effect, if not in design, is to keep the poor people poor.

Business that gets a federal subsidy is not penalized if it makes huge profits. Farmers who are paid not to plant certain crops are not penalized for making as much money on the side as they can. Only the poor are penalized. And the same policy extends to social security paid to those under seventy-two years of age, whose payments are also reduced in proportion to their earnings.

The most devastating weapon of the New Deal was the RFC. This agency was Hoover's creation and an inheritance that FDR greatly exploited. Under Jesse Jones, it bailed out distressed corporations and in its day did a commendable job, free of suspicion of taint or fraud. But the conceptions that it exploited grew and flourished. Business and finance, which were opposed to relief for the poor or even the modest and largely ineffectual WPA, quickly learned that the public trough was an attractive place to wallow. The policy spread, and many other agencies in time became dispensers of the public purse for the rich. By the 1960s and 1970s "socialism for the rich" seemed to have become our way of life.

There are some of my generation who say in retrospect that business in the 1930s was "the enemy." Business was, of course, mainly aligned against FDR in his political campaigns, and big business fought tooth and nail against most New Deal legislation. But business was not the enemy from the point of view of those of us who were the regulators. The Stock Exchange, for example, was cleaned up, but its destruction as an institution was never in our discussions. Nor had we arrived at a point where any talk of its "nationalization" took place. Such talk— when it did occur—was not aimed at business generally but at select key industries such as steel. The few of us who urged FDR in that direction were thinking in terms that the British Labour party later espoused. But we had not advanced as far in our thinking as the late Hugh Gaitskell when he proposed "controlled" stock ownership rather than complete nationalization. Our ideas concerning nationalization were indeed embryonic and we never interested FDR to the point where he said, "Let's have a memo on it."

Deficit spending was a recurring topic of conversation in the New Deal days. I, too, was a Keynesian to the extent that I thought government spending was the only practical political course FDR could take to meet what promised to be a recurring economic crisis. But I did not believe it was the best long-range remedy. FDR and I talked about it. The idea of deficit spending was a worry that kept revisiting him, and when he expressed his concern and asked what I thought, I gave him my views. I told him I thought it was hard to beat the American free enterprise system because it turned loose the genius and energy of hundreds of thousands of people in a frenzy of economic and technological activity. But the concentration of power was a matter of concern. (It was then not nearly as ominous as it is now.) Steel, I pointed out, was even then the fulcrum; automobiles were becoming secondarily critical. My idea was that the federal government would have to sit at the controls at least over steel. How? Not by regulation, for steel would soon run the regulators. The federal government would have to own steel or own a controlling interest in it, so that production would be geared to the public need and not to profit alone.

Moreover, in my view, deficit spending should be used to develop the public sector. We all grew up on—or were fed—the mythology that the private sector was adequate to produce full employment if left alone. Business needed "confidence." Businessmen should not be hampered in their planning. They needed protection from rapacious competition and from the overbearing demands of labor. I felt this business mythology was false.

FDR's refusal to create an economic public sector made the New Deal only a makeshift, compromising arrangement. There was, of course, a big difference under the New Deal in that people no longer starved. They were fed and temporary jobs were created. But no public sector was permanently created, and FDR never entertained the idea seriously.

Neither FDR nor any President who followed him really faced up to the critical problem of unemployment, which has always been part of the American economy except during periods of war. It is, however, a sorry reflection on any society which builds its affluence upon the four to twenty percent of the population which is, at various stages, out of work.

The dimensions of the New Deal soon became clear. It was not a program that was in any sense radical. Rather it was a collection of make-shift devices to shore up the capitalistic system. FDR expressed over and again to me as well as publicly, his amazement at the charges of business that he was its enemy, that he was out to "sovietize" the United States, and so on. He truly thought that he was capitalism's best friend, pointing out the way for its survival. That was indeed the narrow area in which he worked. Rex Tugwell's dream of an America living under a cartel system was in a sense a "planned" society, and FDR was "sold" on it in a superficial way. His immediate reaction was to express criticism of the Court that struck the NRA down. But he soon seemed relieved that Hugh Johnson, the agency's administrator, and his Blue Eagle had been swept out. The new targets became the acute problems such as unemployment insurance, minimum wages, and hours of work.

The radicals were disappointed, but in the long run they for the most part accepted the narrow range of choice of New Deal reforms that Middle America would accept. Though more extreme measures were tendered by communists on the left and fascists on the right, the radicals, I knew, wanted basic reforms to come about by constitutional amendments. They never merited the scary headlines they often received.

There were many conservative influences in the New Deal. Dean Acheson, who served briefly, was one. Bernard Baruch—famous as a Wall Street operator—was another. Baruch nursed his fortune during the Depression and knowing FDR, came to Washington, where he held court every morning in Jackson Park, which faces the White House. Baruch was free and easy with his advice to anyone who would listen. He took a kindly liking to me, and was less vain and more able than most conservatives who took a hand in New Deal affairs. But Bernie was not an idea man, only one who would give you a tranquilizer so that you could see industry or high finance through rosy and sympathetic spectacles.

There were many, many others who lasted through these long years, fighting the New Deal from the inside. The forthright, outgoing reformers did not last long.

Republican Fiorello La Guardia had been in Congress until 1932, but in that election he was swept out in the Roosevelt landslide. He was soon to become mayor of New York, where his voice would still be heard over the land. In Washington, D.C., La Guardia had been a George Norris type of radical—-the George Norris that I came to love. He and Norris got the famous Norris-La Guardia Act through Congress, outlawing the yellow-dog contract. La Guardia called for public works, unemployment insurance, protection of farmers against foreclosures, public power, the forty-hour week. I knew La Guardia and admired him greatly. He was a fiery speaker, flamboyant, smart, and capable of being a demagogue, which he plainly was at times.

My main contact with the radical group in the mid-thirties was Maury Maverick of San Antonio, a lawyer who served in the House as a congressman from Texas from 1935 to 1939. Maury was short and stocky, in that respect very much like La Guardia. Maury also employed the same platform antics—he was flamboyant, cocky, witty, and pugnacious, depending on the need of the situation. He was a radical, not a socialist—and far from being a communist. Maury had his heroes, and they were mine too: Norris and La Follette. He tried to state his radicalism in their idiom. He formed a group of some thirty radicals in the House, one of whom, Mon Wallgren, was from my state, Washington. Mon would mouth Maury's words and ideas, but he soon wilted, carrying the reform banner for only a short time.

Maury admired Huey Long, not for his vicious streak, but for the human causes he championed. Maury used to defend Long, saying the forces he denounced were "the gods of oil and sulphur." As Long's list of gods to be denounced grew and grew, so did Maury's.

Maury Maverick used to tell me his theory of American radicalism: "We Americans want to talk, pray, think as we please—and eat regular."

I suppose I clung to Maury essentially because my own radicalism, if such it could be called, was precisely of his brand. In 1935, when business and finance turned against FDR, it was Maury and his group who told the President that they knew all along that reform could not be based on business support.

Once FDR got that message, he moved ahead with Senator Bob Wagner's labor bill, which guaranteed collective bargaining and established the nature of unfair labor practices; with the Public Utility Holding Company Act; with social security, with unemployment insurance promoted by Secretary of Labor Frances Perkins; with the

Banking Act promoted by Marriner Eccles; and with other related bills putting segments of business under regulation.

I often thought that the real driving force behind this legislation was Hugo Black, who as chairman of a special Senate committee to investigate lobbying (1935-1936), and as head of a special Senate committee investigating ship subsidies and airline subsidies (1933-1934), did more than research historical facts. He used the Congressional hearing as it had never been used before, making it an instrument to achieve reform. He pursued financial chicanery, helped to quicken the conscience of America and to mold public opinion to the need for reforms. He expended an intensity of effort seldom seen.

Black dug deep for facts and was as relentless as a terrier pursuing a rat. He was charged with being unfair, but he never trafficked in innuendoes and slurs, as did some Senate and House investigators who followed him. His standards were high, as they always had been. He did not emerge from Alabama through the usual hierarchy of politics. He announced what he stood for and campaigned relentlessly for it. Hugo Black never tried to destroy a man or a woman, only ideas. And through his investigative committees he exposed ideas that he thought were hostile to democratic principles. It was largely Black who made possible FDR's reforms in the financial world.

The famous Brain Trust of the New Deal was a figure of speech, not a working entity of a fixed group of individuals. Advisors came and went. Hugh Johnson—later to head up the NRA—was in on the ground floor before FDR's election. I knew him only slightly and rated him as a man distinguished only by his invective and by his high-handed management of the draft in 1917. Johnson's mentor was Bernard Baruch.

Ben Cohen—brilliant, retiring, self-effacing—was the brain that put most of the pieces together. Ben was the best and most intelligent man in the New Deal. He put the ideas and the philosophy of the period into legislation. After 1950 his vast talents went largely unused, but he above all others most honored the ethical and intellectual ideals for which FDR stood.

There was no one in FDR's time or later who was better at "unfrocking" a person than Harold Ickes. In 1944, speaking of Tom Dewey running for President and John Foster Dulles running for the Senate from New York, Ickes bellowed over the airwaves, "We are facing one of the most serious times in the history of our country. In a period when we need integrity and reliability, we are confronted by these two synthetic adventurers, Tiptoe Tom and Stepladder John—the DDTs—the Dewey-Dulles twins of American politics."

Harold Ickes was a dear friend of mine who spent his later years writing and rewriting his diary. He was honest and ambitious and hard-hitting. His campaign speeches that came over the radio were masterpieces of political diatribe. Ickes said of Dewey before the nomination in 1944 that Tom "had finally thrown his diaper into the ring." In the 1940 campaign Harold dubbed Willkie a "simple, barefoot Wall Street lawyer." FDR, a good stage director, would send Harold way out to a remote town, say, in Montana, to denounce the opposition—and how Harold loved it. Harold was crotchety and he loved to be called the Old Curmudgeon. He lived near Olney, Maryland, where he and his wife, Jane, raised turkeys. He was a Bull Moose Republican who loved FDR's leadership, and Harold watched over his nest at Interior like a mother hen over her brood.

Another man of the New Deal I greatly admired was Cliff Durr of Alabama. Cliff and his wife, Virginia, were Southern conservatives until Virginia's sister, Josephine, married Hugo Black. Both Cliff and Virginia had come from families with slave-owning backgrounds; they were planters and Presbyterians who were quite paternalistic to Blacks. As Cliff once said, all Blacks at that time "were treated alike, which was very bad, but which all accepted as part of the unchanging order of God."

Cliff had been a Rhodes scholar, studying law at Oxford for three years and returning to work for a firm representing the Alabama Power Company. Cliff Durr and Hugo Black, now related through marriage, began to see a lot of each other. They got into terrific arguments on many occasions, Hugo arguing for public power, higher wages, shorter work weeks, with Cliff being opposed to all. But Cliff and Virginia became slowly convinced they were on the wrong side.

When the Depression of the early thirties hit, Cliff took the position that his law firm should not fire the clerks, stenographers, and younger associates. Rather, it should see the staff through by having the partners reduce their withdrawals of the partnership take. The battle was bitter, and Cliff lost. Not only were the lesser lights discharged, Cliff Durr also was asked to resign, and he found himself out on the street in the middle of the Depression.

Hugo Black was then in the Senate and got Cliff a job at the RFC, where be worked with Stanley Reed on a Save the Banks plan. But as the

New Deal program got under way, Cliff was shocked. People were literally starving all over the nation when Henry Wallace was proposing that corn and cotton be plowed under and that the supply of livestock be reduced by killing little pigs. Cliff had come to Washington resolved to save the system; now he began to think that the Wallace Tugwell-Jesse Jones method of shoring it up was shocking. He lost faith in the system, although he never became socialist or a communist. Like Hugo Black and myself, he became fearful of the concentration of power which socialism could beget. He also believed in freedom of speech and press, due process of law that radiates justice, and law and order in the true meaning of the words. He believed in political and constitutional rights, and in a differently structured economy whereby the basic needs of people would be supplied.

At the RFC, Cliff Durr shifted his interest from banks to defense plants. In 1940 he helped organize a Defense Plant Corporation to help get the country prepared for the war. Jesse Jones was reluctant to sponsor this program because in those days he was saying, "I could do business with Hitler." Defense plans were lagging because the industrialists were on a sit-down strike, so to speak, not wanting to build plants without orders to fill and unless costs and profits were guaranteed. Cliff Durr got FDR to overrule Jesse Jones and defense plants were built.

In 1941 Durr was made a member of the Federal Communications Commission on nomination by FDR. At the FCC he was largely responsible for the creation of an educational radio network, which in time grew into public broadcasting. His creative work at FCC came to an end for a reason most Americans would deem curious.

In January 1943, Eugene Cox of the House introduced a resolution to investigate the FCC. A battle royal followed, in which Cliff Durr forced defeat of the proposal on proof of a charge that Cox had accepted a $2,500 fee to get a constituent's radio license renewed.

In 1943 Martin Dies let loose a barrage against Goodwin B. Watson, chief analyst at FCC, charging Watson with having communist views and affiliations with communist front organizations. Dies also condemned William I. Dodd, Jr., of the FCC, accusing him of being a member of a group which was "subversive." Robert M. Lovett, who worked in the Virgin Islands, was affiliated with numerous communist groups, charged Dies.

The list Dies presented to the House was long. Watson's salary at FCC was $6,500; Dodd's salary there was $3,200. Watson, Dodd, and

Lovett were named in an appropriation bill as not entitled to any salaries under that bill.

Cliff Durr came to the defense of Watson and Dodd, and as a result, an intensive investigation was made of Durr himself. Meanwhile FDR expressed the view that the provision of the bill taking individual employees off the payroll was unconstitutional, but he did not veto the bill because it would have killed other appropriations the government urgently needed. The employees sued in the Court of Claims.

Francis Biddle, the Attorney General, thought the proviso unconstitutional and therefore worked out an arrangement with the Congress to have its own counsel argue the case. The Congress thereupon named John C. Gall to represent it.

The Court of Claims allowed recovery. The Supreme Court took the case on the petition of the United States and affirmed, holding that the bill barring these men from salaried federal positions was a bill of attainder, that is to say, a determination of guilt and the affixing of a stigma on men by a legislative act, not a judicial hearing with all the safeguards of due process.

Under the loyalty and security program launched by Harry Truman, a government agency had to exact a loyalty oath from all its employees. These oaths, designed to catch subversives, were of course meaningless to communists. But Cliff Durr felt they were a monstrous invasion into matters of conscience and belief which are protected by the Constitution. So in 1948, rather than take the oath, Cliff refused reappointment to FCC.

Cliff worked for a while with Jim Patton and the Farmers Union. He testified before Congress, opposing the Truman Doctrine. He was against the Korean War and our conversion of Taiwan into an airport for our bombers, ready to strike Peking. He was opposed to our use of force in the Caribbean.

Durr became ill and returned to Alabama with a severe case of arthritis; he was bedridden for two years. In 1952 he opened a law office in Montgomery, Alabama. At that time he, a white, and two other lawyers, Blacks, were the only ones in the area who would take civil rights cases; and he was one of the stalwarts who supported Martin Luther King in the boycott cases.

Cliff Durr, like Hugo Black, thought that Americans were entitled both to bread and freedom of mind and spirit. He was always worried lest they give up freedom for bread *and* jam. But, as this is written, his health is restored, there is hope in his eyes, and he walks with dignity and pride. He never was tempted by the Golden Gravy Train, and spent his mature years living by his ideals, which were truly Jeffersonian.

Jerry Frank had discovered Norbert Weiner in the late 1930s. Where he had come across him, I do not know, since Weiner was not publishing much before 1948 and one of his earliest books, *The Human Use of Human Beings,* did not appear until 1950. But Jerry Frank found him and brought his ideas into our circle. It was then we began thinking of society in new dimensions—the day when the machine would do the work. Who would own the machine? A cartel? Government? The people? That was the center of our concern.

Beer and radio would not be enough for the new leisure day. An automated society could give to those who had hobbies endless hours of joy. My hobby was the outdoors—hiking, climbing, fishing, botany, geology, the play of sunsets and sunrises, the feel of white waters under me and a canoe at my command. Others would paint or play the fiddle or do carpentry or discover a "green thumb" in gardening. But how about the men and boys I knew who frequented the pool halls and beer joints in Yakima? They liked an occasional woman on the side. They reveled in off-color stories of the barnyard variety. They found that alcohol was an escape—from the nagging wife, from a frustrated ego, from indecision, from defeat in the struggle against the cruel forces of a cruel world. What would happen to them when there were no "productive" jobs? No assembly line positions, no stations in a potato-chip factory, not even a job packing cherries—which women did better than men, after all?

And so we faced the horrible prospect of Norbert Weiner's new society, which we knew was coming. Would the new serfs sell "dope"? Would their new occupation be as procurers? What would this do to society?

The Protestant ethic drilled into me in Yakima as a boy held that industry and hard work won out; that frugality in the long run was rewarding; that a man or woman with high ethical standards eventually prevailed. But we began to think that those endowed with this ethic were doomed as far as work was concerned.

These were some of the most disturbing years in my life. What would become of us? Free enterprise had disappeared, or would soon do so. Automation would make every factory the equivalent of a post office. There might be jobs, but they would be state jobs. Their prospectus would be drawn by bureaucrats, whom the Russians would call "commissars." A man or woman who wanted to be an actor, for example, would have to apply to a government bureau. The bureau, sensitive to political overtones, would be unlikely to hire an offbeat person, perhaps even more unlikely than a director in a capitalist society would be. So the list of unemployables would grow—unless individuals conformed to the state pattern—as many of them probably would.

These were the imponderables Jerry Frank and I discussed in those days. And when we examined the programs of the Manufacturers' Association or the Democratic or Republican National Committee, we realized that they were no more prepared to meet the realities of the modern world than the American Legion had been able to cope with the IWW's whom I had known as a boy.

FDR never debated these issues, but he always listened to us. He felt that America was basically very conservative and our people would not readily embrace new concepts. His judgment of these matters was, I felt, better than mine, but, as I told him, "You can conduct a national seminar by radio and educate the voters."

He never said yes and he never said no. But before long, he spent most of his energies conducting national radio talks not on nationalization of steel or on automation, not on a public sector that would end unemployment, but on the dangers of the Nazis and Adolf Hitler and, soon, the mobilization for actual war.

Brandeis and Black

The time came when I had to tell FDR that I was resigning my SEC position. My salary was $10,000, but with a young family, it cost nearly $15,000 a year to live in Washington. I had been there five years and owed $25,000, largely on my insurance policies. Yale wanted me to return and be dean of the Law School, beginning in the fall of 1939. There was nothing I would have liked more, except one thing and that was being Solicitor General—the lawyer's lawyer. But the list of aspirants for that position was long, and I could not afford to wait it out in Washington. So I gave up any thought of the S.G. job and accepted the deanship at Yale.

The day I told FDR that I would have to leave by June 1939, he said rather wistfully, "We'll see." Our relationship was such that I knew he would have the final word and would probably come up with some distasteful assignment which I would have difficulty declining. I had not the slightest idea I would ever be on the Court. It never was a part of my dreams. I had visited the Court, as I liked to watch it in operation but never once in all my life did it even cross my mind that I might one day sit there.

On occasion I would go across town to hear a case of SEC interest argued. Holmes, whom I last saw as a shriveled, hunched old man, was now gone. There was the Jovian Hughes, the easygoing Roberts, the lean, sour McReynolds, the reserved Sutherland, the professorial Stone, and the bulldog Brandeis.

I visited Stone—my first law professor—regularly at his home, which he had built at 24th Street and Wyoming Avenue, N.W., where he had a spacious office.

I also came to know Brandeis intimately.

I was too modest to search Justice Brandeis out when I went to Washington, though our interests in financial as well as in other matters were so similar. But I had not long to wait to meet him. One day he called—not through a secretary, for he had none. Mrs. Brandeis handled all correspondence that he could not manage by longhand. This call was one he made personally, and in his high resonant voice he asked if I could come by his apartment and see him the next Sunday at four o'clock. He lived on California Street, right off Connecticut, and his apartment, while neat, seemed threadbare.

Nevertheless the Brandeis home was radiant with friendship. The evening meal, when guests were present, was usually soup, followed by boiled chicken from which the soup had been made, and capped with a fruit dessert. The party was over by about ten o'clock, since the Brandeis working day started at five o'clock in the morning.

In those days the Court sat in the old room under the dome of the Capitol. There was no Supreme Court Building, so the Justices worked at home. For his office, Brandeis had an apartment in the same building, on the floor above his residence.

After that first day in 1934, I was with Brandeis about once a week. He drew me to him to find out what was going on. My work interested him above that of anyone in the city, for I dealt in high finance, the subject that had absorbed him in his early days. He commented over and again on the parallelism between my investigation and the one made by the Pujo Committee in 1912 to 1913, with which he had been closely connected. He asked me searching questions, making me recite chapter by chapter what I had discovered. He was fascinated with the anatomy of high finance and commented that the sons of those he had investigated were apparently no better than their fathers had been.

In his early days Brandeis had looked into the affairs of the New Haven Railroad and followed the machinations that seemed to plague that road. He exacted a promise from me: that when I finished work at the SEC and returned to Yale, I would write a book exposing the anatomy of the complex money matters of the New Haven. It was a promise I asked him to relieve me of when I was confirmed for the Court, and he did so. That sad chapter in American finance was never written.

I learned about Zionism from Brandeis and caught some of his zeal for the establishment of a Jewish state. Brandeis belonged to a different school of thought than that of those who eventually created the State of Israel. Chaim Weizmann, the Zionist leader, in time became Brandeis' chief opponent. Brandeis, born in America, was not a product of European ghettos and was not steeped in Jewish culture. His commitment to Israel was intellectual rather than emotional. He thought of building a state based on economic and social measures, with the aid of businessmen, whether they were Zionists or not. The Weizmann school eventually prevailed, based on the principle that Israel should be composed of ardent keepers of the faith. Although Brandeis withdrew from active participation in Israeli matters, the pull of Zionism was evident in every talk he had with me.

Brandeis thought that the area of Palestine should be developed for Jews and non-Jews alike. He was not caught up in what inspired some of the other Zionists—the desperate necessity to save the remnants of the Jewish European community. Modernization, the use of technicians and engineers, creation of a society not restricted to Jews—these were his concerns. I suppose one might say that he was less nationalistic and less concerned with religious matters than other supporters of a Jewish state.

He remained, however, an ardent supporter of the Zionist cause despite criticism of him from other people in the movement. Felix Frankfurter, likewise, was enormously involved in these matters.

I was with Brandeis the day Hitler invaded Poland. He saw his people facing new and horrible ordeals under the Nazis. He paced his apartment, old and bowed, his hands behind his back, whispering, "Will England fight?" The Chamberlain motif "Peace in our time" he knew to be a phony, and he wondered when the world would wake up.

Brandeis was not a philosopher like Cardozo or a salesman like Frankfurter. Brandeis was a modern Isaiah. He was a mighty man of action who, having found the facts and determined the nature and contours of the problem, moved at once. He admired Jefferson and talked to me often about him, not only about Jefferson's interest in the First Amendment but also about his inventive genius in creating useful articles. Brandeis also admired Jefferson's philosophy concerning private ownership, small units of business and agriculture, and an active democracy.

While still in law practice, Brandeis became interested in the promotion of state minimum wage and maximum hour legislation. Oregon had passed a law prohibiting women from working more than ten hours a day in factories and laundries. Brandeis wrote an *amicus* brief in support of the Oregon law when it came before the Supreme Court in 1908. The brief became famous overnight, for it contained not a single citation of legal precedent, only citations to social and economic treatises dealing with the subject.

Brandeis was intent on educating judges as to the facts of life—as to why doctors, social workers, and others thought the maximum hour legislation was essential to the well-being of the workers and of the community where they lived. Why, he asked, should the ultimate wisdom of judges be found in dusty lawbooks? Why should not judges be abreast of life? That type of brief—revolutionary as it was in 1908—came in time to be known as a "Brandeis brief."

While practicing in Boston, Brandeis gave much of his time to public service without payment of a fee—preserving the subway system, devising a sliding scale for the gas system, and promoting the savings-bank life-insurance plan. His investigations into high finance led him to Wall Street, and he teamed up for a while with Samuel Untermeyer to help expose the exploitive power of the money trust. Out of these sorties came his books, *The Money Trust* and *Other People's Money*. He was retained by the Interstate Commerce Commission as special counsel to help it pass on the application of Eastern roads to put into effect a horizontal five percent increase of freight rates.

Brandeis' role as arbiter in the garment industry led to his creation of the famous "protocol" for a permanent government of labor relations in the industry and his promotion of the preferential union shop.

Brandeis' various activities aroused the ire of the Establishment. So when Woodrow Wilson sent his name to the Senate for a seat on the Supreme Court, the powers-that-be moved in to defeat him. Hearings started February 9, 1916, lasted until March 15, 1916, and resumed again May 12, 1916. Brandeis was finally confirmed June 1, 1916: 47 yeas, 22 nays, and 27 not voting.

Brandeis made many notable contributions to the Bar and to the Bench. One of these has gone largely unnoticed. After he took his seat on the Court, Brandeis began to review petitions for *certiorari*. (*Certiorari* is a writ to correct errors in a lower court and, in the Federal system, is discretionary, four of nine justices being necessary for a grant.)

Many of these petitions for *certiorari* raised racial questions. Such questions may involve only state law—as when a state antidiscrimination measure is enforced—and state laws are governed by the state courts. Federal questions are the only issues in state litigation which are reviewable by the Supreme Court. But in order to be reviewed, they must be raised. Thus a federal problem involved in state litigation cannot be reviewed by the Supreme Court unless it has been raised in a state trial, preserved on appeal through the hierarchy of state courts, and then presented to the Supreme Court of the United States. Brandeis soon discovered that many important federal questions presented with clarity and persuasion before our Court had not been properly raised in lower courts and therefore could not be considered.

This failure was explicable on the grounds that the Black lawyer had not been as well trained as his white opponent, since education in the Black law schools of that day was not what it should have been. So Brandeis got hold of Charles H. Houston, a Black Washington, D.C., lawyer who was one of the best ever to appear before our Court, and whose legal training had been at the Harvard Law School.

This was in the late twenties, when Houston was vice-dean of the Howard Law School. While Howard offered no course in Federal Jurisdiction until about ten years later, the Brandeis proposal won instant approval. Houston put the students in his course on constitutional law to work on specific problems, presenting the question as to how to raise, in a trial court, the precise federal constitutional question that would challenge a housing code, or voting barrier, or other racist measure, and how to preserve it on appeal.

Brandeis, like all judges, received a lot of mail asking help in getting a job, pleading that he intervene in some agency proceeding to protect a person, and the like. Brandeis would write on these letters "J.P.P." and they are so marked in the collection of his papers at the University of Louisville. "J.P.P." meant "Judicial Proprieties Prohibit" and Brandeis would pen a letter in his own hand to that effect and send it back to the person who had asked for help.

Brandeis was not unique in being a man of rectitude, but he became more and more unusual as a man who felt that a public office was a public trust and not a position to exploit for private gain.

Brandeis said in the *Olmstead* case in 1928

> *Decency, security and liberty alike demand that government officials shall be subjected to the same rules of conduct that are commands to the citizen. In a government of laws, existence of the government will be imperiled if it fails to observe the law scrupulously. Our government is the potent, the omnipresent teacher. For good or for ill, it teaches the whole people by its example. Crime is contagious. If the government becomes a lawbreaker, it breeds contempt for law; it invites every man to become a law unto himself; it invites anarchy.*

Since that time government has been recurringly lawless as respects entrapment (an agent inciting a crime); wiretaps, where no appropriate warrant is obtained; pilfering of public monies; flouting of election laws; the circulation of scurrilous literature concerning political opponents; and even the burglarizing of private files for political purposes. Lying and deception have grown as practices of government officials— practices that do more to undermine us than the "subversion" against which we have long inveighed.

In American history, lawlessness by government and the great decline in public morality are not new. They have recurred throughout our history. In the last century and in this one the public treasury has been dipped into through direct as well as devious means. Teapot Dome was the high-water mark of this type of corruption.

Ever since World War I our government has been increasingly lawless as it caters to popular fears, and indeed generates them by cries of "subversion" and "un-Americanism." Such manufactured fears have led to constitutional shortcuts of great dimensions. What Mitchell Palmer, Attorney General for Wilson, did to hapless foreigners in New England in the 1920s was a lasting scar, because it flouted constitutional standards. From that time to the present the nation drifted slowly from constitutional government to a government subject to the will of the politicians in power. A notorious example of this neglect of the Constitution is found in the Sacco-Vanzetti trial.

Slowly but perceptibly the end came to justify the means. Government agents incited weak people to commit crimes which were then tolerated by the courts because "deceit" was deemed necessary for effective law enforcement. The persistence with which the third degree has survived is another example. Electronic surveillance has evolved from crude eavesdropping to sophisticated technology.

It is this kind of lawlessness that Brandeis feared the most. Brandeis can be understood not in terms of conservatism or liberalism, but in terms of morality: the end never justifies the means. In the area of law enforcement he included government as well as individuals in pleading for the exercise of moral judgments.

Every official in every branch of government is responsible to the law and to the Constitution. The higher he is, the more important it is that he represent the finest of our constitutional traditions.

To give an example of the wariness a public official must exercise: in 1948, the year Thomas Dewey was running for the Presidency, I was invited to Portland to address the Oregon State Bar Association, which put me up at the Benson Hotel. When I checked out of the hotel, I was told that the bill had been taken care of by the association.

By October of that year I was back in Washington for the opening of Court. The Presidential campaign was getting hotter and hotter, and one day I received a telephone call from a friend, Lindsay C. Warren, the Comptroller General of the United States. He told me he had learned that I had been a guest of the Oregon Bar Association at the Benson Hotel in Portland, and that the association had not paid the bill but had routed it to a shipbuilding company that had a contract with the U.S. Navy. The contractor had in fact paid the hotel bill.

The Comptroller knew about the incident because one of Dewey's own men had been tipped off, and this man checked with Lindsay Warren to make sure the facts were correct. The Comptroller looked into the matter, reported to Dewey that it was all true, and promptly called me. I phoned the Benson Hotel to get the amount of the bill and immediately sent off a check in payment. I also wrote a letter excoriating the president of the Oregon Bar for doing anything that would link a member of the Court with such a highly unethical practice. Although the bill, as I recall, was not much over $50, that story would have made headlines in all the papers. It would even, perhaps, have hurt Truman (who had tried to get me to be his running mate), not because I had done anything immoral but because it could be made to appear that I had. This was politics capitalizing on deceit.

Brandeis thought that people in the public service should be selfless. And so they should be. But there seem to be very few of that breed today. By the time of LBJ personal aggrandizement had become the style. It was, I fear, a part of the return of the herd to a primitive selfishness that could destroy us.

Brandeis would have been appalled to see the use of leverage by a congressman or senator to get a radio or TV license for himself or his family. He would, I think, be appalled at the practice I have mentioned before whereby Pentagon officers step out of their uniforms into positions with private companies doing business with the Pentagon. He would have asked this searching question: "How can an officer who had supervised procurement be a good watchdog for the public if on retirement his reward is going to be a nice, fat job with one of the companies making millions out of government largesse?"

Brandeis would also have been shocked if he had lived to know that William H. Tucker, the man who in 1968 was chairman of the ICC, which approved the Penn-Central merger, shortly resigned and became head of the old New Haven, which was required by the ICC decision to become an integral part of Penn-Central.

Mergers depressed him because they turned entrepreneurs into clerks, independent businessmen into faceless lackeys serving some faceless business bureaucracy. The gravitation of power to the center depressed Brandeis for the same reason. States' rights to him had a very special meaning—they were not to be used as an excuse for the Establishment to keep a minority enslaved. A state was a sovereign political entity, as a member of which the common man had a chance to be heard and to make his views effective.

The computer world would have depressed Brandeis. He saw the forces of disintegration gathering early in this century and it made him sad. The automobile was part of what he disliked. He spoke to me many times about the transformation it was making—not in urban sprawl alone, but in the character of people. An automobile desensitized the driver, making the polite person crude and aggressive. It is the same with any machine. One person in a bomber high above the earth can wipe out thousands of people without sight of blood and without hearing a child's whimper.

Man becomes transformed when a machine separates him from his fellow-man. Man is at his best when he stands on his own feet— accountable to family, to neighbors, to employers, to God. Man is at his worst running with the herd, for then individual responsibility is ignored and individual achievement is not put to the test.

The small men who followed Brandeis in economic affairs mostly ridiculed him for wanting to turn back the clock. But Brandeis' idea was different: he wanted to put the individual and the individual's privacy first, and to establish only the controls that would keep the individual from being regimented.

This line of thought ran through all of Brandeis' opinions, through all his papers, through all his talk. Brandeis had spiritual links with Jefferson as he did with Isaiah, and he lived every day by the faith he acquired from them.

He would be saddened to death if he could see what happened to his dream for this nation.

There is in Brandeis a universal note. We can reach the moon and top all secrets of the universe and yet not survive if we do not serve the soul of man. We serve the soul of man only when we honor individual achievements and respect individual idiosyncrasies. We serve the soul of man only when a man's worth—not his race, creed, or ideology—becomes our basic value.

The nation or the world can be smothered and controlled by a military-industrial complex or by a socialist regime or by some other totalitarian group. But in time the individual will rebel. Man, though presently enmeshed, will seek freedom just as he does today in Russia and in Czechoslovakia, and just as he did in the Watts area of Los Angeles. The struggle is always between the individual and his sacred right to express himself on the one hand, and on the other, the power structure that seeks conformity, suppression, and obedience. At some desperate moment in history, a great effort is made once more for the renewal of individual dignity. And so it will be from now to eternity.

These ideas of freedom did not of course originate with Brandeis. But through his opinions as well as the example of his life, he articulated them and showed they could be practical. That is why Brandeis will always remain a revolutionary symbol.

When I learned, after the event, that Brandeis had gone to FDR and asked that I be named to take his place on the Court when he retired on February 13, 1939, I was the proudest human alive.

I, of course, never served on the Court with Brandeis, but Hugo Black did. For some reason I do not understand, Black and Brandeis were never close. Brandeis came from a more privileged background than either Hugo or I. We two had been exposed to raw-boned experiences. Brandeis did not grow up with policemen shooting at him. Whether that happened in freight yards or in a ghetto, the experience leaves its mark on a man.

Brandeis and Black served together on the Court from October 1937, to February 1939, and perhaps something happened during that time that affected Black's attitudes. Whatever it was, Black kept it to himself.

Yet so far as due process in criminal trials was concerned, and the constitutional impossibility of government ever to play an ignoble role, Black and Brandeis thought pretty much alike. Brandeis probably gave a more robust content to the Fourth Amendment than did Black's construction, but that was a minor difference. They stood together on the First Amendment and on the Fifth.

Hugo Black was fiercely intent on every point of law he presented. He was emphatic, concise, and clear. There was no mistaking where he stood. But there was no fierceness directed to his opposition—only to their ideas. I never heard him say an unkind word about any justice, no matter how deeply opposed the two were. He never indulged in any personal aspersions, no matter how heated the arguments. I think perhaps Bob Jackson at times thought Hugo was personally insulting, but such was never his purpose—and he had only the highest respect for Bob.

When I was rolled on by a horse and sent to Tucson, Arizona, for a long convalescence, Hugo came out to see me, staying a week. He played tennis each day at the university and loafed with me the rest of the time. I came to have a very close relationship with him as a result of that experience.

Hugo loved company and long conversations. His spacious garden in his exquisite Alexandria home was ideal for that purpose during spring and summer. He loved to entertain there; and when, during the Korean War, the Court held on June 2, 1952, that Truman's seizure of the steel mills was unconstitutional, Hugo asked me what I thought of his idea of inviting Truman to his home for an evening after the decision came down. I thought it a capital idea. So in two weeks Hugo extended the invitation and Truman accepted. It was a stag dinner, and only Truman and members of the Court were present. Truman was gracious though a bit testy at the beginning of the evening. But after the bourbon and canapés were passed, he turned to Hugo and said, "Hugo, I don't much care for your law but, by golly, this bourbon is good." The evening was a great step forward in human relations, and to Hugo Black, good human relations were the secret of successful government.

For years Hugo took off for Florida during the winter recess, as he loved the sun on his back. He loved Washington, D.C., in the summer— even its humidity; and he seldom left the city when vacation time came. He read avidly, marking the pages of books with which he disagreed, a practice that misled the minister who preached Hugo's funeral service. Finding passages concerning the virtues of "natural law" all marked in Hugo's books, the minister assumed that "natural law" was Hugo's dish. Natural law, however, was anathema to him, for he felt that it was the source of the judge-made law concerning substantive due process that the old Court had inflicted on the nation between 1882 and 1937.

Clay County, Alabama, his home county, was very close to Hugo's heart. So was the state of Alabama, where he had practiced law, served as prosecutor, and run for the Senate. The dominant opinion in Alabama favored school segregation. As a matter of constitutional law, Hugo was against it—being one of the four, the others being Burton, Minton, and I, who voted to reverse when *Brown v. Board of Education* was first argued in December 1952.

But Alabama rejected that view. When Hugo Black's law class at the university failed to invite him (the outstanding member of the class) to its fiftieth reunion in 1956, Hugo was crushed. He read with tolerant eyes everything his state did, except those matters that seemed to him to trench on constitutional rights. Then he was very upset, but never rancorous or bitter.

Hugo Black was probably the best storyteller of my time. I regret I never took the time to make notes and work the jokes into a brochure. Like the following joke, they usually pertained to Clay County customs or Clay County law practice.

> *It seems that a sharecropper was charged with the crime of stealing the mule of the landlord. The latter was rich and domineering, without many friends among the common people. The evidence against the defendant was overwhelming, so much so that he did not take the stand. The judge charged the jury, laying down the law meticulously. In five minutes the jury returned.*
>
> *"Have you reached a verdict, Mr. Foreman?" asked the judge.*
>
> *'We have, Your Honor."*
>
> *"Then hand it to the clerk."*
>
> *The clerk put on his glasses, took the paper, unfolded it, cleared his throat, and said, 'We the jury find the defendant not guilty, provided that he returns the mule."*
>
> *The judge brought his gavel down sharply, saying, "There is no such verdict in the law. The defendant is either guilty or not guilty." After giving the charge all over again the judge told the jury to retire and come back with a lawful verdict.*

*The jury returned in five minutes and the judge asked the
foreman, "Have you reached a verdict?"*
"We have, Your Honor."
"Then hand it to the clerk."
*The clerk put on his glasses, unfolded the paper, cleared
his throat, and read: "We the jury find the defendant not
guilty. He can keep the mule."*

Hugo Black, like Felix Frankfurter and Harlan Stone, was an ardent
proselytizer of his constitutional views, seeking to convert any "wayward"
Brother on the Court. In his later years that aspect of his character waned,
perhaps due to lack of energy. But in his prime there was no more fervent
evangelist than Hugo Black.

He had been a Sunday School teacher for years in Alabama, and that
background kept surfacing all his life. He had been an active Democrat,
and his personal support of the old historic characters in that party was
whole-hearted. Thus he was offended when I told him that in my view
William Jennings Bryan was a bag of wind. It was not only his party
fealty that made him react in that way. He never had an unkind or
uncharitable thing to say about anyone he had ever known in public
life. In each of them—Democrat, Republican, Socialist—there was some
good, and it was the good that he always mentioned. That is one reason
those who knew him well invariably loved him. And those who loved
him, as I did, would have gone to the very end of the road for him.

When I came on the Court, Hugo Black talked to me about his idea
of having every vote on every case made public. In cases taken and
argued, the vote of each justice was eventually known. But in cases where
appeals were dismissed out of hand or *certiorari* denied, no votes were
recorded publicly. I thought his idea an excellent one and backed it
when he proposed to the conference that it be adopted. But the requisite
votes were not available then or subsequently. As a result he and I started
to note our dissents from denials of *certiorari* and dismissal of appeal
in important cases. Gradually the practice spread to a few other Justices;
and finally I ended up in the sixties noting my vote in all cases where
dismissals or denials were contrary to my convictions.

When Hugo was eighty-one he had some cataracts removed and
seemed to be in good health. He hit tennis balls one hot day with his
wife, Elizabeth, and had a very slight stroke doing so, but when the
1970 term of Court started, be seemed fit. In May 1971, we had a

conference and no one noted that he looked ill. His knees, however, buckled when he was returning to his chambers, and he was put to bed with a high fever. But by the time the Pentagon Papers case was argued on June 26, 1971, he seemed to have regained his old strength and fervor, pouring all of it into one of the best opinions he ever wrote. Shortly thereafter he was in Bethesda Naval Hospital with temporal arteritis, from which he died on September 25, 1971.

Both Black and I were one with Brandeis in his insight into the corporate world and its chicanery. We also stood with Brandeis in his passion to protect small and medium-sized companies and for participatory democracy in which all classes took part.

Brandeis was Wilson's spokesman in support of the Clayton Act. His testimony before Congress on that measure should be required reading in government courses. The Sherman Act had been used by the judiciary to break the Pullman strike and ultimately to put Eugene Debs in jail. The Clayton Act took labor out from under the antitrust laws, declaring, "The labor of a human being is not a commodity or article of commerce."

The other major provision promoted by Brandeis was the prohibition of an acquisition of stock of one corporation by another where the effect "may be to substantially lessen competition" or "tend to create a monopoly in any line of commerce."

The hole that Brandeis and the Clayton Act did not succeed in plugging up was to prohibit the acquisition of assets of one company by another, thus producing a like effect. That was not done until the Celler-Kefauver Act of 1950.

But Black and Brandeis saw eye to eye on that problem. They were indeed brothers under the skin. I have written this account only to state why it is that though all my personal associations on the Court have been warm, congenial, and enduring, I was ideologically closer to Brandeis and to Black than to any others.

Contending Schools of Thought

The Constitution is written in general terms and uses terms like "due process" without definition. Moreover, the policy issues underlying one question or another are often controversial, leading individual Justices to plead for a special construction. During my time the press failed to educate the public as to the nature of the conflicts inside the Court. It usually tried to reduce these disagreements into terms of personal vendetta. But though feelings often ran high, there was never a personal vendetta on the Court in my time.

As I have explained, though the story was current that Felix Frankfurter and I were enemies, that was not the case. Although we differed greatly on the merits of many cases, we were not enemies. Learned Hand once said that Felix was a divisive force in any group of which he was a member. To my mind Felix did indeed stir dissension, but dissension and divisiveness are not synonymous.

I really think that out of the great differences on legal and policy issues coming before the Court there evolved a stronger Court, though, occasionally, the persuasive powers of individual justices may have had undue influence.

Every Justice I have known feels in retrospect that he made mistakes in his early years. The problems sometimes come so fast that the uninitiated is drawn into channels from which he later wants to retreat. That happened to me in the Japanese detention-camp case and to Hugo Black, Frank Murphy and me when the first flag-salute case (*Minersville School District v. Gobitis*) was argued on April 25, 1940. In those days, Felix Frankfurter was our hero. He was indeed learned in constitutional law and we were inclined to take him at face value. We voted with him in the opinion holding that the state could subject the children of Jehovah's Witnesses to compulsory flag salute in public schools.

The Fourteenth Amendment provides that "No state shall ... deprive any person of life, liberty, or property without due process of law." Justice Hughes, writing for a seven-to-two Court in 1931, held that the guarantees of the First Amendment were included in the term "due process" as it was used in the Fourteenth Amendment. The First Amendment guarantees the free exercise of religion as well as free speech and free press absolutely, without reference to due process. Frankfurter, we were later to discover, thought that freedom of speech and of press and the free exercise of religion, as guaranteed against state abridgment by reason of the Fourteenth Amendment, were watered-down versions of those rights as guaranteed by the First Amendment. Why watered-down versions? Because, he maintained, due process as applied to First Amendment freedom meant "due process" free speech, "due process" freedom of the press, "due process" free exercise of religion. Those freedoms could, in other words, be modified or controlled by the states so long as they did not violate due process. What, in his mind, was "due process"? It was a concept of "ordered liberty," a regime of reasonable regulation. Thus, for example, freedom of the press could be abridged, as long as due process was observed.

What does "due process" mean? It is not defined in the Constitution. But the guarantees of the first Eight Amendments—originally applicable only to the federal government—are pretty sturdy standards for "due process." Why not apply them to the states through the Fourteenth Amendment? It was far better we do that than leave "due process" to be defined according to the predilections of individual justices. That was Black's position and mine. That was the position that the Burger court was later to steadfastly reject.

At the time of the first flag-salute case, we had not fully divined Frankfurter's view. We were probably naïve in not catching the nuances of his position from the opinion he had been circulating for some time. No one knew for sure where Stone stood. Finally, on May 31, 1940, the day before the Conference at which Frankfurter's opinion was cleared for Monday release, Stone sent around his dissent. It did not, however, reveal the basic issue, and though Stone vaguely adumbrated his position, he did not, for once, campaign for it. In any case, by this time the vote for Frankfurter's opinion had solidified. It is always difficult, and especially so for a newcomer, to withdraw his agreement to one opinion at the last minute and cast his vote for the opposed view. A mature Justice may do just that; a junior usually is too unsure to make a last-minute major shift. But as the months passed and new cases were filed involving the same or a related problem, Black and I began to realize that we had erred.

Jehovah's Witnesses, the religious sect which had been the defendant in this case, took Exodus 20:4-5 literally. Saluting the flag was to them bowing down to a "graven image." When the issue was again presented in 1942 (*Jones v. Opelika*) and in 1943 (*West Virginia Board of Education v. Barnette*), Black, Murphy and I changed our minds, deserted Frankfurter and, in time, helped constitute a new majority, leaving Frankfurter and his 1940 views in dissent along with Roberts and Reed. The Frankfurter philosophy was finally exposed in that dissent: he held that although free exercise of religion was guaranteed by the First and Fourteenth Amendments, the legislature could nonetheless regulate it by invoking the concept of due process, provided they stayed within reasonable limits.

Stone, who came off a New Hampshire farm and always pronounced Iowa as I-oh-way, never knew how the other half lived, nor had he any speaking acquaintance with the offbeat nonconformists of his time. But during World War I he had an experience that was to influence him throughout his life. He was made a member of the three-man board of inquiry named by the Secretary of War on June 1, 1918, to review the claims of those who had refused military service on the ground of conscientious objection. This board traveled to the various containments, and the contacts, interviews and cross-examinations of the objectors deeply affected Stone. He talked to me a lot about this experience and wrote an account of it. "It may well be questioned," he said in part, "whether the state which preserves its life by a settled policy of violation of the conscience of the individual will not in fact ultimately lose it by the process."

I think it was this experience which made Stone peculiarly sensitive to the claims of Jehovah's Witnesses in the flag-salute case.

The old Court had used the Due Process Clause of the Fourteenth Amendment to strike down social and industrial legislation where there was no explicit guarantee in the Constitution that protected the matter on which the legislation acted.

In 1905 it struck down a maximum ten-hour day in bakeries as an interference with that "liberty" guaranteed by the Fourteenth Amendment *(Lochner v. New York)*. In 1915 it held that a state law could not bar an employer from requiring employees not to become or remain a member of any labor organization *(Coppage v. State of Kansas)*. In 1917 a state law was struck down providing that employment agents were not allowed to receive fees from workers for whom they found jobs, as it interfered with the agents' "liberty" protected by the Fourteenth Amendment *(Adams v. Tanner)*. A minimum-wage law for women in the District of Columbia was likewise invalidated for that reason in 1923 *(Adkins v. Children's Hospital)*. In 1927 a state law forbidding resale of theater tickets at a price in excess of fifty cents above the printed price was held to be an invasion of "liberty" within the meaning of the Fourteenth Amendment *(Tyson and Brother v. Banton)*. In 1928 a state law fixing the fees chargeable by an employment agent met the same fate *(Ribnik v. McBride)*.

This is not a complete catalogue, only illustrative. In one of these earlier cases Justice Holmes wrote in dissent:

> *Some of these laws embody convictions or prejudices which judges are likely to share. Some may not. But a constitution is not intended to embody a particular economic theory, whether of paternalism and the organic relation of the citizen to the State or of laissez faire. It is made for people of fundamentally differing views, and the accident of our finding certain opinions natural and familiar or novel and even shocking ought not to conclude our judgment upon the question whether statutes embodying them conflict with the Constitution of the United States.*

There is nothing in the Constitution that says no state shall abridge "the fixing of prices" or "employment agency fees" or "the right to fix hours of work or wages." The Court coined the phrase "liberty of contract." But as Holmes observed:

> *Contract is not specially mentioned in the text that we have to construe. It is merely an example of doing what you want to do, embodied in the word liberty. But pretty much all law consists in forbidding men to do some things that they want*

to do, and contract is no more exempt from law than other acts.

The Constitution and the Bill of Rights, however, do ban legislation on some things: bills of attainder, religious test oaths, freedom of speech, freedom of press, free exercise of religion, and so on. Are those bans complete or may the legislatures act in those fields if they do not act "unreasonably"? The Frankfurter school of thought answered in the affirmative: either the state—or Congress—has freedom to regulate, the constitutional mandate being construed as only a constitutional admonition for moderation.

While Black, Murphy and I disagreed with the old Court when it sat as a superlegislature reviewing the wisdom of legislation in the social, industrial and financial field, we thought that when the Constitution said in the First Amendment that there should be "no law" abridging a specific right, it did not mean "some law, provided it is reasonable."

The right of free speech, all are agreed, does have its limitations. Statutes which proscribe the use of epithets such as profanity, libel and "fighting" words have generally been excluded from constitutional protection. Such was the case in *Chaplinsky v. New Hampshire,* in which Mr. Chaplinsky addressed the town marshal as being a "damned Fascist" and a "damned racketeer." As Justice Murphy wrote for the Court: "It has been well observed that such utterances are no essential part of any exposition of ideas." They normally do not foster the promotion or discussion of public issues. Their use would in general promote the use of dueling and other forms of violence.

The usual way of stating the difference was that one school of thought was for "balancing" the need for, say, free speech against the need for law and order. The Frankfurter school was for "balancing." Black and I thought that all of the "balancing" had been done by those who wrote the Constitution and the Bill of Rights. They had set aside certain domains where all government regulation was banned. When it came to certain activities, the Constitution had taken government off the backs of men.

That was the great divide between us and the Frankfurter school, which grew wider and wider with the passing years as more and more civil rights clamored for protection.

The broad expansive construction of the Due Process Clause of the Fourteenth Amendment given by the old Court with regard to social and economic legislation was only one of the bones of contention that FDR had with that regime. Another quarrel was over the construction of the Commerce Clause. All that the clause says is: "The Congress shall have power ... to regulate commerce with foreign nations, and among the several states, and with the Indian tribes."

Prior to our Constitution, the states had raised protective tariffs and duties against one another and had taken many forms of retaliatory economic actions against one another. They had treated one another as foreign nations rather than members of a great polity. States lacking seaports were particularly beset. As President Madison said: "New Jersey, placed between Philadelphia and New York, was likened to a cask tapped at both ends; and North Carolina, between Virginia and South Carolina, to a patient bleeding in both arms." This was because duties were assessed on goods coming from abroad and kept by the receiving state. Duties were also collected on merchandise brought in from other states. The problems at that time among the thirteen states were comparable to problems with which many foreign nations these days are wrestling in an effort to provide a common market. It was to this problem that the Commerce Clause was addressed, and the Marshall Court's liberal construction of it laid the foundation for the creation in this country of the greatest common market in the world. That Court in the first place construed "commerce" as broad and all-inclusive. In the second place, it construed the power of Congress to regulate as extensive. Third, it established the principle that a state law regulating commerce in conflict with a federal law was unconstitutional by reason of the Supremacy Clause. In the fourth place, it held that the states may not act in certain fields affecting commerce, even though Congress has failed to pass any statutes governing the same subject matter. That is to say, there are some areas that can be regulated only by Congress.

The states have of course police powers which they may exercise for the health, safety and welfare of their inhabitants, even though those measures may have an incidental effect on commerce. What has to be considered is the magnitude of the effect on commerce, whether the matter is primarily of local concern, allowing for diversity and experimentation, or of national concern requiring uniformity.

These principles were not firmly established by the Marshall Court. They merely appear as the broad outlines of the constitutional contours.

But it was along these lines, projected by the Marshall Court, that the law was to develop: an open economy, a great common market characterized by free trade among the states, but in which the states have the requisite autonomy to deal with peculiar local conditions.

In 1895, however, the power of Congress to regulate commerce was given a narrow construction by an opinion which held that manufacturing, even by units of an interstate complex, was not commerce *(United States v. E. C. Knight Co.)*. That decision had wide ramifications, and in later cases it came to mean that Congress did not have authority even to ban an interstate shipment of goods which were the products of child labor *(Hammer v. Dagenhart)*.

These decisions stood as a great dike against Federal control over many of the pressing economic problems of the 1920s and 1930s. Holmes, in his dissent in the child-labor case, stated the Rooseveltian idea in the following words:

> *The act does not meddle with anything belonging to the States. They may regulate their internal affairs and their domestic commerce as they like. But when they seek to send their products across the state line they are no longer within their rights. If there were no Constitution and no Congress their power to cross the line would depend upon their neighbors. Under the Constitution such commerce belongs not to the States but to Congress to regulate. It may carry out its views of public policy whatever indirect effect they may have upon the activities of the States. Instead of being encountered by a prohibitive tariff at her boundaries, the State encounters the public policy of the United States which it is for Congress to express. The public policy of the United States is shaped with a view to the benefit of the nation as a whole.*

The philosophy of Holmes gradually won out; the narrow construction of the commerce power of Congress announced in 1895 was slowly eroded, many exceptions being created. But the old decision that manufacturing was not commerce was not overruled until 1948 *(Mandeville Farms v. Sugar Co.)*.

The National Labor Relations Act was sustained in 1937 both as respects practices or transactions in the "flow" of commerce and those "'affecting" commerce *(NLRB v. Jones & Laughlin Steel Corp.)*. The marketing program for agricultural products was upheld in 1939 (*Mulford v. Smith*) after a prior defeat of an agricultural program which tried to decrease the quantities of articles produced by increasing the prices *(United States v. Butler)*.

In 1941 the Court, in a unanimous opinion written by Stone *(United States v. Darby)* overruled the old child-labor case and held constitutional an act of Congress which prohibited the shipment in interstate commerce of articles manufactured by employees whose wages were below a stated minimum and whose hours of work were above a prescribed maximum and which prohibited the employment of workers in the production of goods "for interstate commerce" at other than prescribed wages and hours. In upholding the new act, the Court returned to the philosophy of the Marshall Court. Thus Congress once more had the power to stand astride the stream of commerce and impose terms and conditions on those who were producing goods which after manufacture would enter that stream.

The newly restored power under the Commerce Clause reached its outward limits in 1942 when a unanimous Court, under an agricultural marketing act, upheld a sanction against a farmer who raised wheat not for the stream of interstate commerce, but only for consumption on his farm (*Wickard v. Filburn*). The Court said:

> One of the primary purposes of the Act in question was to increase the market price of wheat, and to that end to limit the volume thereof that could affect the market. It can hardly be denied that a factor of such volume and variability as home-consumed wheat would have a substantial influence on price and market conditions. This may arise because being in marketable condition such wheat overhangs the market and, if induced by rising prices, tends to flow into the market and check price increases. But if we assume that it is never marketed, it supplies a need of the man who grew it which would otherwise be reflected by purchases in the open market. Home-grown wheat in this sense competes with wheat in commerce. The stimulation of commerce is a use of the regulatory function quite as definitely as prohibitions or restrictions thereon. This record leaves us in no doubt that Congress may properly have considered that wheat consumed

*on the farm where grown, if wholly outside the scheme of
regulation, would have a substantial effect in defeating and
obstructing its purpose to stimulate trade therein at
increased prices.*

This was a decision that another unanimous Court followed in 1959
when Charles Whittaker was a member *(United States v. Haley)*, though
he later roundly denounced the Court for going to such extremes.

Commerce Clause cases continued to divide the Court, but the reach
of the Commerce power was no longer much in dispute. The
controversies involved construction of commerce legislation and its
ambiguities. They also raised questions of whether a state law could
coexist with a federal law or whether the federal law had pre-empted
the field. These were often important questions, but they never reached
the dimensions of the problems with which the Marshall Court or the
Hughes Court dealt.

The old Court's limitations on the government's power to regulate
social, industrial and business problems and conditions by reason of
the Justices' conception of "liberty" as used in the Due Process Clause
of the Fourteenth Amendment were also slowly eroded. Exceptions
began to appear at least by 1908 *(Muller v. State of Oregon)*. Finally, in
1937, a state law fixing minimum wages was sustained *(West Coast Hotel
v. Parrish)*, the prior contrary decision *(Adkins v. Children's Hospital)*
being overruled. That attitude became a pattern, the new Court
concluding that the wisdom, need or appropriateness of the legislation
was none of its business *(Olsen v. Nebraska)*, and declaring that no law
would be struck down under the Due Process Clause if there was any
rational basis on which it might rest. Most laws survived that test, an
exception being an act of Congress which provided that if a person had
been convicted of a crime of violence and possessed a firearm, it was
presumed that the weapon was received in interstate commerce after
the effective date of the act *(Tot v. United States)*. The Court held that
the presumptions concerning the receipt of the firearms were "violent,
and inconsistent with any argument drawn from experience."

Some laws, however, involved specific guarantees of the Constitution,
such as free exercise of religion or freedom of speech and of the press,
the privilege against self-incrimination, and the like. The question in
those cases was whether those rights could be qualified by legislation—
watered down, so to speak. If it was "reasonable" that free speech be

suppressed or free exercise of religion be qualified, was a law that reached that result constitutional? If that was the test, then the Justices would determine what was "reasonable." In that event they would in a sense sit as a superlegislature. Certainly their views on reasonableness would vary quite widely. We would then have a regime of constitutional law that turned on the subjective attitudes of the Justices rather than on the Constitution. That regime would give the Court vastly more power than it would have if the Constitution were taken more literally.

That was the type of problem posed in the flag-salute cases. It was to appear over and again as civil rights cases mounted. After World War II these cases began to multiply. The work of the Court always mirrors the worries and concerns of the people of a particular age. Since World War II, individual rights have been more and more in balance—as a result of racial tensions, the demands of religious minorities, the trend to conformity and the accompanying revolt, the search for ideological strays in the loyalty and security hearings, the Cold War and the mounting lists of its victims, and many other factors related to the growing power of government and the growing importance of the individual.

The contest within the Court in my early years was between the Frankfurter school, which thought that even specific constitutional guarantees could be watered down by "reasonable" regulations, and those of us, especially Black and myself, who read those specific guarantees more literally as part of the plan of the Framers to take government off the backs of the people when it came to specified civil rights.

With the passage of time the Frankfurter school of thought came to be sponsored by Burger and Blackmun—though they were quite inappropriately called "strict constructionists"—and it will probably endure. Black's death gave this view great momentum. Underlying the differences in the Court on this issue was the more basic conflict that concerned the question of the extent to which the state powers had been restricted by the Fourteenth Amendment. While it established that no state can deny any person life, liberty or property without due process of law, the Amendment does not define due process.

One group on the Court led by Black and me thought that due process in the Fourteenth Amendment meant the prerogatives and procedures set forth in the Bill of Rights. This was the so-called incorporation theory, coming first to a shattering head in 1947, in *Adamson v. California*, in which Frankfurter wrote that the Fourteenth Amendment did not incorporate the Bill of Rights.

Black and I took the opposite view, and in those days we spent many long hours going through the dusty volumes of Civil War history and law trying to ascertain the meanings of the drafters of the Fourteenth Amendment.

The Fourteenth Amendment speaks of the privileges and immunities of citizens, and Black and I could never think of a greater privilege or immunity than the right to speak one's mind or to follow one's own conscience in choosing one's religion. Black wrote a powerful dissent in *Adamson,* in which he laid bare the critical features of the Fourteenth Amendment, supporting the view that Congress, in the recommendation of the Fourteenth Amendment, had in mind making applicable to the states *all* of the provisions in the Bill of Rights which had previously been applicable only to the federal government.

To Frankfurter that was heresy—a wrongful construction of history. Charles Fairman, a Frankfurter disciple who wrote one of the volumes on the Supreme Court in the Holmes series, takes the view that Black was dead wrong and that Frankfurter was dead right. This is an old argument that goes way back into the 1890s. At that time a state condemned the property of a corporation but did not pay just compensation. The question came to the Court, and it ruled that the Just Compensation Clause of the Fifth Amendment was applicable to the states by reason of the Fourteenth Amendment.

If the Due Process Clause in the Fourteenth Amendment makes applicable to property rights the principles and procedures of the Bill of Rights, it is difficult to see why there should be a difference when it comes to individual rights, such as the right to be secure against the police coming in at night to search the house without a search warrant; and why it isn't applicable to the Self-Incrimination Clause contained in the Fifth Amendment.

The great work of the Warren Court was in making the standards of the Bill of Rights applicable to state action. The Fourth Amendment was held to be covered in *Mapp v. Ohio;* the privilege against self-incrimination was also held applicable to the states in *Malloy v. Hogan.*

The ban against cruel and unusual punishment in the Eighth Amendment; the Double-Jeopardy Clause of the Fifth Amendment was treated the same way as was the right to a trial by jury and the right of an accused to be represented by counsel and advised of his rights, as spelled out in the Sixth Amendment and in *Gideon v. Wainwright.*

Indeed, all of the important protective safeguards afforded to the accused by the Bill of Rights have been made applicable to the states. As this was happening a great howl went up in some quarters that states' rights were being abridged and the lives of criminals made easier.

Making the Bill of Rights applicable to the states raised the level of law enforcement practices that states may permissibly use. In *Miranda v. Arizona* we stated that once a person is held by the police in custody and is under examination, that examination as a practical matter is the start of his trial, and that he therefore is entitled to be represented by a lawyer and advised of his constitutional rights. It is indeed difficult to see how a civilized society could demand less. The *Miranda* decision, written by Earl Warren, came in for a lot of abuse and was said to be responsible for increased crime rates. But those knowledgeable in the field know that crime springs from poverty, insufferable living conditions and from involvement in drugs. The presumption of innocence is proclaimed not only for the rich and prestigious members of the community but also for the lowliest members.

Murphy and Rutledge, joining Black's opinion in the Adamson case, filed a separate opinion that said that they thought that the guarantees of due process were not necessarily limited to the provisions of the Bill of Rights but include other privileges and immunities—a decision with which I, in the years to come, was inclined to agree.

The other great cleavage of the Frankfurter school concerned the so-called hands-off policy, by which many Court-made rules promote the policy of judicial abstinence. This tradition meant that the Supreme Court would have symbolic value but little beyond that. That Court would sedulously avoid meeting contentious issues and would sit in resplendent dignity aloof from the issues of the day. That was later to be the Burger philosophy.

Those who take the other view of the role of the Court are called the "activists"; and this was the label that the Harvard cabal used against Brennan, Black, Warren and myself. My view always has been that anyone whose life, liberty or property was threatened or impaired by any branch of government—whether the President or one of his agencies, or Congress, or the courts (or any counterpart in a state regime)—had a justiciable controversy and could properly repair to a judicial tribunal for vindication of his rights.

Men protested that they were being sent to Vietnam to fight when no "war" had been declared by Congress. By the Constitution, only Congress can declare a "war"; the idea of a "presidential war" is foreign to our charter. If "property" is taken in violation of the Constitution, the owner has a justiciable claim. In 1952 the Court so held when Truman seized the steel mills during the Korean "war" (*Youngstown Sheet & Tube Co. v. Sawyer*). Life and liberty are ranked as high as property in the Due Process Clauses. They are indeed the trinity that appears both in the Fifth and in the Fourteenth Amendments. A man whose life may be taken or whose legs may be shot off in Vietnam has as high a right to judicial protection as did the steel mills in the Korean "war."

I wrote numerous opinions stating why we should take these cases and decide them. Once or twice Potter Stewart and Bill Brennan joined me. But there was never a fourth vote. I thought then—and still think—that treating the question as a "political" one was an abdication of duty and a self-inflicted wound on the Court.

If the judiciary bows to expediency and puts questions in the "political" rather than in the justiciable category merely because they are troublesome or embarrassing or pregnant with great emotion, the judiciary has become a political instrument itself. Courts sit to determine questions on stormy as well as on calm days. The Constitution is the measure of their duty. And it is the Constitution, not the judges' individual preferences, that marks the line between what is justiciable on the one hand and, on the other, what is political and therefore beyond the reach or competence of courts. A question is "political" only if the Constitution has assigned it to one of the other two departments for solution.

Franklin D. Roosevelt

As I have mentioned, soon after I came on the Court, FDR began to call me, asking me to take one assignment after another. One summer he had several jobs for me as an administrative assistant at the White House. In June 1942 he asked me to spend the summer there. My job would be to knock department heads together so as to (a) expedite decisions and (b) resolve conflicts or differences of view.

I talked with both Roberts and Black about it and they agreed that I should decline the invitation. Hugo said, "If you do an effective job, you will get into a first-class row with some vested interest in twenty-four hours. If you don't get into a row, you'll be a flop."

I wrote FDR that "since last December I have often thought that I should enter the Army or the Navy. Except for such a major war move, I thought I should stay on the Court." I added: "I am inclined to the view that any real undertaking on my part to iron out difficulties between department heads who have authority and who in many instances have a real hostility would not prove to be helpful and might injure the Court."

My countersuggestion to FDR was that he designate for the job three or four men on a permanent basis with definite authority and responsibility, adding that they might be able to do "what department heads ought to do on their own 90 per cent or more of the time without any intercession."

Advising a President while being a Justice leads to complications, as Abe Fortas and many other Justices have discovered. The norm is not necessarily a true separation of powers, for every Justice is part of the town, of the nation, of the world, and is bound to play more of a role than that of passive onlooker. The difficulty lies in the disqualifications that may arise when future cases are before the Court. I saw that problem enveloping my projected advice to FDR and I therefore never undertook to serve in that role.

In my day I felt there was no room for a Justice in the executive branch. So I rejected all of FDR's requests for advice except one—to serve as a committee to recommend a person to head up the Office of Manpower.

Sidney Hillman, Paul McNutt and others were vying for the job, and I gave FDR the benefit of my views. He kept coming back, again and again, with other jobs. I saw him often, played poker with him, helped him on speeches, but I declined his overtures to put me to work in the White House, as I did not think I should undertake that work unless I resigned from the Court.

Finally, on a hot September night in 1941, he asked me to do just that. I was at the rodeo in Pendleton, Oregon, when a resourceful White House operator tracked me down; I took the call in a phone booth and heard FDR say that the Court was not the place for me. I must resign.

In September 1941, FDR had in mind the creation of the War Production Board, which actually took place on January 16, 1942. In the meantime an office was vacant—Coordinator of National Defense Purchases, established by the Counsel of National Defense but soon to be transferred to the Executive Office of the President. FDR wanted me to take it over and create what in time became the War Production Board. Bernard Baruch had recommended me, the President said, and I must do it.

"Is this a draft—a real draft, Mr. President?"

"A real draft," he replied.

'Then I'll do it."

"Wonderful," he boomed back. "Call me the minute you get here."

I was back in Washington in a week and reported to the White House operator. I was sick at heart, for I did not want to leave the Court, but the Old Man could not be denied. No White House message came that day and none the next. None came that week. Soon I picked up a morning paper to read that Donald Nelson had been named for the office. I was greatly relieved. FDR never mentioned the matter when I saw him next. He looked like the cat that had swallowed the canary; but he never told me what had happened. The technique of complete silence was one of FDR's accomplishments.

I soon learned that Harry Hopkins, whose star was rising, had persuaded FDR to make the switch from me to Donald Nelson. Harry Hopkins was a sick man; and the sicker he got, the closer FDR pulled the man to him. Dr. Draper thought it was the "identity" FDR felt for Hopkins, both being invalids and both getting worse. While FDR's general level of health was good, he walked less and less. "The braces kill me these days," he would say. He was putting on weight; and his lack of leg exercises practically immobilized him.

Harry Hopkins was very much in the center of White House activities by 1941. He was indeed a physically sick man, his face being that of a cadaver at FDR's funeral. He had great personal ambitions—to succeed FDR. He was therefore instinctively jealous of anyone whom FDR liked. Warfare around a throne has always been acrimonious. Harry, whom I liked, saw me as a rival—which I was not in terms of personal ambition; but he treated me accordingly. He must have gloated over his shunting me aside and replacing me with Don Nelson. He and I never discussed the episode, though I always felt grateful for Harry's decapitation of me for that job, since it was one of the most thankless of them all.

When war came, on December 7,1941, I was giving a luncheon at my home. Dr. Draper was there, and so was Henry Wallace. As a matter of fact I had seated them at the same cardtable, as Draper had been curious about Wallace. Draper's opinion of Wallace, I later found out, was very revealing: "I'd keep him on the faculty but I'd never make him Dean." Which in Draper language meant that Wallace as an idea man was outstanding; as an administrator, not very good.

Robert P. Patterson, former federal judge and now Undersecretary of War, was also there. It was about one o'clock when my butler, Rochester (after whom Jack Benny was to name a famous radio and movie character), whispered to me that Judge Patterson was wanted by the White House operator. Bob shortly returned and told us he had an announcement to make. The room became silent and he said, 'The Japanese have just attacked Pearl Harbor." Then he quickly left for the Pentagon.

FDR had been alarmed when Hitler became Chancellor on January 30, 1933; and I always thought that FDR's recognition of Russia on November 16, 1933, was the first conscious power move on his part in reaction to Hitler. It did indeed lay the basis for the final combination that was fatal to Hitler. I think that the prospect of a global engagement began to take definite shape in FDR's mind no later than 1937. His well-known "quarantine" speech, in which he denounced international terrorism, was made in Chicago in October 1937, and his "dagger in the back" speech on the Italian invasion of France was made in Charlottesville in June 1940. FDR in those three years often talked of "neutrality," but he was, as Rex Tugwell once put it, "the least neutral of all Americans." In 1937 the Ludlow Resolution, a proposal to require a popular referendum before Congress could declare war, was debated. It was defeated in the House in 1938 by a vote of 209 to 188 after FDR had sent a message that "it would cripple any President in his conduct of our foreign relations, and it would encourage other nations to believe that they could violate American rights with impunity."

My view of the conduct of foreign affairs is that the Constitution provides that it is Congress which has the power to "declare war" and that all diplomacy, short of that, is under the guidance of the President. That was my interpretation in 1937 when the Ludlow Resolution was debated as it was my view during the Nixon Vietnam war.

Hitler annexed Austria in March 1938, and then, after the "peace in our time" accord with the British Chamberlain government, took Czechoslovakia. The year 1939 saw Poland invaded. I was at the Polish embassy that night, and the Polish ambassador, both proud and valiant, took me aside to assure me that this was Hitler's greatest error, that the Polish army would cut the Germans to ribbons. I raised a glass to Polish victory but left the embassy with a heavy heart.

FDR's policy in these years and continuing into 1940 was to help the victims of the aggressors. He still talked of the defeat of Hitler by means "short of war"; and in 1939 he had, I think, a hope that Mussolini could be persuaded to stay out of war.

Throughout 1939 and 1940 he talked peace, peace, peace. Yet, as Hitler invaded nation after nation, he denounced those acts of aggression.

In 1939 he had proclaimed the neutrality of the United States in the war between Germany and Poland, France and the United Kingdom. In 1940 he was urging that we build up our armed defenses; and he was releasing surplus stocks of airplanes, artillery and munitions to Great Britain. In 1940, while dedicating the Great Smoky Mountains Park, he spoke mostly of the dangers of aggressive war. On December 29, 1940, he told the nation, "The Nazi masters of Germany have made it clear that they intend not only to dominate all life and thought in their own country, but also to enslave the whole of Europe and then to use the resources of Europe to dominate the rest of the world." It was then he declared we should be "the great arsenal of democracy."

On the Fourth of July of that year, he had warned the country that "the United States will never survive as a happy and fertile oasis of liberty surrounded by the cruel desert of dictatorship." On August 14, 1941, came the momentous Atlantic Charter announcing the new enduring compact between this country and England. And the next day came the joint Roosevelt-Churchill message asking for a Moscow conference. On September 1, 1941, he stated, "We shall do everything in our power to crush Hitler and his Nazi forces." On September 11, 1941, he told the country again about the Nazi danger, saying, "When you see a rattlesnake poised to strike, you do not wait until he has struck before you crush him." On October 13, 1941, he announced that aid was being rushed to Russia.

On December 6, 1941, he sent word to the Japanese ambassador, saying that the concentration of Japanese forces in Vietnam was the cause of great concern and asked for their withdrawal. Then came December 7, "a date which will live in infamy," and the declaration of war on December 8.

These are merely the well-known highlights of Roosevelt's policies toward the growing war. In between were dozens upon dozens of measures taken by FDR, building a mosaic of civilian and military agencies, all equipped with power to deal with the pressing problems of war, should it come. So, despite the Pearl Harbor disaster, we were, thanks to FDR's foresight, well prepared.

FDR did not cut many constitutional corners. He recognized that the source of his power was Congress. In his first inaugural he said, "I shall ask the Congress for the one remaining instrument to meet the crisis—broad Executive power to wage a war against the emergency, as great as the power that would be given to me if we were in fact invaded by a foreign foe."

In 1941 FDR did impound money appropriated by Congress for the building of highways to offset the increase in military expenditures, which aroused some critics, as did later impoundments by FDR.

He did by-pass Congress in 1940 when he made a deal by which, in exchange for our destroyers, England gave us bases in the Atlantic. But he acted in reliance on an opinion of his Attorney General and after consulting with Democratic and Republican leaders in Congress. The Lend-Lease Act was debated and passed by Congress. His earlier proposal to reform the Supreme Court was submitted to Congress.

FDR was criticized and denounced for starting a "presidential war" against Hitler—an alleged precedent for the later "presidential war" against Vietnam. All of FDR's sympathies and prejudices were for England's cause. He could not constitutionally have reacted otherwise. Hence, after close consultation with Churchill he started a vast rearmament program into which we had committed about $100 billion before war was declared.

Congress, prior to December 8, 1941, did not declare war on Germany or Japan. It was, however, active in authorizing the establishment of defense posts far from our shores and in readying America for any assaults. These preliminary moves by both FDR and Congress, in the eyes of some people, amounted to an undeclared war. I never thought it was. They involved a readiness to risk hostilities, but they never committed America to an all-out undertaking to destroy Hitlerism. A declaration of war would envisage a total effort against another power—the kind which the "presidential war" in Vietnam launched. FDR certainly believed in a strong presidency, but it was not a secretive one. He held press conferences twice a week, even through most of the war. He believed in participatory democracy and was constantly in touch with diverse people with diverse views, seeking enlightenment for himself and a consensus among the people.

I had a little to do with these policy decisions. During these days FDR would mull over his problems in the evenings, and he used me as a sounding board. The ugly character of the Nazi regime was a recurring theme as the persecution of the Jews loomed larger and larger. Those barbaric acts and the barbaric quality of the Nazis themselves were the main forces shaping FDR's policies.

I saw FDR on December 8, 1941, and he was indeed greatly relieved that the long period of waiting was over. I think that by the fall of 1941 he had hoped we would get into the war and throw our massive weight against Hitler and the Japanese. I think he would have asked for a declaration of war before December 8, 1941, if he could have managed it politically.

That day as I left the White House I realized that an armament program leads irresistibly to war. The reasons are partly subconscious perhaps. In any event, the pressures mount to use newly collected weapons and manpower. The military are bent on flexing their muscles; a theater of war is a place where promotions come fast.

The presence of a big whopping military establishment puts immeasurable pressures on Presidents, senators, congressmen, Cabinet officers. They begin to think more and more in military terms. The mass media are attracted to shining armor, like flies to honey. In time the nation is saturated with military news, military hopes, military thinking.

Preparedness, I realized that December day in 1941, no more stops war than the death penalty stops murders. Man is basically predatory, and preparedness excites the base instincts that propel man to killing.

There never was a "credibility gap" when FDR was in the White House. Feeling as he did that we would be drawn into the European maelstrom, he undertook to educate the people. But he never played tricks on them, nor did he give them false figures or pretend one thing while doing another. He tried to get the people to see the needs and the dangers, but he never manufactured facts, nor used verbal razzle-dazzle to create false issues and to utter half-truths. He did, however, have a high regard for human rights and knew that they were in the crucible.

The route he traveled was indeed a delicate one, for there was still a hard core of isolationism in the country and he had to educate the people on the menace of Hitler. Many voices helped him in that cause, particularly those of Winston Churchill and of Edward R. Murrow and Raymond Swing, whose factual radio reporting out of a bombed and battered London helped condition the American mind to the world of reality. And so far as the written word was concerned, no one had deeper insight and understanding than Dorothy Thompson, one of the first to give us a picture of the anatomy of Nazism.

FDR had resolved that the world should be rid of unilateral military action. During the war he talked with me many times about Woodrow Wilson and his ill-fated League of Nations. He talked about Wilson's mistakes. FDR thought that if we were to have collective security, the plans for it must be laid in advance of victory. He desired to capitalize on the spirit of unity and cooperation, dominant in wartime between the Allies, to lay the foundation of a new world agency providing for collective security.

"We'll call it the United Nations," he said.

And so he arranged the Dumbarton Oaks Conference, where the delegations of the United States, the United Kingdom, the Soviet Union and China met during 1944, completing their conversations on October 7. Their proposals outlined the general structure of what later became the United Nations, and they received FDR's blessing, on October 9, 1944:

This time we have been determined first to defeat the enemy,
assure that he shall never again be in a position to plunge the
world into war, and then to so organize the peace-loving
nations that they may through unity of desire, unity of will,
and unity of strength be in a position to assure that no other
would-be aggressor or conqueror shall even get started. That
is why from the very beginning of the war, and paralleling
our military plans, we have begun to lay the foundations for
the general organization for the maintenance of peace and
security.

Dean Acheson, as Undersecretary of State under Cordell Hull, lobbied the Senate for approval of the UN Charter. But he said in 1970, "I never thought the United Nations was worth a damn. To a lot of people it was a Holy Grail, and those who set store by it had the misfortune to believe their own bunk." But whatever its limitations, it was a step toward a Rule of Law—man's only hope for escape from total annihilation.

As the war progressed, missions came and went, all secretly. Harry Hopkins became a courier between FDR and Churchill and he executed his assignments faithfully. I saw FDR frequently at night. He maintained that I made the best dry martinis of anyone in town. He liked them dry—six to one—and very cold, with lemon peel. After dinner we would often see a movie, usually alone, sometimes with others. One night William Bullitt, who had been our first ambassador to the Soviet Union, was there holding forth on the need to set up democratic underground organizations in Eastern Europe, a proposal that FDR vetoed.

Another night FDR sketched the architectural design for the Bethesda Naval Hospital, and the structure, as built, largely followed that design. Another night FDR talked of his successor. He was thinking of the election in 1948, for he had, I think, no premonition of his early demise. I asked him what men had emerged in the war effort who were of presidential caliber. After a long silence he replied, "George Marshall is the best of all who have crossed the screen." He went on to extol Marshall's many virtues and to explain why he thought he had the stature to lead the nation in the postwar world and deal with the multi-ideological problems that were certain to arise.

William (Wild Bill) Donovan, for whom I had once worked on a bankruptcy investigation, was then head of the Office of Strategic Services under the Joint Chiefs of Staff and was recruiting men for it.

He came to see me, inviting me to resign from the Court, go to a training school and serve in the Asian theater. I was then too heavily committed, emotionally and otherwise, to the Court to leave it.

Admiral William F. Halsey was in town from the Pacific making speeches that caused the audiences to howl when he called the Japanese "yellow-bellied bastards." Admiral Chester W. Nimitz was going silently and efficiently about his business, and General Carl (Tooey) Spaatz was thrilling the nation with his aeronautical wonders. General Dwight D. Eisenhower was home on personal business. Admiral William D. Leahy at the White House was a strong and steady influence. I knew them all except Eisenhower, and admired each one for his particular talents. It was a great team that FDR had assembled.

But even the great were bogged down in paperwork. Memoranda were produced in greater numbers than bullets. They flooded the departments. On one of my regular lunch dates with Forrestal, I said, "Why don't you write a two-page memo and put in between the two sheets a half-dozen pages of the same size containing excerpts from the *Odyssey* or *Iliad*?"

The next time I saw him, Forrestal was laughing when he told me that he had done it and "the whole thing came back initialed by everyone, including George Marshall."

As the months passed, the alphabetical agencies multiplied and people poured into the capital to work for the government. Office space was at a premium. One day at lunch, FDR was talking about it. I suggested that he move the Supreme Court to Denver, Colorado. I pointed out that Denver is not far from the geographical center of the United States—a point north of Rapid City, South Dakota, not far from the Wyoming line. With the Court in Denver he could put hundreds of tables in the hallways of the court building in Washington, creating a regular assembly line for memoranda and other paperwork.

He pretended to think the idea was excellent but added, "How can I keep my eye on you all if you are way out there?"

The war produced a great spate of litigation.

War in the constitutional sense is more than a state of hostilities. As I discuss elsewhere, in the sixties Johnson carefully avoided asking

Congress to declare "war" against Vietnam. Yet editors and people generally talked loosely about the "war." Some said that those who dissented against our Vietnam policy were guilty of "treason."

When does dissent become treason? Article III, Sect. 3, of the Constitution defines "treason" as follows: "Treason against the United States, shall consist only in levying war against them, or in adhering to their enemies, giving them aid and comfort."

This comes into play when there is "war," and "war" comes into being by a "declaration" by Congress, as provided in Article 1, Sect. 8. The difference between "war" and a state of hostilities is tremendous—as constitutional students know.

So it is a form of illiteracy to talk about "treason" and "war" in the constitutional sense, when speaking of those who voiced their dissent against our Vietnam policies.

But the objection goes even deeper. Proof of "treason" requires proof of "overt" acts. Jefferson, who fought bitterly to exclude "constructive treason" in the old English sense from our Constitution, would turn in his grave at the suggestion that speech could be an "overt" act.

Sedition, of course, is quite a different thing. Whether speech alone could ever qualify is a very moot question. It was so condemned in one case in which "war" had been declared and was in process.

It was condemned in another case in which there was a "conspiracy" to teach the noxious creed even though there was no "war" in existence. But there were qualifications originally stated by Mr. Justice Holmes in the "clear and present danger" test.

The terms "treason" and "war" as used in the Constitution are words of art. The truck drivers and field hands of the nation cannot be expected to understand subtle constitutional nuances. But news editors who mold public opinion have a special trust, a special responsibility not to misuse terms.

The war power is a pervasive one. As Hughes once wrote: "The power to wage war is the power to wage war successfully." People are regimented in ways that defy peacetime notions of liberty. Property is controlled and regulated in fashions severe by normal standards. Great restraints are permissible, for the very life of the country is at stake.

When Tomoyuki Yamashita, the Japanese general, was captured and an American military tribunal was named to try him for violating the law of war—letting his troops commit atrocities against the civilian population and prisoners of war—we held that no constitutional questions were presented. And when an Allied military court was set up by MacArthur in Japan to sit in judgment on alleged Japanese war criminals, our Court held we had no jurisdiction even to entertain a petition for a writ of habeas corpus on behalf of a prisoner held or tried by that tribunal, since it was multinational in character, not solely American. But I felt and still feel that the Court had jurisdiction over the American member of that tribunal, since he was bound by the American Constitution.

The Japanese cases are another illustration of the way in which a state of "war" affects civil rights. Those cases are little understood. They reached the Court in 1943 and 1944, but they arose in 1942 when no one knew where the Japanese army and navy were. Actually they were starting their invasion of Malaya and Burma. But our Pacific defenses were so slight at that time that, as I have mentioned, the Pentagon advised us on oral argument that the Japanese army could take everything west of the Rockies if they chose to land. Evacuation of the entire population would of course have been permissible by constitutional standards pertaining in time of war. Was it constitutional to evacuate only citizens of Japanese ancestry? That was an issue hotly contested both in the curfew case *(Hirabayashi v. United States)* and in the evacuation case *(Korematsu v. United States)*.

The Pentagon's argument was that if the Japanese army landed in areas thickly populated by Americans of Japanese ancestry, the opportunity for sabotage and confusion would be great. By doffing their uniforms they would be indistinguishable from the other thousands of people of like color and stature. It was not much of an argument, but it swayed a majority of the Court, including myself. The severe bite of the military evacuation order was not in a requirement to move out but in the requirement to move out of the West Coast and move into concentration camps in the interior. Locking up the evacuees after they had been removed had no military justification. I wrote a concurring opinion, which I never published, agreeing to the evacuation but not to evacuation *via* the concentration camps. My Brethren, especially Black and Frankfurter, urged me strongly not to publish. "The issue of detention is not here," they said. "And the Court never decides a constitutional question not present." The latter was of course not true, as John Marshall's famous *Marbury v. Madison* shows. In that landmark case, Chief Justice Marshall established the concept of judicial review of congressional acts by declaring section 13 of the Judiciary Act of

1789 unconstitutional. He did so in spite of the fact that the question brought before the Court was not the constitutionality of the act, but whether or not Secretary of State Madison should be compelled to deliver the judicial appointment papers left over by his predecessor in office. Technically, however, the question of detention was not presented to us. Yet evacuation via detention camps was before us, and I have always regretted that I bowed to my elders and withdrew my opinion.

On the same day that we decided the evacuation case we held that there was no authority to detain a citizen, absent evidence of a crime (*Ex parte Endo*). Meanwhile, however, grave injustices had been committed. Fine American citizens had been robbed of their properties by racists—crimes that might not have happened if the Court had not followed the Pentagon so literally. The evacuation case, like the flag-salute case, was ever on my conscience. Murphy and Rutledge, dissenting, had been right.

The cases were not myriad but they were numerous, and from them comes the story that the "war power" is a broad, pervasive, concurrent power which gives Congress authority to do things it would never dream of doing in days of peace.

FDR did have a lingering grudge against the Court as an institution. He never really got over the defeat of his Court-packing plan. He mentioned it again when I proposed that the Court move to Denver. This time he asked why lawyers were so conservative, why they turned out to be stodgy judges. He mentioned no names, but he obviously had been disappointed at some of his own judicial appointees. I told him that there was nothing in the Constitution requiring him to appoint a lawyer to the Supreme Court.

"What?" he exclaimed. "Are you serious?"

I answered that I was.

He lit a cigarette, leaned back and after a moment's silence said, "Let's find a good layman." He became expansive and enthusiastic and held forth at length, going over various names.

"You'll have to pick a member of the Senate," I said. "The Senate will never reject a layman as a nominee who is one of their own."

His face lit up and he said excitedly, "The next justice will be Bob La Follette." There was no vacancy then, and none occurred before FDR died. But a plan had been laid to shake the pillars of tradition and make the Establishment squirm by putting an outstanding, liberal layman on the Court.

As the years passed, the unpopularity of Henry Wallace grew. Though he, as Vice President, was President of the Senate and presided over that body, he had few friends there. He was never a hail-fellow, nor much of a mixer. By and large, he stayed aloof and remote. While he had a popular following in the country, he had few political friends in Washington. That feeling about him became a powerful factor in rejecting him for renomination in 1944. Everyone close to FDR knew that the President was a sick man. Some of us close to him thought he had suffered a slight stroke, though Ross McIntyre, his physician, denied it. Many of us felt he would not live through another four years. So the sentiment grew that Wallace must go and a new running mate be selected.

There was a mounting sentiment for me as FDR's running mate in 1944. 1 did nothing to encourage the movement and indeed did not covet the job. I had many talks with my friend Senator Frank Maloney about it. He was going to the Convention and wanted to make the nominating speech, but I gave him a letter of refusal to be read at the convention in case some of my exuberant friends put me in nomination.

Frank said with all of the emotion an Irishman can muster, "They simply won't take Wallace. And Truman? Who is he? My colleague of course. But he's nobody. If I put your name before the convention, there would be a stampede."

Once, as June 1944 came near, Ed Murrow and Eric Sevareid came to see me. They wanted "the word" from me. They were friends and would treat the news discreetly—my resignation to run for Vice President as soon as the Court adjourned. But I shook my head.

Some of my friends were indeed dead serious about making me FDR's running mate. Henry Hess, later U.S. Attorney in Oregon and a famous trial lawyer, had a nomination speech which I had difficulty avoiding. He was an old friend and I loved him like a brother, and I could not get through his head that politics was not my bent. George Killion of California, later president of the U.S. President Line, was another unquenchable character with only that one mission in life.

Cal Cook of California was a third. I had known him at Whitman College and he was in the outer ring of Governor Culbert L. Olson politics in California. He was at the time in the dry-cleaning business and flew north, tracked me down in Oregon, and walked the trails there, trying to convince me to take the plunge.

On the way West that summer I had stopped in San Francisco for a few days to see Max Radin, the professor of law at Berkeley who selected my law clerk for years. I greatly enjoyed Max's scintillating mind, and it was refreshing to be exposed to him after a stodgy winter in the capital. On this 1944 trip Max gave me a stag dinner at a famous restaurant noted for its pheasant. Phil Gibson, Chief Justice of the California Supreme Court, was there; George Killion, Earl Warren and Cal Cook were also present. We had a special dining room with no other people within shouting distance. I left early, at about ten o'clock, as I was rising at dawn driving north. I had checked my hat and coat in the lobby of the restaurant near the entrance. I presented the check, waited a moment for the two articles, left a tip in a saucer and turned to leave. At that instant a flashlight bulb went off. To my right was the photographer; to my left was a blonde I had never seen. Where the two had come from I do not know. But it obviously was a frame-up to give WOD some nasty publicity. Cal Cook, who had followed me out, jumped the photographer, knocked him down, seized his camera and actually crushed it with his feet. He then called a cab for me, muttering some obscenities about the San Francisco press.

There were others in Washington—Abe Fortas and other SEC allies— who were really a stout band of campaigners for me; and if politics had been my dish, I'd have had as backers men who would have walked the last mile. I was grateful; I was impressed by their sincerity; my old analyst Dr. Draper thought it would be the best thing possible for the country. But the truth is, I never had the Potomac Fever and could not be excited about catching it.

Later I tried to get a copy of the longhand note refusing the nomination which I had given Frank Maloney. He had died prematurely; his wife, Martha, shortly following. They left a son, Bobby, who had all of his father's papers in a trunk. But by the time I caught up with Bobby the trunk had been in a flood and all the papers destroyed.

Despite my supporters, my decision was made—to stay on the Court. I thought that if a member of the Court were going to get into the Convention struggle, he should resign from the Court, as Hughes had done in 1916.

After the Democratic National Convention in 1944, which was held in Chicago, I learned that FDR had preferred that I run with him. I did not know it at the time; he had never broached the matter to me. But Grace Tully, who was then his secretary, tells how he dictated the famous letter on his railroad car in the Chicago switchyards. He did not repudiate Henry Wallace, as he did not want to alienate that bloc of votes. But he did not prefer Wallace and knew that the pros would never accept Wallace. This was true, for FDR was failing and those on the inside knew that the Vice President would likely take over before 1948. The pros kept demanding that FDR give them a clue as to his wishes. Finally he dictated the letter to Grace Tully saying he would be happy to run "with either Bill Douglas or Harry Truman." She gave the letter to Bob Hannegan, who was chairman of the Democratic National Committee and was Truman's manager at the 1944 convention. Hannegan was so upset over the letter that he turned the names around before he released it to the convention. So the convention delegates believed that Truman was FDR's first choice. I was at my cabin in the Wallowa Mountains of Oregon, miles removed from telephones and roads, and knew nothing of those shenanigans. An FDR "draft" would have been difficult to resist. I am glad I never had to face up to it in 1944.

That fall I met Bob Hannegan at a cocktail party. Bob was jubilant over the way in which he had steered Truman through the convention, and he laughed when he said, "Bill, we really did you in."

I put my arm around him, for I greatly liked him, and said, "Bob, if I ever did run for anything, I'd want you as my manager." In spite of Hannegan's great effort on Truman's behalf, when Hannegan died a couple of years later, Truman didn't go to his funeral because Hannegan's questionable financial dealings had come to light in the meantime.

After the returns of the 1944 election were in and the year 1945 approached, FDR faded quickly. The look of death crept into his face. He was pallid and listless. In January 1945 I sent him a birthday present, a martini mixer. As I have mentioned, he liked his martinis dry and very cold, and the perennial problem that I, his bartender, had was to make sure they were not too "watery." This particular gift solved that problem, for the ice was in a separate chamber in the center of a bowl whose walls were an excellent transmitter of cold. Off it went and back came the message:

> Dear Bill:
>   Ever so many thanks for that fine birthday gift. I haven't seen anything like it in a very long time, so it is particularly welcome. I look forward to "launching" it soon and you were good to think of me! With my warm regards,
>   As ever,
>   Franklin Roosevelt

This note was written March 22, 1945. I lunched with him a few days before he died. He had always dominated the table, tossing bits of conversation to each person. This day he tossed nothing to anyone. I kept up a chatter, and he would raise his head to nod concurrence. But then he would drop his head and stay utterly silent as he consumed his food like an automaton. All the Rooseveltian gaiety, humor, deviltry, laughter, teasing, taunting had gone. The man was alive but doomed. I could hardly see him for my tears when we shook hands and said goodbye. I knew I would probably never see him again, for he was leaving that day for Warm Springs, Georgia.

When he died he was with Lucy Mercer, whom I did not know. Apparently, he had fallen in love with her when she was Eleanor Roosevelt's social secretary. At that time FDR was Assistant Secretary of the Navy under Josephus Daniels. George Draper had told me the story years earlier and had related how there was a showdown between FDR and his wife over Lucy Mercer. According to Draper, Eleanor was ready to leave her husband unless the ties with Lucy were broken. FDR's friends advised him to break them—if he wanted a political future. In those days divorce was an ugly word, and a person tarnished by such an event was deemed ineligible for public office. By and by the public mood changed, but at the time FDR bowed to it and gave Eleanor the necessary reassurances. But as Joe Kennedy once remarked, "An association so old and so intimate as that one simply could not be completely broken."

April 12,1945 ... I was alone in the late afternoon driving my car west on Constitution Avenue. A friend pulled alongside, sounded his horn and pointed to his radio. I turned mine on and out of the ether came the stark news—FDR had just died. I parked the car and walked for hours, trying to adjust myself to the great void that his death had created.

On April 14 the Court was at Union Station to meet the funeral train coming north from Warm Springs, Georgia. We followed the funeral cortege. Soldiers marched; great horses pulled the casket majestically up Pennsylvania Avenue. The multitudes lined the street. All was silent except for the distant sound of muffled drums, the scuffing of the feet of the soldiers, the sound of the horses' hooves, the impact of steel-rimmed wheels on the pavement, and the quiet sobbing of the spectators.

People loved FDR. He was the one who had banished Fear. Now that he was gone, Fear had returned to their hearts—and the people wept without restraint.

The Court, including former Chief Justice Hughes, attended the service in the East Room of the White House, and on Sunday, the fifteenth, the Court went by train to Hyde Park. FDR was buried in his garden behind a ten-foot-high hemlock hedge that was one hundred and forty years old. The peonies were just coming out; the pansies were blooming in all their glory.

Here was the house where FDR's mother had planned to keep him tethered as a stamp collector after polio had paralyzed him. Here was the scene of his greatest personal victory.

There were the customary twenty-one salutes—and Fala, his constant companion, barked at each one. As I watched and listened, the words of a New Hampshire lawyer came back to me. I had spent the summer of 1932 in that state and felt the mounting heat of the campaign as September arrived. One day in Wolfeboro I asked a prominent lawyer how the national election was progressing. Shaking his finger, he said, "America will never put a cripple in the White House."

Then I remembered Draper saying, "Franklin, it's your head and your heart, not your legs, that are important. Your head and heart can put you in the Governor's mansion in Albany and in the White House. Franklin, people will remember you for what you are, for what you do—not for your legs."

People around the world knew this instinctively. FDR heralded the strength of the spirit of man over all his handicaps.

His life had become the symbol of a cooperative world regime founded on unity in diversity, mutual help and friendship—the symbol which we rather quickly dissipated by making the Cold War our new crusade. That is one theme of this book—to show why it was that my generation became politically bankrupt.

FDR gave the nation the kind of leadership I admired. We seemed to lose stature and greatness in his passing, becoming petty and greedy and small where we had known magnanimity, altruism and humanism.

On October 21, 1944, looking ahead to the end of World War II and a new world order, FDR said that it "must depend essentially on friendly human relations, on acquaintance, on tolerance, on unassailable sincerity and good will and good faith."

Truman was to take a different stance. In August 1945 he dropped our atomic bombs on Hiroshima and Nagasaki—civilian targets. By that act he introduced America to the world in a new image—a modern Genghis Khan bent on ruthless destruction.

PART THREE

Civil Libertarian

In the foreword to his book, *Mr. Lincoln and the Negroes: The Long Road to Equality,* Douglas tells of having participated in 1961 in a "Free Africa" rally, where he read from the Declaration of Independence and presented Lincoln's commentary from the Second Inaugural. He was later challenged by a State Department official for having misread the Declaration, which, in that official's view, claimed only that Americans were equal to the British. Douglas decided that it was time to review the history of the struggle for racial equality in the United States. The chapter included here pays particular attention to the legal and constitutional dimensions of the struggle, while showing also Douglas's understanding of the political and social facts that constitute the critical context for legal action.

The decade after the end of World War II brought a series of important free speech cases to the Court. As the conflict with the Soviet Union grew to full-scale ideological warfare, public authorities sought to silence dissenting voices on both the right and the left. Douglas, usually joined by Black, was a persistent champion of the importance of free speech and open discussion as the critical distinguishing feature of democratic government. Three of his opinions are reproduced here.

In *Terminiello v. Chicago,* Douglas wrote for the Court in striking down the disorderly conduct conviction of a speaker who had delivered an intentionally provocative and racist discourse to a crowd in a hall, while his opponents were gathered on the outside. In Douglas's view, part of the office of speech in a democracy was to stir unrest. The fact that speech was provocative could not alone deprive it of the protection of the First Amendment.

In *Dennis v. United States*, Douglas dissented from the conviction of eleven top leaders of the Communist Party of the United States, under the Smith Act. The majority had confirmed the conviction under a watered-down version of the "clear and present danger test," according to which a very small risk of a very large harm was enough to warrant punishment. Douglas the Legal Realist stepped forward, finding the communists the "miserable merchants of unwanted wares," and insisting that some real danger must be present to warrant the punishment of unpopular ideas.

Beauharnais v. Illinois brought another Douglas dissent, as the majority sustained a conviction under a law that prohibited publications which portray "depravity, criminality, unchastity, or lack of virtue of a class of citizens of any race, color, creed or religion." The danger, in Douglas's eyes, lay in allowing the legislature to choose which messages should not be heard in public.

In all these cases, Douglas was locked in a dispute with Justice Frankfurter. In *Brandenburg v. Ohio* the Court approached the Douglas position by requiring that speech, to be punishable, must be both directed at producing imminent lawless action and likely to produce that result. Even then, Douglas was not entirely satisfied.

In 1963, Justice Douglas delivered the James Madison Lecture at the New York University Law School; his speech was printed in the school's law review as *The Bill of Rights Is Not Enough*. Drawing on examples from both foreign and domestic contexts, he argued forcefully for the importance of law to the preservation of liberty, while recognizing that the success of the enterprise depended on a people committed to embracing both.

In his later years, Douglas chafed under the constraints associated with living in an ever more crowded and complex society. Perhaps the most eloquent statement in this regard was his summer retreat to the Cascades every year, often before the Court was entirely through with its work for the term. But just as he created space for himself by returning to the mountains, so he sought to secure room for his fellow citizens to pursue their own views of the good, through his interpretation of the Constitution. Here, in "The Right to be Let Alone," from *The Right of the People*, he speaks of the right to privacy, suggesting the foundations for his opinion in *Griswold v. Connecticut*, which follows.

In the early years of the twentieth century, the Supreme Court had invalidated a wide range of government regulations of business, on the ground that they violated the "liberty of contract" implicitly protected by the Due Process Clause of the Fourteenth Amendment. One of the hallmarks of the New Deal Court was its abandonment of that doctrine, in favor of a view that due process required only that regulation be reasonably adapted to achieving a legitimate government purpose. Douglas was among the most forceful critics of the old Court's ways, but he also insisted that certain values, not explicitly mentioned in the text of the Constitution, were nonetheless protected against government interference. The most controversial of these values, and certainly the one most dear to Douglas, was the right to privacy, which provided the foundation for the Court's judgment in *Roe v. Wade*, protecting a woman's right to choose an abortion. In *Griswold*, Douglas articulates the right to privacy as a necessary implication from certain other rights explicitly protected by the Bill of Rights.

Themes that had always figured strongly in Douglas's writings—concern for the disadvantaged, the corruption of the "Establishment," the need for the people to take control of their own destiny—came together in *Points of Rebellion*, a little volume published at the height of agitation against the war in Vietnam. Some saw it as an effort by Douglas to pander to the activists of the anti-war movement, or at least to associate himself with them. The activists had likely drawn inspiration from the civil rights movement and from a Court which, for a time, took constitutional commitments to freedom and equality seriously. As always, Douglas was a visionary with his feet on the ground, working as much with facts as with ideals, in the Realist tradition.

Mr. Lincoln and the Negroes

Lincoln often spoke of the Declaration of Independence and its statement that "all men are created equal." To him those words were "the electric cord … that links the hearts of patriotic and liberty-loving men together, that will link those patriotic hearts as long as the love of freedom exists in the minds of men throughout the world."

Early in his public life he had pointed out that slavery was not consistent with the Declaration of Independence. "We began by declaring that all men are created equal; but now from that beginning we have run down to the other declaration, that *some* men to enslave *others is* a 'sacred right of self-government.' … If it had been said in Old Independence Hall, seventy-eight years ago, the very door-keeper would have throttled the man, and thrust him into the street."

In the debates of the 1850s some declared that, when the Declaration of Independence stated that all men are created equal, it meant only that "British subjects on this continent" were "equal to British subjects born and residing in Great Britain." Lincoln's answer was that in that view "the French, Germans, and other white people of the world are all gone to pot" along with the blacks, browns, and yellows. The opposition then changed its position and maintained that the equality clause of the Declaration of Independence meant "white men, men of European birth and European descent, and had no reference either to the Negro, the savage Indians, the Fiji, the Malay, or any other inferior and degraded race."

The man who maintained that all men, irrespective of race, creed, or color, were equal before the law called the Declaration of Independence the "immortal emblem of Humanity" because it gave "to the whole great family of man" the right to life, liberty, and the pursuit of happiness. He maintained that it "applies to the slave as well as to ourselves, that the class of arguments put forward to batter down that idea, are also calculated to break down the very idea of a free government, even for white men, and to undermine the very foundations of a free society."

He said, "The Saviour, I suppose, did not expect that any human creature could be perfect as the Father in Heaven; but He said, 'As your Father in Heaven is perfect, be ye also perfect.' He set that up as a standard, and he who did most towards reaching that standard, attained the highest degree of moral perfection. So I say in relation to the principle that all men are created equal, let it be as nearly reached as we can. If we cannot give freedom to every creature, let us do nothing that will impose slavery upon any other creature."

In Lincoln's day the Know-Nothings were opposed to Negroes, foreigners, and Catholics. As early as 1855, he denounced the Know-Nothings. "As a nation," he wrote, "we began by declaring that 'all *men are created equal.*' We now practically read it 'all men are created equal, *except negroes.*' When the Know-Nothings get control, it will read 'all men are created equal, except negroes, *and foreigners, and Catholics.*' When it comes to this I should prefer emigrating to some country where they make no pretense of loving liberty—to Russia, for instance, where despotism can be taken pure, and without the base alloy of hypocrisy."

The Declaration of Independence would give men courage in distant days "to renew the battle which their fathers began—so that truth and justice and mercy and all the humane and Christian virtues might not be extinguished from the land, so that no man would hereafter dare to limit and circumscribe the great principles on which the temple of justice was being built." Early in his life Lincoln spoke of the force and power of the Declaration of Independence:

> *Of our political revolution of '76, we all are justly proud. It has given us a degree of political freedom, far exceeding that of any other of the nations of the earth. In it the world has found a solution of that long mooted problem, as to the capability of man to govern himself. In it was the germ which has vegetated, and still is to grow and expand into the universal liberty of mankind.*

That germ has yet to take root in most areas and had not done so even in the North during the Civil War. Negroes in the Union Army suffered discrimination. Colored troops were segregated from white troops, yet made to serve under white officers. The Negro soldiers did not receive the same pay as white soldiers, whites receiving $13 a month plus allowances for clothing and the Negroes $7 a month. In 1862, the Negroes' salary was raised to $10 a month. Finally, in 1864, Congress provided that all Negroes who were free before April 19, 1861—the date the first call for troops was made—were to receive the same pay as white soldiers. On March 3, 1865, all Negroes who had been taken into the Army on assurance by the President or Secretary of War that they would get equal pay were granted it. The Civil War ended, however, without all Negroes in military service receiving the same pay as the whites rendering the same service.

That inequality in treatment cast a long shadow across the pages of American history. The Negro, though freed, suffered discrimination even when he was a soldier or sailor. Not until the 1940s were steps taken to end the practice of segregating Negroes in the Armed Services. Not until 1954 was segregation in the Armed Services completely and finally uprooted—a provision that has not, however, been extended to the National Guard.

The end of that regime of segregation has had continuous, as well as immediate benefits, as summarized by the 1961 United States Commission on Civil Rights Report on Employment:

> *The Armed Forces of the United States offer work opportunities second in quantity only to the civilian establishment of the Federal Government. In breadth of training opportunities they are second to none, offering training in almost every type of skill and learning either through their own facilities or through reimbursement to private institutions. To the Negro, who is often discriminatorily denied such opportunities as a civilian, enlistment in the Armed Forces is particularly attractive. Thus many Negroes have elected to become military career men. Others have acquired skills through military training which have enabled them to qualify for civilian jobs— particularly those requiring technical skills—which would not otherwise have been open to them.*

After the Civil War, the northern states opened inns, theaters, and other public facilities to all races. By 1870, Illinois had extended the franchise to Negroes. But though most of the states made racial discrimination unlawful, discrimination continued in various forms throughout the nation—from the 1860s to the 1960s.

After the Civil War some southern states provided that there should be no segregation in public schools. Those laws, however, were soon repealed; and segregation became the way of life, fortified by custom and by law. Public facilities—such as parks, railroad cars, restaurants, theaters, schools, waiting rooms, and toilets—were racially segregated by state laws. The validity of those laws was squarely presented to the Court over thirty years after the Civil War was ended. At that time the Court was composed of Chief Justice Fuller of Illinois, Field of California, Gray of Massachusetts, Brewer of Kansas, Brown of Michigan, Shiras of Pennsylvania, White of Louisiana, Peckham of New York, and Harlan of Kentucky. Of the nine, only White was from the South. Harlan, from the Border State of Kentucky, was once a slaveowner. All of the judges from the North plus White, the sole Southerner, joined in *Plessy v. Ferguson* to decide on May 18, 1896, that a state's segregation of the races in passenger trains was not a denial of "equal protection of the laws" within the meaning of the Fourteenth Amendment. The opinion was written by Brown, who commented for the Court on the meaning of that clause:

> *The object of the amendment was undoubtedly to enforce the absolute equality of the two races before the law, but in the nature of things it could not have been intended to abolish distinctions based upon color, or to enforce social, as distinguished from political equality, or a commingling of the two races upon terms unsatisfactory to either. Laws permitting, and even requiring, their separation in places where they are liable to be brought into contact do not necessarily imply the inferiority of either race to the other, and have been generally, if not universally, recognized as within the competency of the state legislatures in the exercise of their police power. The most common instance of this is connected with the establishment of separate schools for white and colored children, which has been held to be a valid exercise of the legislative power even by courts of States where the political rights of the colored race have been longest and most earnestly enforced.*

It was argued that if a state legislature could segregate the races in railroad coaches, it could enact laws "requiring colored people to walk upon one side of the street, and white people upon the other, or requiring white men's houses to be painted white, and colored men's black, or their vehicles or business signs to be of different colors, upon the theory that one side of the street is as good as the other, or that a house or vehicle of one color is as good as one of another color." The Court answered by saying that every exercise of the police power of a State must be "reasonable" and enacted "for the promotion of the public good and not for the annoyance or oppression of a particular class." Thus it rejected *apartheid* carried to its ultimate end as in South Africa. It upheld segregation of the races in public facilities provided the "separate" facilities granted the Negroes were "equal" to those used by the whites. (A phrase coined by the dissenter.) A state, the Court ruled, could put its weight behind the racial bias or prejudice of the dominant group in the community, making that bias or prejudice the state's policy.

The first Mr. Justice Harlan was the sole dissenter. He stated what was to become sixty years later the prevailing construction of the Equal Protection Clause of the Fourteenth Amendment:

> *in view of the Constitution, in the eye of the law, there is in this country no superior, dominant, ruling class of citizens. There is no caste here. Our Constitution is color-blind, and neither knows nor tolerates classes among citizens. In respect of civil rights, all citizens are equal before the law. The humblest is the peer of the most powerful. The law regards man as man, and takes no account of his surroundings or of his color when his civil rights as guaranteed by the supreme law of the land are involved.*

He added:

> *The destinies of the two races, in this country, are indissolubly linked together, and the interests of both require that the common government of all shall not permit the seeds of race hate to be planted under the sanction of law. What can more certainly arouse race hate, what more certainly create and perpetuate a feeling of distrust between these races, than state enactments, which, in fact, proceed on the*

ground that colored citizens are so inferior and degraded that they cannot be allowed to sit in public coaches occupied by white citizens?

Negroes have also been discriminated against at the polls. By the 1960s the percentage of Negroes registered as voters was only about 4 percent of all voting-age Negroes in Mississippi and 40 percent in Florida, with an overall average of 28 percent as compared with an overall average of 56 percent for southern whites.

Various devices were used to keep the Negro from voting. Racial gerrymandering (which the courts in time struck down) reduced the proportionate weight of Negro votes or eliminated them entirely from municipal affairs. There were other deterrents. Some states, including northern ones, have used poll taxes to raise money for the support of the government. These taxes are laid upon persons without regard to their occupations or property and may amount to one dollar a year or more. States that collected poll taxes customarily required the poll tax to be paid before a person could vote; and that requirement was sustained, since in our federal system the qualifications of voters are determined by the states, save as the Constitution restrains them. While the tax for each year might not be great, arrears had to be paid; and the total amount due might be $15, $20, $25, or more. The pinch of the poll tax was on the poor; and since Negroes were usually poor, the poll tax discouraged them from voting. Congress finally adopted a resolution in 1962 proposing a Constitutional Amendment that would abolish the poll tax as a condition to voting in a Presidential election or in an election for Senator or Representative in Congress.

Literacy is not synonymous with intelligence. Even illiterate, unsophisticated people can vote intelligently. India, under Nehru, is an example. In spite of an overall illiteracy rate of 78 percent, Indians have voted with discernment in municipal, state, and national elections. Seldom have they been seduced by the wiles of the Communist party; they have kept India solidly in the democratic ranks.

Under our constitutional system qualifications of voters have been entrusted to the states. There are exceptions—the Fifteenth Amendment denies a state the power to withhold voting rights on account of race, color, or previous condition of servitude, and the Nineteenth bars denial of voting rights on account of sex. If a literacy test is not used as a cloak to bar a person from voting because of race or sex, it is constitutional.

Such legislation may not be wise; but the power to prescribe literacy requirements has been sustained.

It has at times been used only as a cloak for violating the Fifteenth Amendment.

In some areas the Citizens Councils—organized to prevent assertion by Negroes of their rights—comb through registration records looking for Negro registrations that might be challenged on the grounds of illiteracy. A Negro registrant is easy to detect, since the color of the registrant is often disclosed on the card. Once these files are combed, many minor errors—both on the parts of whites and blacks—can be found. The Negro who makes a mistake is stricken from the rolls while a white voter is not. One Negro woman was removed because her age was incorrectly computed by one day if the date on which the registration card was executed was counted. A Negro man was removed because he misspelled the county of his birth. Yet those who challenged him themselves spelled the word "misspelled" incorrectly. A Negro who in describing his color used the letter "C" rather than the word "Colored" was stricken, though a white person who used the letter "W" was not. All Negro registrants in some wards were challenged, while none of the whites were; overall 100 or 150 Negro registrants were examined while only two or three white ones were. Moreover, more than 60 percent of the white registrations had deficiencies on their cards like those for which Negroes were challenged. Yet white voters went unchallenged while Negroes were stricken.

Laws were passed in some states which qualified as a voter anyone whose ancestor was eligible to vote on January I, 1866. All whites were therefore qualified, provided their grandfathers were not aliens, criminals, and the like. A twentieth-century Negro's grandfather, however, had probably been a slave. Even though "free" in 1866 he had not been allowed to vote. So his grandson or granddaughter, unlike the white voter, was required to take a literacy test. These laws were held unconstitutional.

In some states the primary election (where candidates are chosen to run in the general election) is a vital election, as the person who wins the Democratic primary is practically certain of winning in the general election. Some states enacted laws that only white people could vote in their primaries. Those laws were finally held unconstitutional.

Yet, in spite of discrimination, Negro votes at times have been a decisive factor in close elections. They caused Louisiana and Tennessee to go Republican in 1956, and provided a margin of victory in a number of counties in other states. Negro votes gave Kennedy his 9,561-vote victory over Nixon in North Carolina in 1960. Negroes were elected to public office in Georgia, South Carolina, North Carolina, Tennessee, Texas, and Virginia in the 1950s and 1960s. These Negro office holders constitute a very small minority; yet they are scattered throughout many local units, including school boards and planning commissions. Though the white voters in the South outnumber the Negro voter by over 12 to 1, the whites have promised Negroes equality in employment and other civil rights. For the Negro vote, once purchased by politicians, has become more and more conscious of its power, and candidates are catering more and more to Negro interests.

Poor educational facilities for the Negro have proved to be his greatest deterrent, as Booker T. Washington forecast in *Up from Slavery.*

The lack of good educational facilities is reflected in statistics showing that service and other nonskilled, nonfarm occupations employ about 47 percent of Negro workers and 14 percent of white workers. Only 12 percent of Negro workers are in professional, managerial, and white collar occupations, compared to about 42 percent of white workers. The median family income for Negroes is about 30 percent below the median for the whites. The rate of unemployment for Negroes is double that for whites.

Through the years, discrimination as respects education has been notorious. Usually the Negro school has been inferior to the white school both in instruction and educational standards. Negroes sued in the courts claiming that the segregated schools, which they were required to attend, were not equal to the white schools. Over and again the courts ruled that the facilities were not equal and that therefore the Negroes should be admitted to the white schools. Some states tried to solve the problem by giving Negroes scholarships to attend out-of-state schools. The courts ruled that this was a subterfuge and not allowable. Some white schools, after admitting a Negro, under compulsion, required him to sit in a row apart from the whites or to use only a segregated part of the school library. The courts held that this device was not constitutional. Finally cases arose where it was contended that the schools of Negroes in fact were equal to those of the whites. And so the question was presented, were the old decisions (holding segregation constitutional if "separate but equal" facilities were made available to Negroes) still valid?

If state laws had required segregation in public schools of Jews and Gentiles, who would have been so bold as to maintain that those laws were constitutional? But the background of slavery had long plagued the Negro and put his case in a different frame of reference.

Finally, the Court in 1954 decided *Brown v. Board of Education of Topeka*, holding that the "separate but equal" doctrine was unconstitutional; that neither a state nor the federal government could require the races to be segregated in public schools; that the American Constitution was "color blind." Segregation, it was said, was not that "equal protection" of the law that the Fourteenth Amendment guarantees every person against hostile state action.

By coincidence the Court that decided the *Brown* case also had on it only one Southerner—Hugo L. Black—and one from Kentucky, Stanley Reed. While *Plessy v. Ferguson* was decided in favor of segregation eight to one, the *Brown* case was decided the other way in a unanimous opinion.

Some criticized the Court for overruling a sixty-year-old precedent. But the Court has never viewed constitutional decisions as permanent fixtures beyond the power of recall. It has frequently overruled cases construing the Constitution, since the oath a justice takes is to support the Constitution, not the gloss that some predecessor put on it. In 1938 the Court overruled an earlier constitutional decision having nothing to do with racial problems and which had been decided ninety-six years earlier. Between 1937 and 1949 the Court had in fact overruled thirty prior constitutional decisions. What the Court did in the *Brown* case was therefore in a great tradition. The practice of courts undoing their own wrongs is a healthy one. It heeds Shakespeare's warning in *The Merchant of Venice:*

> *'Twill be recorded for a precedent;*
> *And many an error by the same example*
> *Will rush into the state.*

In spite of progress made in complying with the 1954 decision, there were at the end of 1961 over two thousand school districts in the South that had not even started to comply with it. There was also school segregation in the North, East, and West, resulting largely from neighborhood schools that served residential concentrations of Negroes. But the South is not alone in noncompliance. In Chicago segregation in the schools increased from 85 percent to 92 percent between 1958 and 1962. Some communities used gerrymandering to fix boundaries of school districts so as to produce segregated schools; and those projects, when challenged in the courts, were set aside.

Meanwhile, suits were brought by Negroes claiming they were denied sleeping accommodations on interstate railroads or were required to sit apart on interstate buses. In other suits Negroes complained that they had been denied the right to vacant seats in railroad dining cars, or denied access to public parks, public beaches, public golf courses. These cases, like those involving public schools, were decided in favor of the Negroes. Yet not until 1961 was segregation of races on interstate trains and buses and in interstate terminals banned by an all-inclusive regulation of the Interstate Commerce Commission.

Negroes have not been given equal opportunity, even in work. Prior to 1961 there was no Negro physician on the *regular* staff of any *private* New York City hospital, though a few extended courtesy privileges to Negro physicians. Up to 1941 most of the public hospitals in New York City did not allow Negroes on their in-staffs. Negroes were not allowed to eat in white restaurants in the nation's capital until 1953.

In 1945, New York and New Jersey passed comprehensive laws forbidding discrimination in employment on account of race, creed, color, or national origin. Some twenty states had adopted that kind of law by the1960s. In 1961 President Kennedy issued a comprehensive executive order banning discrimination based on race, creed, color, or national origin both in federal employment and in employment by contractors or sub-contractors doing work for the federal government.

By the mid-1950s most unions had opened their membership to Negroes as well as whites. But, as we entered the 1960s, one of the largest unions barred them from membership.

Even when Negroes are not admitted to membership in a union, the union is often the bargaining agent for all employees—white and black. The union must therefore, the Courts say, act impartially and not discriminate against one race and in favor of the other.

The average annual income of a Negro family is not much more than 50 percent of the average annual income of the white family. When unemployment comes, Negroes are among the first to be affected. The unemployment figures for the early 1960s in some of the leading cities show that Negro unemployment comes close to national unemployment in the days of the Great Depression. With automation and other technological developments, more skilled labor may be required and by the same token the unskilled laborers will find it increasingly difficult to get jobs. Yet a Negro unskilled laborer has difficulty moving up the escalator into a skilled job.

Some forty national and international unions have civil rights committees to make sure that there is no discrimination in employment. Yet discrimination persists. A 1961 report showed that of the 3,500 apprentices in all trades in Newark, New Jersey, only two were Negroes. A 1961 Chicago study showed that, while 25 percent of that city's population was Negro, less than 1 percent of all apprentices in Chicago were Negroes. In Detroit only one Negro had ever participated in the automobile workers' apprentice program. In the North, while vocational training is open to all, few Negroes have become skilled mechanics for the reason that craft unions in practice would not admit them. Thus even in the North vocational training has largely been for the whites, the Negroes being trained for more menial tasks, such as shoe repairing, tailoring, and plastering. Even when a Negro was admitted to a craft union, he was assigned lower-paid work or no work at all. And even though he was a union member, when he moved from one section of the country to another, the union would often not recognize his union card.

As we entered the 1960s many communities still barred Negroes from jury duty; in others they were excluded from white restaurants, white parks, white movies—although decisions of the Court make clear that any segregation enforced as a matter of municipal policy is unconstitutional.

Segregation in housing is still the rule, not the exception. Many deeds to real estate located in residential areas long provided that the property would not be sold to Negroes, to Mexicans, to Jews. The courts by the 1950s had refused to enforce these restrictions. Yet in many areas real estate brokers still will not sell Negroes property in white residential areas; in some cities zoning boards have refused permits to build schools that were to be integrated.

The prejudices of property owners have been encouraged by real estate brokers, builders, and the financial community upon which mortgage financing depends. Those groups, with few exceptions, have maintained that only a "homogeneous" neighborhood assures economic soundness. Seventeen states and a number of cities have adopted laws and ordinances to eliminate racial discrimination in housing. But at the beginning of the 1960s the federal government, though heavily involved in financing housing and related projects, had done very little to remove racial discrimination in that area. In Chicago residential segregation increased from 92 percent to 93 percent between 1950 and 1960.

The cause of equality of the races which Lincoln espoused as an American ideal has not been wholly fulfilled either in the North or South or East or West. Abroad, Americans are often chided about it. After World War II, Mrs. Edith Sampson, a Negro lawyer from Chicago, visited India and was questioned by members of an audience: "Why do they lynch Negroes in America? Why are they not given a fair trial?" She shook her finger at the inquirer, saying, "I fight for the rights of the Negroes at home. But here in India let me say this: no minority race has made greater progress than the American Negro since the Civil War."

The Negro has indeed made greater progress in this nation than any racial minority in a like length of time in any other nation in any area of the world.

The classless society of the Second Inaugural exists in very few areas of the world. Equality among men is today more often than not dishonored on the other continents. The new Constitution of India abolishes legal distinctions based on caste, but caste prejudice, deeply rooted in custom, still continues. In some Asian countries—Indonesia, the Philippines, and Thailand—Chinese are barred from certain industries and from many trades. Overseas Chinese in Southeast Asia are sometimes not even allowed to vote, to own land, or to hold office.

In South Africa, Negroes are segregated, deprived of civil rights, and relegated to an inferior citizenship.

In Communist countries, class lines are strictly drawn. The preferred class is made up of party members. They get the extra ration coupons, the largest apartments, the automobiles. In southern Russia—which is made up of minority races—there is a segregated school system. In southern Russia, a Russian gets 130 percent of the salary which a member of a minority race receives for doing the same work. Friendship University in Moscow was organized in order to segregate Asian and African students from Russian students. In Russia the identification papers of a Jew are stamped "Jew"; and it is a crime to teach the Hebrew language.

Some Moslem nations relegate Hindus and Jews to second-class citizenship. Turkey, modern both in political organization and in technology, bears down fiercely on her Kurdish minority and even bars the use of the Kurdish language. In northern Iran the same despised minority, the Kurds, though nominally given equal protection of the laws, is in practice not admitted to public office. Christians in Pakistan, though not persecuted, have a keen sense of outlawry.

Religious differences cut deeply into some political structures. The partition of India had much the same separatist influence as would an attempt to partition the United States into Catholic America and Protestant America. The electoral register system—introduced by England into India—is used in Lebanon today. That nation is divided into Moslem, Druse, and Christian districts from which only a Moslem, a Druse, or a Christian respectively can be elected. The qualification for office is therefore a religious one, not a candidate's experience and general capabilities.

Hitler's idea of the master race is the foundation of *apartheid* in South Africa; and the fanatical Negroes who sponsor the Muslim League in America make the same claim to Black Supremacy. Racism is sometimes founded on economics. The Armenian, the Jew, the Greek, the Chinese is often despised by those who do not have the same acquisitive nature or ability. Those not so able in business and finance find themselves out of a job because of their astute competitors; or they may end up working for the persons who outdistance them in that kind of contest. The latter is true in Indonesia and Malaya, where the local people awakened to the fact that most of the wealth was owned by the Chinese. The hatred and suspicion that resulted are not peculiar to the rampant animosity that the browns often show toward the yellows. It explains a good deal of the anti-Semitism that has plagued the world. And, in the Fiji Islands, I learned that the local people hate the Indian landowners for much the same reason. At home, the unskilled white laborer often fears the competition of the Negro.

Racism, when openly discussed, is usually placed in terms of "superiority" versus "inferiority."

Even the anthropologists quarrel over those terms. At first glance, there may seem to be widespread racial differences. The Chinese, for example, who had to withstand severe winters and droughts, developed a resourcefulness that Malays living in a more benign environment did not need. But whether this was due to heredity or environment has never been proven.

In the United States, the major controversy has centered on the alleged difference between the Negro and the white. Those who would attempt to prove innate differences have relied chiefly on IQ tests and on their own ideas of what constitutes "civilization." The great majority of social scientists and physical anthropologists, however, agree that it is impossible to draw meaningful conclusions from tests which cannot take into account the very real cultural and environmental factors which have handicapped Negroes taking those tests. Scores are significantly lower where children have been educated in poorer schools, or in states where less money is spent on the school budget. Neither innate differences nor innate equality is capable of being proven—race by race.

There are those who would run the nation on a basis of the proved achievements of one race. John C. Calhoun, who advocated that theory, has modern followers. In theory, one would then have the Republic of Plato, where instead of democracy, with each man having an equal say in government, one would have oligarchy: government by those innately fit to rule over those innately fit to serve. This is the type of government which Lincoln rejected. Today equality must mean equality of education, of work, of opportunity to travel and to assimilate all aspects of the world's cultures. The idea of "superior" and "inferior" races is usually a man-made distinction to serve a political or social end, and misses the point of equal opportunity to which Lincoln was dedicated.

Mr. Justice Holmes wrote in 1913:

> *as I grow older I grow calm. If I feel what are perhaps an old man's apprehensions, that competition from new races will cut deeper than working men's disputes and will test whether we can hang together and can fight; if I fear that we are running through the world's resources at a pace that we cannot keep; I do not lose my hopes. I do not pin my dreams for the future to my country or even to my race. I think it probable that civilization somehow will last as long as I care to look ahead—perhaps with smaller numbers, but perhaps also bred to greatness and splendor by science. I think it not improbable that man, like the grub that prepares a chamber for the winged thing it never has seen but is to be—that man may have cosmic destinies that he does not understand. And so beyond the vision of battling races and an impoverished earth I catch a dreaming glimpse of peace.*

When two races are brought together in the same community, they in time either blend or one is eventually exterminated. Extermination was the fate of many aborigines in Australia. Settlers in Tasmania, for example, hunted down the aborigines as we hunted down wolves. None of the aborigines of Tasmania survived. Survival or amalgamation seems to be the fate of each race. It may be romantic to think of the future in terms of blue-eyed, fair-haired people. But it is not a reliable article of faith. As the years pass, the amalgamation of the races increases. Malays and Chinese—Negroes and whites—whites and browns—yellows and whites. The full-bloods among the American Indians steadily decrease. In Panama, where Indian, Spaniard, and Negro have lived for years, those without Negro blood are less than 10 percent.

The fear of racial amalgamation is the unstated premise of much of the opposition to integration of schools, parks, buses, trains, waiting rooms, and other public facilities. It has caused the phrase "with malice toward none" to be rewritten. Yet Lincoln's rejection of "malice" and his embrace of "charity" have a potent influence in the world even a century after his death.

"I shall do nothing in malice. What I deal with is too vast for malicious dealing."

Today he represents the democratic ideal to uncounted millions who have never known justice, who have never experienced equality. The most enduring monument a person can have, he once said, is not made of marble; it is "in the hearts of those who love liberty, unselfishly, for all men."

The underprivileged peoples of all continents have enshrined him in their hearts.

His symbol now is different from the one his deed and words warrant. In Africa especially he has become the champion of every black still denied first-class citizenship and equal justice under law.

Three Free Speech Cases

Terminiello v. Chicago   337 U.S. 1 (1949)

MR. JUSTICE DOUGLAS DELIVERED THE OPINION OF THE COURT.

Petitioner after jury trial was found guilty of disorderly conduct in violation of a city ordinance of Chicago and fined. The case grew out of an address he delivered in an auditorium in Chicago under the auspices of the Christian Veterans of America. The meeting commanded considerable public attention. The auditorium was filled to capacity with over eight hundred persons present. Others were turned away. Outside of the auditorium a crowd of about one thousand persons gathered to protest against the meeting. A cordon of policemen was assigned to the meeting to maintain order; but they were not able to prevent several disturbances. The crowd outside was angry and turbulent.

Petitioner in his speech condemned the conduct of the crowd outside and vigorously, if not viciously, criticized various political and racial groups whose activities he denounced as inimical to the nation's welfare.

The trial court charged that "breach of the peace" consists of any "misbehavior which violates the public peace and decorum"; and that the "misbehavior may constitute a breach of the peace if it stirs the public to anger, invites dispute, brings about a condition of unrest, or creates a disturbance, or if it molests the inhabitants in the enjoyment of peace and quiet by arousing alarm." Petitioner did not take exception to that instruction. But he maintained at all times that the ordinance as applied to his conduct violated his right of free speech under the Federal Constitution. The judgment of conviction was affirmed by the Illinois Appellate Court and by the Illinois Supreme Court. The case is here on a petition for *certiorari* which we granted because of the importance of the question presented.

The argument here has been focused on the issue of whether the content of petitioner's speech was composed of derisive, fighting words, which carried it outside the scope of the constitutional guarantees. We do not reach that question, for there is a preliminary question that is dispositive of the case.

As we have noted, the statutory words "breach of the peace" were defined in instructions to the jury to include speech which "stirs the public to anger, invites dispute, brings about a condition of unrest, or creates a disturbance..." That construction of the ordinance is a ruling on a question of state law that is as binding on us as though the precise words had been written into the ordinance.

The vitality of civil and political institutions in our society depends on free discussion. As Chief Justice Hughes wrote in *De Jonge v. Oregon,* it is only through free debate and free exchange of ideas that government remains responsive to the will of the people and peaceful change is effected. The right to speak freely and to promote diversity of ideas and programs is therefore one of the chief distinctions that sets us apart from totalitarian regimes.

Accordingly a function of free speech under our system of government is to invite dispute. It may indeed best serve its high purpose when it induces a condition of unrest, creates dissatisfaction with conditions as they are, or even stirs people to anger. Speech is often provocative and challenging. It may strike at prejudices and preconceptions and have profound unsettling effects as it presses for acceptance of an idea. That is why freedom of speech, though not absolute, is nevertheless protected against censorship or punishment, unless shown likely to produce a clear and present danger of a serious substantive evil that rises far above public inconvenience, annoyance, or unrest. There is no room under our Constitution for a more restrictive view. For the alternative would lead to standardization of ideas either by legislatures, courts, or dominant political or community groups.

The ordinance as construed by the trial court seriously invaded this province. It permitted conviction of petitioner if his speech stirred people to anger, invited public dispute, or brought about a condition of unrest. A conviction resting on any of those grounds may not stand.

Dennis v. United States   341 U.S. 494 (1951)

Mr. Justice Douglas, dissenting.

If this were a case where those who claimed protection under the First Amendment were teaching the techniques of sabotage, the assassination of the President, the filching of documents from puʰlic files, the planting of bombs, the art of street warfare, and the like, I would have no doubts. The freedom to speak is not absolute; the teaching of methods of terror and other seditious conduct should be beyond the pale along with obscenity and immorality. This case was argued as if those were the facts. The argument imported much seditious conduct into the record. That is easy and it has popular appeal, for the activities of Communists in plotting and scheming against the free world are common knowledge. But the fact is that no such evidence was introduced at the trial. There is a statute which makes a seditious conspiracy unlawful. Petitioners, however, were not charged with a "conspiracy to overthrow" the Government. They were charged with a conspiracy to form a party and groups and assemblies of people who teach and advocate the overthrow of our Government by force or violence and with a conspiracy to advocate and teach its overthrow by force and violence. It may well be that indoctrination in the techniques of terror to destroy the Government would be indictable under either statute. But the teaching which is condemned here is of a different character.

So far as the present record is concerned, what petitioners did was to organize people to teach and themselves teach the Marxist-Leninist doctrine contained chiefly in four books: Stalin, *Foundations of Leninism* (1924); Marx and Engels, *Manifesto of the Communist Party* (1848); Lenin, *The State and Revolution* (1917); *History of the Communist Party of the Soviet Union* (B.) (1939).

Those books are to Soviet Communism what *Mein Kampf* was to Nazism. If they are understood, the ugliness of Communism is revealed, its deceit and cunning are exposed, the nature of its activities becomes apparent, and the chances of its success less likely. That is not, of course, the reason why petitioners chose these books for their classrooms. They are fervent Communists to whom these volumes are gospel. They preached the creed with the hope that some day it would be acted upon.

The opinion of the Court does not outlaw these texts nor condemn them to the fire, as the Communists do literature offensive to their creed. But if the books themselves are not outlawed, if they can lawfully remain on library shelves, by what reasoning does their use in a classroom become a crime? It would not be a crime under the Act to introduce these books to a class, though that would be teaching what the creed of violent overthrow of the Government is. The Act, as construed, requires the element of intent—that those who teach the creed believe in it. The crime then depends not on what is taught but on who the teacher is. That is to make freedom of speech turn not on *what is said,* but on the *intent* with which it is said. Once we start down that road we enter territory dangerous to the liberties of every citizen.

There was a time in England when the concept of constructive treason flourished. Men were punished not for raising a hand against the king but for thinking murderous thoughts about him. The Framers of the Constitution were alive to that abuse and took steps to see that the practice would not flourish here. Treason was defined to require overt acts—the evolution of a plot against the country into an actual project. The present case is not one of treason. But the analogy is close when the illegality is made to turn on intent, not on the nature of the act. We then start probing men's minds for motive and purpose; they become entangled in the law not for what they did but *for what they thought;* they get convicted not for what they said but for the purpose with which they said it.

Intent, of course, often makes the difference in the law. An act otherwise excusable or carrying minor penalties may grow to an abhorrent thing if the evil intent is present. We deal here, however, not with ordinary acts but with speech, to which the Constitution has given a special sanction.

The vice of treating speech as the equivalent of overt acts of a treasonable or seditious character is emphasized by a concurring opinion, which by invoking the law of conspiracy makes speech do service for deeds which are dangerous to society. The doctrine of conspiracy has served divers and oppressive purposes and in its broad reach can be made to do great evil. But never until today has anyone seriously thought that the ancient law of conspiracy could constitutionally be used to turn speech into seditious conduct. Yet that is precisely what is suggested. I repeat that we deal here with speech alone, not with speech *plus* acts of sabotage or unlawful conduct. Not a single seditious act is charged in the indictment. To make a lawful speech unlawful because two men conceive it is to raise the law of conspiracy to appalling proportions. That course is to make a radical break with the past and to violate one of the cardinal principles of our constitutional scheme.

Free speech has occupied an exalted position because of the high service it has given our society. Its protection is essential to the very existence of a democracy. The airing of ideas releases pressures which otherwise might become destructive. When ideas compete in the market for acceptance, full and free discussion exposes the false and they gain few adherents. Full and free discussion even of ideas we hate encourages the testing of our own prejudices and preconceptions. Full and free discussion keeps a society from becoming stagnant and unprepared for the stresses and strains that work to tear all civilizations apart.

Full and free discussion has indeed been the first article of our faith. We have founded our political system on it. It has been the safeguard of every religious, political, philosophical, economic, and racial group amongst us. We have counted on it to keep us from embracing what is cheap and false; we have trusted the common sense of our people to choose the doctrine true to our genius and to reject the rest. This has been the one single outstanding tenet that has made our institutions the symbol of freedom and equality. We have deemed it more costly to liberty to suppress a despised minority than to let them vent their spleen. We have above all else feared the political censor. We have wanted a land where our people can be exposed to all the diverse creeds and cultures of the world.

There comes a time when even speech loses its constitutional immunity. Speech innocuous one year may at another time fan such destructive flames that it must be halted in the interests of the safety of the Republic. That is the meaning of the clear and present danger test. When conditions are so critical that there will be no time to avoid the evil that the speech threatens, it is time to call a halt. Otherwise, free speech which is the strength of the Nation will be the cause of its destruction.

Yet free speech is the rule, not the exception. The restraint to be constitutional must be based on more than fear, on more than passionate opposition against the speech, on more than a revolted dislike for its contents. There must be some immediate injury to society that is likely if speech is allowed. The classic statement of these conditions was made by Mr. Justice Brandeis in his concurring opinion in *Whitney v. California.*

> *Fear of serious injury cannot alone justify suppression of free speech and assembly. Men feared witches and burnt women. It is the function of speech to free men from the bondage of irrational fears. To justify suppression of free speech there must be reasonable ground to fear that serious evil will result if free speech is practiced. There must be reasonable ground to believe that the danger apprehended is imminent. There must be reasonable ground to believe that the evil to be prevented is a serious one. Every denunciation of existing law tends in some measure to increase the probability that there will be violation of it. Condonation of a breach enhances the probability. Expressions of approval add to the probability. Propagation of the criminal state of mind by teaching syndicalism increases it. Advocacy of law-breaking heightens it still further. But even advocacy of violation, however reprehensible morally, is not a justification for denying free speech where the advocacy falls short of incitement and there is nothing to indicate that the advocacy would be immediately acted on. The wide difference between advocacy and incitement, between preparation and attempt, between assembling and conspiracy, must be borne in mind. In order to support a finding of clear and present danger it must be shown either that immediate serious violence was to be expected or was advocated, or that the past conduct furnished reason to believe that such advocacy was then contemplated.*
>
> *Those who won our independence by revolution were not cowards. They did not fear political change. They did not exalt order at the cost of liberty. To courageous, self-reliant men, with confidence in the power of free and fearless reasoning applied through the processes of popular government, no danger flowing from speech can be deemed clear and present, unless the incidence of the evil apprehended is so imminent that it may befall before there is opportunity for full discussion. If there be time to expose through discussion the falsehood and fallacies, to avert the*

evil by the processes of education, the remedy to be applied is more speech, not enforced silence." (Bold italics added.)

I had assumed that the question of the clear and present danger, being so critical an issue in the case, would be a matter for submission to the jury. It was squarely held in *Pierce v. United States* to be a jury question. Mr. Justice Pitney, speaking for the Court, said, "Whether the statement contained in the pamphlet had a natural tendency to produce the forbidden consequences, as alleged, was a question to be determined not upon demurrer but by the jury at the trial." That is the only time the Court has passed on the issue. None of our other decisions is contrary. Nothing said in any of the nonjury cases has detracted from that ruling. The statement in *Pierce v. United States* states the law as it has been and as it should be. The Court, I think, errs when it treats the question as one of law.

Yet, whether the question is one for the Court or the jury, there should be evidence of record on the issue. This record, however, contains no evidence whatsoever showing that the acts charged, *viz.*, the teaching of the Soviet theory of revolution with the hope that it will be realized, have created any clear and present danger to the Nation. The Court, however, rules to the contrary. It says, "The formation by petitioners of such a highly organized conspiracy, with rigidly disciplined members subject to call when the leaders, these petitioners, felt that the time had come for action, coupled with the inflammable nature of world conditions, similar uprisings in other countries, and the touch-and-go nature of our relations with countries with whom petitioners were in the very least ideologically attuned, convince us that their convictions were justified on this score."

That ruling is in my view not responsive to the issue in the case. We might as well say that the speech of petitioners is outlawed because Soviet Russia and her Red Army are a threat to world peace.

The nature of Communism as a force on the world scene would, of course, be relevant to the issue of clear and present danger of petitioners' advocacy within the United States. But the primary consideration is the strength and tactical position of petitioners and their converts in this country. On that there is no evidence in the record. If we are to take judicial notice of the threat of Communists within the nation, it should not be difficult to conclude that *as a political party* they are of little consequence. Communists in this country have never made a respectable or serious showing in any election. I would doubt that there is a village, let alone a city or county or state, which the Communists could carry. Communism in the world scene is no bogeyman; but Communism as a political faction or party in this country plainly is. Communism has been so thoroughly exposed in this country that it has been crippled as a political force. Free speech has destroyed it as an effective political party. It is inconceivable that those who went up and down this country preaching the doctrine of revolution which petitioners espouse would have any success. In days of trouble and confusion, when bread lines were long, when the unemployed walked the streets, when people were starving, the advocates of a short-cut by revolution might have a chance to gain adherents. But today there are no such conditions. The country is not in despair; the people know Soviet Communism; the doctrine of Soviet revolution is exposed in all of its ugliness and the American people want none of it.

How it can be said that there is a clear and present danger that this advocacy will succeed is, therefore, a mystery. Some nations less resilient than the United States, where illiteracy is high and where democratic traditions are only budding, might have to take drastic steps and jail these men for merely speaking their creed. But in America they are miserable merchants of unwanted ideas; their wares remain unsold. The fact that their ideas are abhorrent does not make them powerful.

The political impotence of the Communists in this country does not, of course, dispose of the problem. Their numbers; their positions in industry and government; the extent to which they have in fact infiltrated the police, the armed services, transportation, stevedoring, power plants, munitions works, and other critical places—these facts all bear on the likelihood that their advocacy of the Soviet theory of revolution will endanger the Republic. But the record is silent on these facts. If we are to proceed on the basis of judicial notice, it is impossible for me to say that the Communists in this country are so potent or so strategically deployed that they must be suppressed for their speech. I could not so hold unless I were willing to conclude that the activities in recent years of committees of Congress, of the Attorney General, of labor unions, of state legislatures, and of Loyalty Boards were so futile as to leave the country on the edge of grave peril. To believe that petitioners and their following are placed in such critical positions as to endanger the Nation is to believe the incredible. It is safe to say that the followers of the creed of Soviet Communism are known to the F. B. I.; that in case of war with

Russia they will be picked up overnight as were all prospective saboteurs at the commencement of World War II; that the invisible army of petitioners is the best known, the most beset, and the least thriving of any fifth column in history. Only those held by fear and panic could think otherwise.

This is my view if we are to act on the basis of judicial notice. But the mere statement of the opposing views indicates how important it is that we know the facts before we act. Neither prejudice nor hate nor senseless fear should be the basis of this solemn act. Free speech—the glory of our system of government—should not be sacrificed on anything less than plain and objective proof of danger that the evil advocated is imminent. On this record no one can say that petitioners and their converts are in such a strategic position as to have even the slightest chance of achieving their aims.

The First Amendment provides that "Congress shall make no law... abridging the freedom of speech." The Constitution provides no exception. This does not mean, however, that the Nation need hold its hand until it is in such weakened condition that there is no time to protect itself from incitement to revolution. Seditious conduct can always be punished. But the command of the First Amendment is so clear that we should not allow Congress to call a halt to free speech except in the extreme case of peril from the speech itself. The First Amendment makes confidence in the common sense of our people and in their maturity of judgment the great postulate of our democracy. Its philosophy is that violence is rarely, if ever, stopped by denying civil liberties to those advocating resort to force. The First Amendment reflects the philosophy of Jefferson "that it is time enough for the rightful purposes of civil government, for its officers to interfere when principles break out into overt acts against peace and good order." The political censor has no place in our public debates. Unless and until extreme and necessitous circumstances are shown, our aim should be to keep speech unfettered and to allow the processes of law to be invoked only when the provocateurs among us move from speech to action.

Vishinsky wrote in 1938 in *The Law of the Soviet State*, "In our state, naturally, there is and can be no place for freedom of speech, press, and so on for the foes of socialism."

Our concern should be that we accept no such standard for the United States. Our faith should be that our people will never give support to these advocates of revolution, so long as we remain loyal to the purposes for which our Nation was founded.

Beauharnais v. Illinois 343 U.S. 250 (1952)

MR. JUSTICE DOUGLAS, DISSENTING.

Hitler and his Nazis showed how evil a conspiracy could be which was aimed at destroying a race by exposing it to contempt, derision, and obloquy. I would be willing to concede that such conduct directed at a race or group in this country could be made an indictable offense. For such a project would be more than the exercise of free speech. Like picketing, it would be free speech plus.

I would also be willing to concede that even without the element of conspiracy there might be times and occasions when the legislative or executive branch might call a halt to inflammatory talk, such as the shouting of "fire" in school or a theatre.

My view is that if in any case other public interests are to override the plain command of the First Amendment, the peril of speech must be clear and present, leaving no room for argument, raising no doubts as to the necessity of curbing speech in order to prevent disaster.

The First Amendment is couched in absolute terms—freedom of speech shall not be abridged. Speech has therefore a preferred position as contrasted to some other civil rights. For example, privacy, equally sacred to some, is protected by the Fourth Amendment only against unreasonable searches and seizures. There is room for regulation of the ways and means of invading privacy. No such leeway is granted the invasion of the right of free speech guaranteed by the First Amendment. Until recent years that had been the course and direction of constitutional law. Yet recently the Court in this and in other cases has engrafted the right of regulation onto the First Amendment by placing in the hands of the legislative branch the right to regulate "within reasonable limits" the right of free speech. This to me is an ominous and alarming trend. The free trade in ideas which the Framers of the Constitution visualized disappears. In its place there is substituted a new orthodoxy—an orthodoxy that changes with the whims of the age or the day, an orthodoxy which the majority by solemn judgment proclaims to be essential to the safety, welfare, security, morality, or health of society. Free speech in the constitutional sense disappears.

Limits are drawn—limits dictated by expediency, political opinion, prejudices or some other desideratum of legislative action.

An historic aspect of the issue of judicial supremacy was the extent to which legislative judgment would be supreme in the field of social legislation. The vague contours of the Due Process Clause were used to strike down laws deemed by the Court to be unwise and improvident. That trend has been reversed. In matters relating to business, finance, industrial and labor conditions, health and the public welfare, great leeway is now granted the legislature, for there is no guarantee in the Constitution that the status quo will be preserved against regulation by government. Freedom of speech, however, rests on a different constitutional basis. The First Amendment says that freedom of speech, freedom of press, and the free exercise of religion shall not be abridged. That is a negation of power on the part of each and every department of government. Free speech, free press, free exercise of religion are placed separate and apart; they are above and beyond the police power; they are not subject to regulation in the manner of factories, slums, apartment houses, production of oil, and the like.

The Court in this and in other cases places speech under an expanding legislative control. Today a white man stands convicted for protesting in unseemly language against our decisions invalidating restrictive covenants. Tomorrow a Negro will be haled before a court for denouncing lynch law in heated terms. Farm laborers in the West who compete with field hands drifting up from Mexico; whites who feel the pressure of orientals; a minority which finds employment going to members of the dominant religious group—all of these are caught in the mesh of today's decision. Debate and argument even in the courtroom are not always calm and dispassionate. Emotions sway speakers and audiences alike. Intemperate speech is a distinctive characteristic of man. Hotheads blow off and release destructive energy in the process. They shout and rave, exaggerating weaknesses, magnifying error, viewing with alarm. So it has been from the beginning; and so it will be throughout time. The Framers of the Constitution knew human nature as well as we do. They too had lived in dangerous days; they too knew the suffocating influence of orthodoxy and standardized thought. They weighed the compulsions for restrained speech and thought against the abuses of liberty. They chose liberty. That should be our choice today no matter how distasteful to us the pamphlet of Beauharnais may be. It is true that this is only one decision which may later be distinguished or confined to narrow limits. But it represents a philosophy at war with the First Amendment—a constitutional interpretation which puts free speech under the legislative thumb. It reflects an influence moving ever deeper into our society. It is notice to the legislatures that they have the power to control unpopular blocs. It is a warning to every minority that when the Constitution guarantees free speech it does not mean what it says.

The Right to Be Let Alone

Government exists for man, not man for government. The aim of government is security for the individual and freedom for the development of his talents. The individual needs protection from government itself—from the executive branch, from the legislative branch, and even from the tyranny of judges. The Framers of the Constitution realized this and undertook to establish safeguards and guarantees. Some of these concern the procedure that must be followed if government undertakes to move against the citizen. Others concern substantive rights such as freedom of religion and freedom of assembly.

There is, indeed, a congeries of these rights that may conveniently be called the right to be let alone. They concern the right of privacy—sometimes explicit and sometimes implicit in the Constitution. This right of privacy protects freedom of religion and freedom of conscience. It protects the privacy of the home and the dignity of the individual. Under modern conditions it involves wire-tapping and the use of electronic devices to pick up the confidences of private conversations. It also concerns the problem of the captive audience presented in *Public Utilities Commission v. Pollak,* where the Court held that streetcars could play radio programs to their captive audiences and that the passenger, no matter how offended he might be by the program, could only sit and listen—or walk to work.

I should also mention the right to travel—a right that today lies in the vague penumbra of the law because the final word has not yet been written. The Court has shown intolerance toward state restrictions against the free movement of people within the nation (*Edwards v. California*). But whether the government may prevent a citizen from traveling abroad because, for example, he has unpopular political beliefs is a phase of the problem yet unresolved.

This right to be let alone is a guarantee that draws substance from several provisions of the Constitution, including the First, the Fourth, and the Fifth Amendments. It was described in comprehensive terms by Mr. Justice Brandeis in his dissent in *Olmstead v. United States:*

The makers of our Constitution undertook to secure
conditions favorable to the pursuit of happiness. They
recognized the significance of man's spiritual nature, of his
feelings and of his intellect. They knew that only a part of the
pain, pleasure and satisfactions of life are to be found in
material things. They sought to protect Americans in their
beliefs, their thoughts, their emotions and their sensations.
They conferred, as against the Government, the right to be
let alone—the most comprehensive of rights and the right
most valued by civilized men.

We often boast of our advance over the totalitarian regimes. We have tremendous advantages that they do not enjoy. Those advantages are not in material things such as technology and standards of living. They relate to matters of the mind and the spirit. They relate to the inalienable rights of man proudly proclaimed in our Declaration of Independence, and in part engrossed in our Constitution. Some call them legal rights; some natural rights. Natural rights were often invoked by the *laissez-faire* theorists of the late nineteenth and twentieth centuries to protect the nation's economy against governmental control. Conspicuous is the case of *Lochner v. New York,* holding unconstitutional a New York law setting ten hours as the work day of bakery employees, a decision that led Mr. Justice Holmes to say in dissent, "The Fourteenth Amendment does not enact Mr. Herbert Spencer's Social Statics."

The natural rights of which I speak are different. They have a broad base in morality and religion to protect man, his individuality, and his conscience against direct and indirect interference by government. Some are written explicitly into the Constitution. Others are to be implied. The penumbra of the Bill of Rights reflects human rights which, though not explicit, are implied from the very nature of man as a child of God. These human rights were the products both of political thinking and of moral and religious influences. Man, as a citizen, had known oppressive laws from time out of mind and was in revolt. Man, as a child of God, insisted he was accountable not to the state but to his own conscience and to his God. Man's moral and spiritual appetite, as well as his political ideals, demanded that he have freedom. Liberty was to be the way of life—inalienable, and safe from intrusions by government. That, in short, was our beginning.

Much of this liberty of which we boast comes down to the right of privacy. It is reflected in the folklore, which goes back at least as far as Sir William Staunford, that "my house is to me as my castle." But this right of privacy extends to the right to be let alone in one's belief and in one's conscience, as well as in one's home.

This right—the right to be let alone—has suffered greatly in recent years. Dr. A. Powell Davies recently pointed out how far we have gone in investigating opinions and beliefs:

> *Whatever an individual has thought or done—or even may have thought or done—should be discovered, if possible, to determine whether it has—or conceivably might seem to have—some bearing upon that individual's reliability as a citizen of the United States. Let us admit it: we now have in this country a system of investigation similar to that of the communists. It is not as harsh—not in most respects—but it has the same objects and uses some of the same methods. To a communist society, such a system is appropriate: it protects communism. To a free society, it can never be appropriate: it does not protect freedom, it destroys it.*

We have entered this forbidden field out of a legitimate concern for the problem of subversion. These days the problem of the subversive centers around communism. There can be no denying the fact that communism and the Communist Party present special problems. Some countries have dealt with it in a special way. Thus the Constitution of the Republic of Vietnam, adopted in 1956, provides: "All activities having as their object the direct or indirect propagation or establishment of Communism in whatever form shall be contrary to the principles embodied in the present Constitution." That provision in effect withdraws the protection of free speech and a free press from this area. We have no such constitutional provision. Our theory from the beginning has been that our society is not so fragile that we must ban any discourse by any political party.

Yet the Communist Party is not just another political party. It is not indigenous to America; it has international connections and affiliations. Indeed, some legislatures have declared (and courts have sustained the finding) that the Communist Party of this country is part of an international conspiracy. Today the American Communist Party, following a change in its constitution, professes not to sanction the use of force and violence. But that profession is a recent one. Classically the Communist Party has advocated force and violence as political weapons.

These differences between the Communist Party and other political parties should not, however, blind us to four further considerations:

First, joining is an innate American habit. Men like Emerson fought it; but the habit grew and grew and became distinctly American. It is indeed the source of much of the power of self-help that appears and reappears in all phases of our life. This "passion for joining," as Professor Schlesinger once put it, has roots not only in our habits but in the First Amendment. Joining is one method of freedom of expression; it is a form of free inquiry; it is an exercise of the right of free assembly.

Second, for most of the years since World War I the Communist Party has been a wholly lawful party, not being outlawed by the States. In the election years from 1924 to 1940 it ran candidates for President, and one year it collected votes in thirty-seven States. As of 1955, the Communist Party was outlawed in only four States, all of those statutes being passed since 1950.

Third, guilt is personal under our system. A man can be punished for what he does, not for the acts of his friends, his associates, or his family. Joining the Communist Party does not necessarily indicate approval of all for which that organization stands, just as all who belong to the Presbyterian Church, the American Legion, or the American Bar Association do not necessarily endorse every tenet of those organizations. Prior to World War II, people joined the Communist Party for a number of reasons. As the Court recently said, speaking through Mr. Justice Black, in *Schware v. Board of Bar Examiners,*

> *During the depression when millions were unemployed and our economic system was paralyzed, many turned to the Communist Party out of desperation or hope. It proposed a radical solution to the grave economic crisis. Later the rise of fascism as a menace to democracy spurred others who feared this form of tyranny to align with the Communist Party. After 1935, that Party advocated a "Popular Front" of "all democratic parties against fascism." Its platform and slogans stressed full employment, racial equality and various other political and economic changes.*

During that war, when Russia was our ally, many others joined the Communist Party. From reading many records in cases involving communists, I gather that many who joined may not have had subversion as a purpose. Some seemed to be sheer sentimentalists; others seemed utterly confused. Yet there has been a readiness to identify all who joined the party at any period of its existence with all of the aims espoused by it. That is guilt by association—a concept which is foreign to our history.

Fourth, is the command of the First Amendment which decrees that government has no concern with thoughts and beliefs. The search for political heresy which the threat of communism has engendered too readily identifies all unorthodox thought and expression as communistic. We have been too willing to sacrifice the rights of the unorthodox thinker to the search for communists. We have been too quick to identify someone who supports any portion of the party line— from political ownership of the means of production to equal rights for Negroes—as a communist. In short, the fear of communism has created an atmosphere which is antagonistic to a climate of tolerance for unorthodox thought and free communication of ideas which is so vital to a democracy.

We have witnessed in recent years a search for subversives which has not conformed to these American precepts. We have looked not only for the active, dedicated communists but also for those who once were communists, for those who associated with communists or who had communist relatives, for those who had sympathy with some of the reforms which communists promoted, and even for those whose ideas were unorthodox.

This search for subversives, like the search for heretics in an earlier age, led to excesses. The abuses caused the late Albert Einstein to say in 1954:

> *If I would be a young man again and had to decide how to make my living, I would not try to become a scientist or scholar or teacher. I would rather choose to be a plumber or a peddler in the hope to find that modest degree of independence still available under present circumstances.*

Right to Privacy

Griswold v. Connecticut   *381 U.S. 479 (1965)*

MR. JUSTICE DOUGLAS DELIVERED THE OPINION OF THE COURT.

Appellant Griswold is Executive Director of the Planned Parenthood League of Connecticut. Appellant Buxton is a licensed physician and a professor at the Yale Medical School who served as Medical Director for the League at its Center in New Haven—a center open and operating from November 1 to November 10, 1961, when appellants were arrested.

They gave information, instruction, and medical advice to *married persons* as to the means of preventing conception. They examined the wife and prescribed the best contraceptive device or material for her use. Fees were usually charged, although some couples were serviced free.

The statutes whose constitutionality is involved in this appeal are §§53-32 and 54-196 of the General Statutes of Connecticut (1958 rev.). The former provides:

> *Any person who uses any drug, medicinal article or instrument for the purpose of preventing conception shall be fined not less than fifty dollars or imprisoned not less than sixty days nor more than one year or be both fined and imprisoned.*

Section 54-196 provides:

> *Any person who assists, abets, counsels, causes, hires or commands another to commit any offense may be prosecuted and punished as if he were the principal offender.*

The appellants were found guilty as accessories and fined $100 each, against the claim that the accessory statute as so applied violated the Fourteenth Amendment.

Coming to the merits, we are met with a wide range of questions that implicate the Due Process Clause of the Fourteenth Amendment. Overtones of some arguments suggest that *Lochner v. New York* should be our guide. But we decline that invitation as we did in *West Coast Hotel Co. v. Parrish, Olsen v. Nebraska, Lincoln Union v. Northwestern Co., Williamson v. Lee Optical Co., Giboney v. Empire Storage Co.* We do not sit as a super-legislature to determine the wisdom, need, and propriety of laws that touch economic problems, business affairs, or social conditions. This law, however, operates directly on an intimate relation of husband and wife and their physician's role in one aspect of that relation.

The association of people is not mentioned in the Constitution nor in the Bill of Rights. The right to educate a child in a school of the parents' choice—whether public or private or parochial—is also not mentioned. Nor is the right to study any particular subject or any foreign language. Yet the First Amendment has been construed to include certain of those rights.

By *Pierce v. Society of Sisters,* the right to educate one's children as one chooses is made applicable to the States by the force of the First and Fourteenth Amendments. By *Meyer v. Nebraska* the same dignity is given the right to study the German language in a private school. In other words, the State may not, consistently with the spirit of the First Amendment, contract the spectrum of available knowledge. The right of freedom of speech and press includes not only the right to utter or to print, but the right to distribute, the right to receive, the right to read and freedom of inquiry, freedom of thought, and freedom to teach— indeed the freedom of the entire university community. Without those peripheral rights the specific rights would be less secure. And so we reaffirm the principle of the *Pierce* and the *Meyer* cases.

In *NAACP v. Alabama* we protected the "freedom to associate and privacy in one's associations," noting that freedom of association was a peripheral First Amendment right. Disclosure of membership lists of a constitutionally valid association, we held, was invalid "as entailing the likelihood of a substantial restraint upon the exercise by petitioner's members of their right to freedom of association. In other words, the First Amendment has a penumbra where privacy is protected from

Justice Douglas. Photographer: Harris and Ewing. Collection of the Supreme Court of the United States.

governmental intrusion. In like context, we have protected forms of "association" that are not political in the customary sense but pertain to the social, legal, and economic benefit of the members. In *Schware v. Board of Bar Examiners*, we held it not permissible to bar a lawyer from practice, because he had once been a member of the Communist Party. The man's "association with that Party" was not shown to be "anything more than a political faith in a political party" and was not action of a kind proving bad moral character.

Those cases involved more than the "right of assembly"—a right that extends to all irrespective of their race or ideology. The right of "association," like the right of belief, is more than the right to attend a meeting; it includes the right to express one's attitudes or philosophies by membership in a group or by affiliation with it or by other lawful means. Association in that context is a form of expression of opinion; and while it is not expressly included in the First Amendment its existence is necessary in making the express guarantees fully meaningful.

The foregoing cases suggest that specific guarantees in the Bill of Rights have penumbras, formed by emanations from those guarantees that help give them life and substance. Various guarantees create zones of privacy. The right of association contained in the penumbra of the First Amendment is one, as we have seen. The Third Amendment in its prohibition against the quartering of soldiers "in any house" in time of peace without the consent of the owner is another facet of that privacy. The Fourth Amendment explicitly affirms the "right of the people to be secure in their persons, houses, papers, and effects, against unreasonable searches and seizures." The Fifth Amendment in its Self-Incrimination Clause enables the citizen to create a zone of privacy which government may not force him to surrender to his detriment. The Ninth Amendment provides: "The enumeration in the Constitution, of certain rights, shall not be construed to deny or disparage others retained by the people."

The Fourth and Fifth Amendments were described in *Boyd v. United States* as protection against all government invasions "of the sanctity of a man's home and the privacies of life." We recently referred in *Mapp v. Ohio* to the Fourth Amendment as creating a "right to privacy, no less important than any other right carefully and particularly reserved to the people."

The present case, then, concerns a relationship lying within the zone of privacy created by several fundamental constitutional guarantees. And it concerns a law which, in forbidding the *use* of contraceptives rather than regulating their manufacture or sale, seeks to achieve its goals by means having a maximum destructive impact upon that relationship. Such a law cannot stand in light of the familiar principle, so often applied by this Court, that a "governmental purpose to control or prevent activities constitutionally subject to state regulation may not be achieved by means which sweep unnecessarily broadly and thereby invade the area of protected freedoms." Would we allow the police to search the sacred precincts of marital bedrooms for telltale signs of the use of contraceptives? The very idea is repulsive to the notions of privacy surrounding the marriage relationship.

We deal with a right of privacy older than the Bill of Rights—older than our political parties, older than our school system. Marriage is a coming together for better or for worse, hopefully enduring, and intimate to the degree of being sacred. It is an association that promotes a way of life, not causes; a harmony in living, not political faiths; a bilateral loyalty, not commercial or social projects. Yet it is an association for as noble a purpose as any involved in our prior decisions.

Points of Rebellion

There always have been—and always will be—aggrieved persons. The lower their estate the more difficult it is to find a right to fit the wrong being done. Part of our problem starts at that point. In New York City a housing complaint must go to one of the nineteen bureaus that deal with those problems. It takes a sharp and energetic layman or lawyer to find the proper desk in the bureaucracy where the complaint must be lodged.

The finance company's motion for summary judgment might be defeated if the borrower had a lawyer who could show that the hidden charges, when cumulated, resulted in usurious charges.

But since no one appears in defense, a judgment is entered which is shortly used to garnishee the wages of the defendant.

The landlord's motion for eviction might be defeated, if the tenant had a lawyer who could prove that the real basis of eviction was the tenant's activities on civil rights. Perhaps he refused to pay rent until the landlord made repairs. Normally that is no defense. The historic rule disallows the failure to make repairs as a defense to the failure to pay rent. The theory was that the duty to pay rent was dependent on the conveyance of the agreed-upon space irrespective of its condition. But in recent years lawyers have pressed the opposite position and have sometimes won. The fact is that a person with a competent lawyer has some chance; one without a lawyer has only a little chance.

The examples are as numerous as the woes and complaints of people. Most cases—civil, certainly, and many criminal ones also—are lost and neglected in the onrush of daily life for lack of any spokesmen for indigents before courts or administrative agencies.

There are at least thirty million people in this category in the country. It was to service them that the Office of Economic Opportunity established Neighborhood Legal Services in some 250 centers. In 1968 NLS processed cases involving from 750,000 to 1,000,000 people in a total of 500,000 cases. But the need is astronomical: it is estimated that the annual caseload produced by the poor alone is somewhere between five million and fifteen million.

The demand for an Ombudsman—especially in metropolitan areas—constantly recurs, and reflects a complaint of rich and poor alike that the laws have become much too complex. What is irritating to the rich is often suffocating to the poor.

Our fourth Chief Justice, John Marshall, who served from 1801 to 1834, said:

> *The very essence of civil liberty certainly consists in the right of every individual to claim the protection of the laws, whenever he receives an injury.*

Finding a right to correct a wrong is, however, the least of all the modern pressing problems. If poor and rich alike had lawyers to assert their claims, we would still be left with staggering problems.

The vital problems will require a great restructuring of our society. Many issues will emerge. The most immediate, though perhaps minor in the overall picture, concern two important areas.

First is the problem of reallocating our resources.

Second is the problem of creating some control or surveillance over key administrative agencies.

The most explosive issues involve the reallocation of resources. For example, the $80 billion budget of the Pentagon poses inflammatory problems:

If we prepare for wars, which ones are we to fight?

Should we prepare for war or for cooperative international programs designed to prevent war and to provide suitable substitutes for it?

Should not domestic problems—racial discrimination, housing, food for the hungry, education, and the like—receive priority?

The Pentagon is ready to start constructing the ABM system and is helping scientists prepare their articles praising it. The electronics industry is firmly entrenched in the Pentagon and that industry will reap huge profits from ABM which started as a five billion dollar item, quickly jumped to ten billion and two hundred billion and even four hundred billion. Congress has approved this program, though by a slim majority. The voices and pressures of the military-industrial complex seem always to suffocate the pleas of the poor as well as the pleas of those who want to be done with wars and create a cooperative world pattern for the solution of international problems.

Does social and economic justice always serve a secondary role in our society?

General David M. Shoup of the Marines has called the Pentagon and the defense industry "a powerful public opinion lobby." War has become to American civilians "an exciting adventure, a competitive game, and an escape from the dull routine of peacetime."

Our whole approach to world problems has changed. We now have what General Shoup calls the "military task force" type of diplomacy. We have eight treaties to help defend forty-eight nations if they ask us—or if we choose to intervene. Our militarism threatens to become more and more the dominant force in our lives. This is an inflammatory issue; and dissent on it will not be stilled.

The advances of technology present the problem of increasing disemployment in the private sector. We brag about our present low unemployment. But that is due to Vietnam. Without Vietnam we would have 15 per cent or more unemployment. Must we fight wars to have full employment?

Technology is in the saddle and displaces manpower. The old problem of unemployment has become the new problem of disemployment. How many of the present eighteen-year-old men and women will be permanently disemployed? Thoughts such as these fill the hearts of the young with dismay.

Automation is more complete in the petrochemical industry than in any others. From the mid-1950s on, there has been an almost steady decline in the number of "all employees" in petroleum refineries; and the same is true of "production workers"—from 147,000 in 1953 to 90,000 in 1967. An ever-increasing quantity of food and industrial goods is produced by a rapidly decreasing fraction of workers. Those displaced sometimes end up making what is called "redundant" goods, items and services of value, but quite secondary or even needless measured by basic human requirements. Those engaged in various aspects of the moon project are an illustration. Most "redundant" goods projects do not produce what the people need, e.g. more hospital beds, urban projects that replace dirty ghettos, and the like.

Some who are presently "on welfare" represent the third generation in one family on the relief rolls. There is no work available and some of these people now think they are caught as victims of a system that pays people to be poor.

Training for industrial work can take care of a portion of these people, but with the great onrush of population, private industry—unless aided by wars—will not be able to meet the employment needs.

The answer, of course, is the creation of a public sector in which people will do more than rake leaves or sell apples on street corners.

A Senate Subcommittee in 1968 proposed that 1.2 million socially useful jobs be created within the next four years in the public sector. But the proposal seemed to die there.

Where is the blueprint for a public sector?

How do the disadvantaged go about the promotion of such a blueprint?

If history is a guide, the powers-that-be will not respond until there are great crises, for those in power are blind devotees to private enterprise. They accept that degree of socialism implicit in the vast subsidies to the military-industrial complex, but not that type of socialism which maintains public projects for the disemployed and the unemployed alike.

I believe it was Charles Adams who described our upside down welfare state as "socialism for the rich, free enterprise for the poor." The great welfare scandal of the age concerns the dole we give rich people. Percentage depletion for oil interests is, of course, the most notorious. But there are others. Any tax deduction is in reality a "tax expenditure," for it means that on the average the Treasury pays 52 per cent of the deduction. When we get deeply into the subject we learn that the cost of public housing for the poorest 20 per cent of the people is picayune compared to federal subsidy of the housing costs of the wealthiest 20 per cent. Thus, for 1962, Alvin Schoor, in *Explorations in Social Policy*, computed that, while we spent $870 million on housing for the poor, the tax deductions for the top 20 per cent amounted to $1.7 billion.

And the 1968 *Report of the National Commission on Civil Disorder* tells us that during a thirty-year period when the federal government was subsidizing 650,000 units of low-cost housing, it provided invisible supports, such as cheap credit and tax deductions, for the construction of more than ten million units of middle- and upper-class housing.

The big corporate farmer who has varied business interests has a large advantage over the small farmer. The farm corporation can write off profits from non-farm enterprises against farm losses. Moreover, it gets a low capital gains rate of tax in situations such as the following: a corporation buys cattle and keeps them for several years, taking the maintenance costs as a farming loss and thereby reducing its profits from other sources. Then it sells the herd and any profit on the sale is taxed at 25 per cent.

Like examples are numerous in our tax laws, each marking a victory for some powerful lobby. The upside down welfare state helps the rich get richer and the poor, poorer.

Other subsidies receive a greater reverence. Railroads, airlines, shipping—these are all subsidized; and those companies' doors are not kicked down by the police at night.

Publishers get a handsome subsidy in the form of low second-class mail rates, and publishers' rights are meticulously honored.

The subsidies given farmers are treated, not as gratuities, but as matters of entitlement.

The airspace used by radio and TV is public property. But the permittees are not charged for the use of it.

Of all these only the welfare recipient is singled out for degrading supervision and control. Moreover, the poor man's welfare may be cut off without any hearing.

Mr. Justice Holmes uttered a careless dictum when he said that no one has "a constitutional right to be a policeman." The idea took hold that public employment was a privilege, not a right, and therefore conditions could be attached to it. The notion spread to public welfare: a needy person could be denied public help if he did not maintain the type of abode the welfare worker approved; a person on welfare has no Fourth Amendment rights: the police are empowered to kick down the door of his home at midnight without any search warrant in order to investigate welfare violations.

But the largesse granted the radio and TV industry through permits issued may not be revoked without meticulous regard for procedural due process.

The specter of hunger that stalks the land is likely to ignite people to violent protest.

Families that make less than $3,000 a year number thirteen million.

Families making less than $2,000 a year, one million.

Families making less than $1,000 a year, five million.

The condition is not peculiar to any particular State, but is nationwide. Of course, a rural family making in the neighborhood of $3,000 a year may be relatively well-off—-if it has a cow, chickens, and vegetable garden. But, as the poor are driven from the land by the technological revolution in agriculture and pile up in the urban centers, these statistics on our "poor" become ominous.

The federal food program is not responsive to that growing need. It is designed by the agribusiness lobby to restrict production, keep prices high, and assure profits to the producers. That lobby controls the Department of Agriculture, which as a result has made feeding the poor a subordinate and secondary function.

In one year Texas producers, who constitute .02 per cent of the Texas population, received $250 million in subsidies, while the Texas poor, who constitute 28.8 per cent of the Texas population, received $7 million in food assistance.

Of the thirty million poor, less than six million participate in either the national food stamp program or the surplus commodity program.

A pilot food stamp project was established in two counties of South Carolina in 1969. If a poor family makes under $360 a year, it gets food stamps free under that pilot project. A poor family making more than that but less than $1,000 a year pays for food stamps, even though the family income is not sufficient to meet family necessities. Nationwide, 17 per cent of the family budget goes for food—*on the average.* The poor who buy food stamps pay much more.

A family of four makes, say, $1,000 a year and pays $40 a month for food stamps that are worth $70. That helps; but the families still cannot afford it. Moreover, these food stamp programs do not exist as a matter of right. While the federal government pays some of their costs, the state or local government, not Washington, D. C., must initiate the food stamp program.

What do local people think of their poor? That they are a worthless lot? That hard work and industry would cure their lot? That if the local poor are well-fed they may stay; but if they are left on their own, they may emigrate and settle down in some metropolitan ghetto?

The local agencies also determine what families are "eligible" for food stamps. Their word is the law, for there are no procedures and no agency or surveillance to make sure that people are not made "ineligible" because of race, creed, or ideological views. Retailers who may receive food stamps and turn them into the local bank for cash have prescribed remedies if they are discriminated against. But the faceless, voiceless poor have no such recourse.

The hungry people have to go to the County Courthouse to be processed for "eligibility." This chore, an easy one for the sophisticated, is very nearly a barrier to the illiterate poor. Getting to town, some thirty or forty miles away, is one difficulty. Standing in line a day or more and being interrogated on personal affairs by complete strangers is another barrier. If the food program is to be effective, the agency people must take it into the hovels of the poor.

One aspect of the hunger problem concerns school lunches, originally started to help dispose of surpluses and thus protect the producers against declines in the market. They are now part of a "feeding the hungry" project. Official reports give glowing accounts of the progress made; and there has been some. But, again, whether there are school lunches in any community depends on the local school board. In schools where there are few poor students, the poor are fed. In schools where most children are poor, the school board often does not supply enough money to feed them all.

The person who must pick those allowed to eat on the limited budget is the principal. The result is that some hungry children go without lunches—80.8 per cent in Virginia, 70.4 per cent in West Virginia, 73.5 per cent in Pennsylvania, and 86.8 per cent in Maryland. Overall, the national figures show that at least two out of three needy children do not receive school lunches.

Yet, the total number of school children from families at the rock-bottom poverty level is six million.

We do not know how the two million is chosen from the six. But we do know that at times the principal disqualifies a hungry child based on his judgment of the moral character of the parents, not on the child's need.

And there is no way for the parents or the child to review that ruling of the principal.

Ninety-nine of the 253 counties in Texas took no part in the federal food program in 1968. Texas has the largest farm subsidy total in the nation but denies food aid to more poor people than any other State.

In Tuscaloosa, Alabama, forty-nine producers divided $605,000 for not growing crops, while 21,409 poor people had no access to the federal food program.

Some States—notably New York, Louisiana, Massachusetts, and South Carolina—contribute to the cost of school lunches. But in the other States the local contribution is minor. The federal government pays about one-third of the cost of lunches (if donated food is included); the children pay the rest.

No matter what the propagandists say, hungry school children who have had lunches, in the main, either pay for the food themselves or are beneficiaries of the meager amount the federal government has put into the program.

In 1968 when Resurrection City was erected in Washington, D. C., there were Congressional hearings on this problem. An American of Mexican ancestry testified:

> *We are here with brothers of other races, here in unity, in love for each other. We are all poor. We speak for the oppressed, for the hungry thousands that exist in this country, to the tortures of many kinds that have been applied to us.*
>
> *We have become immune and still exist, because our pride and honesty keep us going. We are the ghosts, the sons of chiefs, gods, kings and revolutionists, here to haunt you for what is rightfully ours—the human right to exist. We come here with the same problems and the same objectives. We are a proud race of people in a racist society. We look, we feel, we eat sometimes, we sleep, we walk, we love, and we die the same.*
>
> *If we are to be heard here and across the country today— it has taken a long time for you to hear the complaints up to now but don't forget we Mexican-American people have waited four hundred years to be heard—if you intend to help us, do so now. Don't pass the buck or stall any longer.*

The problem of hunger—like the ghetto problem and the racial problem—has festered for years. The Puritan ethic that hard work and thrift will take anyone to the top has conditioned much of our thinking and has made us slow to deal with the problems of hunger and ghettos. Those problems suddenly loom large and ominous because of the mounting population and the growing dependence of people on government.

Property has assumed a different form. To the average man it is no longer cows, horses, chickens, and a plot of land. It is government largesse—farm subsidies, social security, veterans' benefits, unemployment insurance, old-age pensions, medicare, and the like. Even business has a towering stake in government largesse, as witness the $80 billion budget of the Pentagon.

The political struggles ahead are for increasing shares of government largesse. The opposed forces are numerous. On one side are powerful lobbies such as the industrial-military complex, the agro-business lobby, and the highway lobby. These have powerful spokesmen. The poor, the unemployed, and the disemployed are opposed—and they are not well organized.

The use of violence as an instrument of persuasion is therefore inviting and seems to the discontented to be the only effective protest.

Our second great task is to control the American bureaucracy. As the problems of the nation and the states multiplied, the laws became more prolix and the discretion granted the administrators became greater and greater. Licenses or permits are issued if the agency deems it to be "in the public interest." Management of national forests and national parks is left to federal agencies which in turn promulgate regulations governing the use of these properties but seldom allow a public voice to be heard against any plan of the agency.

The examples are legion and they cover a wide range of subjects from food stamps, to highway locations, to spraying of forests or grasslands to eliminate certain species of trees or shrubs, to the location of missile bases, to the disposal of sewage or industrial wastes, to the granting of off-shore oil leases.

Corporate interests, as well as poor people—unemployed people as well as the average member of this affluent society—are affected by these broad generalized grants of authority to administrative agencies. The corporate interests have been largely taken care of by highly qualified lawyers acting in individual cases and by Bar Associations proposing procedural reforms that define, for example, the "aggrieved" persons who have standing to object to agency orders or decisions. But the voices of the mass of people are not heard; and the administrative agencies largely have their own way.

Moreover, the Establishment controls those agencies. That control does not come from corrupt practices or from venality. It results from close alliances made out of working relations, from memberships in the same or similar clubs, from the warp and woof of social relations, and from the prospects offered the administrator for work in the ranks of the Establishment, *if* he is the right and proper man. The administrative office is indeed the staging ground where men are trained and culled and finally chosen to the high salaried posts in the Establishment that carry many desirable fringe benefits. The New Dealers mostly ended up there. Under Lyndon Johnson there was lively competition for administrative men who would in two years have made a million working for the Establishment. That is a powerful influence among many agencies; and it results in those who have agency discretion exercising it for the benefit of those who run the corporation state. And those people are by and large the exploiters.

Anyone who opposes one of those federal agencies whose decision may destroy a lake or river or mountain knows something about the feeling of futility that is abroad in the land.

Agencies—notably the Forest Service and Bureau of Land Management—spray public lands to get rid of a shrub like the sagebrush or a tree like the mesquite. It is said that riddance of those species increases the supply of grass. The driving force behind the scene is the cattle baron who grazes his stock on public lands.

Neither his request for spraying nor the agency's decision to authorize it is put down for a hearing. Though Rachel Carson's *Silent Spring* has been out some years and though the dangers of pesticides are increasingly known, the agency has no "control" plot where the precise effect of the particular herbicide on our ecology has been studied. The agency, in other words, goes at the problem blindly. It will learn what damage the spray does only years after the spraying has been completed. Moreover, the public is not allowed to protest at a hearing or tender expert testimony as to what this particular spray will do to the environment. This is public land. Why should not members of the public have a right to be heard? No satisfactory answer has been given—only the desire of the agency to be rid of all outside interference.

Once in a blue moon a hearing is held. Early in 1969 the Forest Service's proposal to spray the Dry Fork in the Big Horn National Forest in Wyoming was put down for a hearing so that Norma Ketchum—but no other member of the public—could be heard. Why only that one lady? Senator Gale McGee at her request spoke to the Forest Service about the project. Because of his political pressure, this one lady was heard.

But spraying regularly takes place with no one being heard.

Private persons, as well as government agencies, do this spraying. Why should a private owner not be required to put his spraying project down for a public hearing? He may own the mesquite trees; but he does not own the wildlife that comes and goes across his property.

In 1968 and 1969 great stretches of the Sonora Desert in Arizona were sprayed to kill mesquite in order to help the cattlemen. Such a large number of kangaroo rats and other rodents were killed that the horned owls left the country for lack of food.

Does not the horned owl have value to the environment?

I remember an alpine meadow in Wyoming where willows lined a clear, cold brook. Moose browsed the willow. Beaver came and made a dam which in time created a lovely pond which produced eastern brook trout up to five pounds. A cattle baron said that sagebrush was killing the grass. So the Forest Service sprayed the entire area. It killed the sagebrush and the willow too. The moose disappeared and so did the beaver. In time the dam washed out and the pond was drained. Ten years later some of the willow was still killed out; the beaver never returned; nor did the moose.

Why should a thing of beauty that hundreds of people enjoy be destroyed to line the pockets of one cattle baron?

The agency decision that destroys the environment may be the cutting of a virgin stand of timber or the construction of a road up a wilderness valley. Hundreds of actions of this kind take place every year; and it is the unusual case on which the public is heard.

In 1961-1962 the Forest Service made plans to build a road up the beautiful Minam River in Oregon—one of the few roadless valleys in the State. It is choice wilderness—delicate in structure, sparse in timber, and filled with game. We who knew the Minam pleaded against the road. The excuse was cutting timber—a poor excuse because of the thin stand. The real reason was road building on which the lumber company would make a million dollars. The road would be permanent, bringing automobiles in by the thousands and making a shambles of the Minam.

We spoke to Senator Wayne Morse about the problem and he called over Orville Freeman, Secretary of Agriculture, the agency that supervises the Forest Service. Morse pounded the table and demanded a public hearing. One was reluctantly given. Dozens of people appeared on the designated day in La Grande, Oregon, not a blessed one speaking in favor of the plan. Public opposition was so great that the plan was suffocated.

Why should not the public be heard whenever an agency decides to take action that will or may despoil the environment?

The design of a highway, as well as its location, may be ruinous to economic, aesthetic, scenic, recreational, or health interests.

By highway design and construction the Bureau of Public Roads has ruined fifty trout streams in the Pacific Northwest. Gravel and rocks have been dumped in the streams, making the water too fast for trout or salmon. Rivers have been dredged, with the result that they have become sterile sluiceways.

Why should not the public be allowed to speak before damage of that character is done?

Racial problems often are the key to a freeway crisis. In Washington, D. C., the pressure from the Establishment was so great on the planners that the natural corridor for the freeway was abandoned and the freeway laid out so it would roar through the Black community. That experience was not unique. Many urban areas have felt the same discrimination. The Blacks—having no voice in the decision—rise up in protest, some reacting violently.

Why should not all people—Blacks as well as Whites—be allowed to appear, by right, before a tribunal that is impartial and not a stooge for the powerful Highway Lobby, to air their complaints and state their views?

Why should any special interest be allowed to relocate a freeway merely to serve its private purposes?

The Highway Lobby makes the Bureau of Public Roads almost king. In 1968, when Alan Boyd proposed hearing procedures before federally supported highways were either *located* or *designed,* public hearings on the proposed regulations were held. Every one of our fifty governors appeared or sent word *opposing* the regulations. Why? Because the national highway lobby and the state highway departments have such a close working partnership that nothing should be done to disrupt it. That means that they think that individuals should have no voice in planning. Yet the location of a highway may: (a) ruin a park, as those in Washington, D.C., know from the repeated threats to Glover Archbold Park; (b) ruin the scenic values of a river; (c) needlessly divide a unitary suburban area into separate entities; (d) ruin a trout stream (as some fifty highways have done in the Pacific Northwest); (e) have an ugly racial overtone, as where a freeway is diverted by the Bureau from a white area and sent roaring through the middle of a Black section.

The values at stake are both aesthetic and spiritual, social and economic; and they bear heavily on human dignity and responsibility. Is a faceless bureaucrat to tell us what is beautiful? Whether a particular type of highway is more socially desirable than the country's best trout stream? Whether a particularly described highway is more desirable than a wilderness park? Whether the Blacks should be sent scurrying so that the whites can live in peace and quiet? Where do the Blacks go but into more crowded neighboring slums, as there are no suburban slums yet created?

Offshore leasing of oil lands has become another explosive issue. Offshore oil wells may result in leakages that ruin a vast stretch of beaches, as recently happened at Santa Barbara. Conservationists, if heard, could have built a strong case against the permits. Without any hearings, Secretary of the Interior Udall was allowed to do the bidding of the oil companies and knuckle under to the pressure of President Johnson to start more money coming into the federal treasury to wage war in Vietnam. The result was that the beaches of Santa Barbara were ruined by one man's *ipse dixit.*

The tragedies that are happening to our environment as a result of agency actions are too numerous to list. They reach into every State and mount in intensity as our resources diminish.

People march and protest but they are not heard.

As a result, Congressman Richard L. Ottinger of New York has recently proposed that a National Council on the Environment be created and granted power to stay impending agency action that may despoil the natural resources and to carry the controversy into the courts or before Congress, if necessary.

Violence has no constitutional sanction; and every government from the beginning has moved against it.

But where grievances pile high and most of the elected spokesmen represent the Establishment, violence may be the only effective response.

In some parts of the world the choice is between peaceful revolution and violent revolution to get rid of an unbearable yoke on the backs of people, either religious, military, or economic. The Melville account from Guatemala is in point. Thomas R. Melville and Arthur Melville are two Maryknoll Fathers and Marian P. Bradford, a nun, who later married Thomas.

These three worked primarily among the Indians who make up about 56 per cent of the population of Guatemala. They saw the status quo, solidly aligned against the Indians, being financed by our Alliance For Progress and endowed with secret intelligence service to ferret out all "social disturbers." Between 1966 and 1967 they saw more than 2,800 intellectuals, students, labor leaders, and peasants assassinated by right-wing groups because they were trying to combat the ills of Guatemalan society. Men trying to organize unions were shot, as were men trying to form cooperatives. The Melvilles helped the Indians get a truck to transport lime from the hills to the processing plant, an operation historically performed by Indians who carried one hundred-pound packs on their backs. A truck would increase the production of the Indians and help raise their standard of living. But the powers-that-be ran this truck off the road into a deep canyon and did everything else possible to defeat this slight change in the habits of the Indians.

And so the Indians faced the issue of whether the use of violence in self-defense was justified. The simple question they asked their priests was whether they would go to hell if they used violence.

The Melvilles said:

> *Having come to the conclusion that the actual state of*
> *violence, composed of the malnutrition, ignorance, sickness*
> *and hunger of the vast majority of the Guatemalan*
> *population, is the direct result of a capitalistic system that*
> *makes the defenseless Indian compete against the powerful*
> *and well-armed landowner, my brother and I decided not to*
> *be silent accomplices of the mass murder that this system*
> *generates.*
>
> *We began teaching the Indians that no one will defend*
> *their rights if they do not defend them themselves. If the*
> *government and oligarchy are using arms to maintain them*
> *in their position of misery, then they have the obligation to*
> *take up arms and defend their God-given right to be men.*

Their final conclusion was "Our response to the present situation is not because we have read either Marx or Lenin, but because we have read the New Testament."

That is also what Dom Helder Camara, Archbishop of Recife, Brazil, was telling the world in 1969. "My vocation," he said, "is to argue, argue, argue for moral pressure upon the lords." The "lords" are the "slavemasters"—the Establishment in Brazil and the United States, now dedicated to crushing any move towards violent upheaval. Though violence is not open to Archbishop Camara, he said, "I respect the option for violence."

Guatemala and Brazil are token feudal situations characteristic of the whole world. They represent a status quo that must be abolished.

We of the United States are not in that category. But the risk of violence is a continuing one in our own society, because the oncoming generation has two deep-seated convictions:

First—The welfare program works in reverse by syphoning off billions of dollars to the rich and leaving millions of people hungry and other millions feeling the sting of discrimination.

Second—The special interests that control government use its powers to favor themselves and to perpetuate regimes of oppression, exploitation, and discrimination against the many.

There are only two choices: A police state in which all dissent is suppressed or rigidly controlled; or a society where law is responsive to human needs.

If society is to be responsive to human needs, a vast restructuring of our laws is essential.

Realization of this need means adults must awaken to the urgency of the young people's unrest—in other words there must be created an adult unrest against the inequities and injustices in the present system. If the government is in jeopardy, it is not because we are unable to cope with revolutionary situations. Jeopardy means that either the leaders or the people do not realize they have all the tools required to make the revolution come true. The tools and the opportunity exist. Only the moral imagination is missing.

If the budget of the Pentagon were reduced from $80 billion to $20 billion it would still be over twice as large as that of any other agency of government. Starting with vast reductions in its budget, we must make the Pentagon totally subordinate in our lives.

The poor and disadvantaged must have lawyers to represent them in the normal civil problems that now haunt them.

Laws must be revised so as to eliminate their present bias against the poor. Neighborhood credit unions would be vastly superior to the finance companies with their record of anguished garnishments.

Hearings must be made available so that the important decisions of federal agencies may be exposed to public criticism before they are put into effect.

The food program must be drastically revised so that its primary purpose is to feed the hungry rather than to make the corporate farmer rich.

A public sector for employment must be created that extends to meaningful and valuable work. It must include many arts and crafts, the theatre, industries; training of psychiatric and social workers, and specialists in the whole gamut of human interest.

The universities should be completely freed from CIA and from Pentagon control, through grants of money or otherwise. Faculties and students should have the basic controls so that the university will be a revolutionary force that helps shape the restructuring of society. A university should not be an adjunct of business, nor of the military, nor of government. Its curriculum should teach change, not the status quo. Then, the dialogue between the people and the powers-that-be can start; and it may possibly keep us all from being victims of the corporate state.

The constitutional battle of the Blacks has been won, but equality of opportunity has, in practice, not yet been achieved. There are many, many steps still necessary. The secret is continuous progress.

Whatever the problem, those who see no escape are hopelessly embittered. A minimum necessity is measurable change.

George III was the symbol against which our Founders made a revolution now considered bright and glorious. George III had not crossed the seas to fasten a foreign yoke on us. George III and his dynasty had established and nurtured us and all that he did was by no means oppressive. But a vast restructuring of laws and institutions was necessary if the people were to be content. That restructuring was not forthcoming and there was revolution.

We must realize that today's Establishment is the new George III. Whether it will continue to adhere to his tactics, we do not know. If it does, the redress, honored in tradition, is also revolution.

Poets and authors have told us that our society has been surfeited with goods, that our people are mostly well-fed, that marketing and advertising devices have put into our hands all manner and form of gadgets to meet any whim, but that we are unhappy and not free.

The young generation sees this more clearly than their parents do. The youngsters who rise up in protest have not formulated a program for action. Few want to destroy the system. The aim of most of them is to regain the freedom of choice that their ancestors lost, to be free, to be masters of their destiny.

We know by now that technology can be toxic as well as tonic. We know by now that if we make technology the predestined force in our lives, man will walk to the measure of its demands. We know how leveling that influence can be, how easy it is to computerize man and make him a servile thing in a vast industrial complex.

This means we must subject the machine—technology—to control and cease despoiling the earth and filling people with goodies merely to make money. The search of the young today is more specific than the ancient search for the Holy Grail. The search of the youth today is for ways and means to make the machine—and the vast bureaucracy of the corporation state and of government that runs that machine—the servant of man.

That is the revolution that is coming.

That revolution—now that the people hold the residual powers of government—need not be a repetition of 1776. It could be a revolution in the nature of an explosive political regeneration. It depends on how wise the Establishment is. If, with its stockpile of arms, it resolves to suppress the dissenters, America will face, I fear, an awful ordeal.

PART FOUR

Internationalist

In 1953, Douglas traveled throughout Southeast Asia, including Vietnam. He was never one to settle for the canned tour for visiting dignitaries. He took off through the countryside, talking to whoever he could, from the most exalted of officials to the most ordinary peasants. "Vietnam—Nation in Disintegration," from *North from Malaya*, and "Vietnam" from *The Court Years* provide descriptions of the political situation in Vietnam that could have served as a primer for American leaders who, a decade later, started the escalation that led to that most infamous of U.S. military adventures. Douglas always insisted on the unconstitutionality of the war. Formally, the war did not have the Congressional declaration required by Article I of the Constitution. Reading these accounts, one might conclude that it also failed Douglas's test on a less formal, but more fundamental level—it was nothing more than an extension of French colonialism, therefore wrong for a nation committed to freedom and equality.

Vietnam – Nation in Disintegration

A Phantom Army

Rugged mountains with a tumbled mass of peaks rising over 7,000 feet form the northern and western borders of Vietnam. Their dense vegetation, harsh limestone cliffs, and narrow defiles have made them somewhat of a barrier against the invader, somewhat of a refuge for minority tribes. But these mountains have never been much of a protection against China on the north. They have passes which served as the pathways for the human migrations which peopled the countries of Southeast Asia. They have long been the traditional haunts of tigers, elephants, panthers, and malarial mosquitoes. Now they are also the refuge of Communist guerrillas. Today they furnish Red China and the Communists of Vietnam (the Viet Minh) the staging grounds for an unrelenting military action. Red China has secretly united with the Viet Minh to drive the French out of Vietnam and to take over the government. It is from this mountain stronghold that strong Communist forces make their great assaults.

These mountains are the source of the Red River and many other fingers of water that run southeast to the Gulf of Tonkin. The Red River delta is rich in rice. Wherever one looks there is wet paddy. The rice fields run to the horizon—unbroken except for an occasional lone tree and clusters of villages. From the delta the mountain strongholds of the Communists look like the low broken hills of western Connecticut. Their lines are soft; and on a clear evening they stand silhouetted against the sky like relics of ancient ranges.

Up to the fall of 1950 the French held most of these hills by a line of forts along the Chinese border. But the Communists drove them out. Today the Viet Minh occupies them and from that strategic position commands most of the delta. The Red River delta is a narrow coastal plain, hemmed in by mountains on the west and on the north. The French have placed their uneasy lines at the head of this delta. Should the Viet Minh break through, all of Vietnam might fall. For there are not many natural defense positions to the south.

Far to the south are other Viet Minh forces. They are scattered through the rich delta near the mouth of the Mekong River in Cochin China.

The Mekong, which rises with the Yangtze and Salween in southeastern Tibet, flows 2,800 miles to the sea in southern Vietnam. Its rich delta of swamps, rice lands, palm trees, and mangroves gives ideal hiding grounds to the guerrillas. These guerrillas are smaller in number and weaker in strength than those up north. They are far from the Chinese border and are therefore more on their own. But they are strongly entrenched, and recently they have extended their operations into the neighboring state of Cambodia.

There are strong political as well as military reasons why the Viet Minh concentrates its efforts on the Red River delta in the north and the Mekong River delta in the south. Those are the two rich areas of the country, the Mekong River delta being one of the richest rice-producing regions in all of Southeast-Asia. The Red River delta in the north and the Mekong River delta in the South are the food baskets of Vietnam. They hang, as it were, on either end of a long pole, the pole being the range of Annamite Mountains that runs north and south for the length of the country.

When I was in Vietnam the Mekong River delta was deep in floods, so I did not visit it. I traveled instead the Red River delta, far to the north.

A macadam road, built high to serve as a dike in time of floods, streaks north from Hanoi. It is pock-marked from the pounding of trucks and from land mines. When I traveled it in August 1952, it was heavy with traffic. Dozens of American-made trucks filled with soldiers were moving north.

Up front were white-kepied French Legionnaires (mostly Polish and German) with hard-bitten faces. I had seen some of them on leave in Hanoi, carefree, relaxed, swaggering. I had talked with some in the lounge of the Hotel Metropole, and they were sure this business of war would be over and done with in a year and that they would be on their way home. And when I had asked, "The French will win in a year?" there was only a shrug of the shoulders.

Next in the caravan came young Vietnamese troops, as nondescript and as expressionless as the peasants in the rice fields.

In the rear came truck after truck filled with Senegalese troops. They wore broad-brimmed hats. And their smiles were almost as wide. I had seen them on guard at bridges outside Hanoi. They were always smiling or mimicking. Once when I stopped to take a picture of a sentry, he dropped his gun, held his hands above his head, and, feigning solemnity, said, "I surrender, monsieur." The Senegalese who were present had roared with laughter. About the only smiles I had seen in this country were the smiles of the Senegalese. They have roots perhaps deeper in the country than any other foreign race. Many of them in the Tonkin area have almost become members of the peasant families. They serve the role of big brother. Their attachments are close and enduring. And this day they waved and shouted at me from the trucks which carried them to the front lines a few miles north—the thin lines that stand between Hanoi and the Viet Minh army.

We were slowed to a few miles an hour by this caravan of trucks until we came to a left-hand fork in the road a few miles out of Hai Duong. There we bore off to the northwest, leaving the troops. The day was hot and muggy; not a breath of air stirred; no ripple touched the high stand of brightly green rice; paddies were empty of people and of animals. The rural scene was as peaceful as any New England could offer.

But war and peace are a strange mixture in Vietnam. What seemed to be a calm and placid countryside quickly exploded with violence. As I rounded a curve in the Jeepster I was right in the middle of a battle. A dozen French soldiers were charging across a field toward a squat mud hut by a lone palm tree. A half dozen men opposed them, rising from the grass and firing. One man fell, a wisp of smoke floated above him, and then the sound of the guns was lost in the screech of my tires.

Vietnam knows war as few countries have known it. She has been in the throes of bloody civil war for six years. Ho Chi Minh, the tubercular Communist who has had a more powerful hold on the people than any leader in modern times, has been a fugitive since late 1946. Since then he has been hiding in the mountains on the Chinese border, organizing his army and marshaling his propaganda. The Chinese set up military training schools for him. Russia sent instructors from Czechoslovakia, many mortars, and some $2^{1}/_{2}$-ton trucks. China supplied carbines, machine guns, bazookas, anti-aircraft guns, mortar, and artillery—much of it American equipment that originally had been given Nationalist China or that was captured in Korea. China has had no tanks, no planes, and only a few trucks to give Ho Chi Minh. But she has been furnishing

3,000 tons of ammunition a month. And recently she has started to supply political commissars to Ho Chi Minh's army.

This war material has to be carted over the mountains from China. There is little motor transport and only primitive roads. Ho Chi Minh answered that problem in logistics through the mass use of slave labor. He has conscripted all men between eighteen and forty-five for the army and for his labor battalions. With China's help he has mustered as high as 600,000 coolies for some of his operations. They are his supply line, moving hundreds of miles over the mountains with food, supplies, and ammunition for the Viet Minh army. Yet without much motor transport Ho Chi Minh waxes strong. Opposed to him are nearly 400,000 troops (150,000 French) with tanks, planes, artillery, and all the modern implements of war. But Ho Chi Minh's armies, though vastly inferior in arms and equipment, are a stand-off to the French and Vietnamese. They are so strong that for the most part they hold the initiative. Their estimated total is 300,000 men, with a central unit composed of 50,000 hard and seasoned troops. These soldiers are probably as good as any in Asia. Ho Chi Minh carefully conserves them. He has committed them to battle only twice. He holds them in reserve, using unorthodox warfare to undermine the opposition.

(1) There are few direct assaults. The tactics are one of infiltration behind the lines in an effort to harass and annoy the opposition and to keep it off balance.

(2) The Communist orders are never to meet a superior force head on, but to give way. These orders go further and direct the soldiers to dissolve before a stronger force, to conceal their weapons, to take off their uniforms and assume the role of peasants, and days or weeks later to reassemble at a designated point.

(3) Troops seldom move in the classical way. There is no convoy, no body of men marching down a road, no sweeping movements of mechanized troops. The soldiers travel at night—behind or in oxcarts, across rice paddies on foot, or in unsuspecting trucks. They may also move by daytime in the guise of peasants. A cart full of grass may conceal their carbines; loads of banana wood may contain sticks that have been hollowed out and filled with hand grenades. Thousands of soldiers often sift through a countryside silently and mysteriously, suddenly to appear far in the rear of their enemy.

(4) In the hills the troops are dug in, and the defense runs miles in depth. There is no "front line" in the conventional sense. Dugouts twenty

feet or more deep hold a few men. These dugouts are so widely dispersed and so well concealed that they offer no military target either for artillery, mortar, or aerial bombs.

(5) Dispersion extends to supplies and ammunition dumps. For example, aerial reconnaissance will show no enemy artillery within range. Yet under cover of night thousands of coolies pull guns dozens of miles to points within range of the "front" and before dawn wheel them back again.

The success of these tactics depend primarily on two conditions. First, there must be great reservoirs of expendable man power. Second, there must be a sympathetic, co-operative community of the same race as the enemy army. In other words, the enemy must have popular support far to the rear of the lines that are supposed to defend the nation.

The army of the Viet Minh employs the tactics Mao Tse-tung used in China. It never attacks until it has a vastly superior force in the field. It gives way before overwhelming power, its army becoming peasants. Until the strategic hour to strike arises, it harasses the opposition, infiltrates his rear, keeps him constantly off balance, and takes a heavy toll of his men.

The battle I passed through this August day, though a minor skirmish, was illustrative of these Communist tactics. It took place about twenty miles behind the French lines. How contact happened to be made I do not know. A handful of Viet Minh troops was apprehended deep in French territory where under cover of night it had been wreaking destruction on communications.

The examples of this operation are frequent and dramatic. Hué, a town of about thirty thousand, is some three hundred miles south of Hanoi and over one hundred miles below the Viet Minh stronghold in the provinces of Thanh-hoa and Vinh. It is the ancient capital of Annam. On August 26, 1952, the day before I reached there, a regiment of Viet Minh troops (about three thousand) suddenly appeared below Hué. Their appearance was more startling than General Jubal A. Early's arrival at the back door of Washington, D.C., on July 11, 1864, during the Civil War. Early had brought his cavalry cross-country through Maryland on a hard, fast ride. These Viet Minh troops traveled silently and quietly. They drifted down from the north singly and in small groups, traveling at night and sleeping in huts of sympathetic villagers by day. It took them days on end to work their way south of Hué, where a rendezvous had been arranged. Yet in spite of the time it took, the necessary reliance that was placed upon the villagers along the way, the distance covered, the number of people who must have known of the movement, not a word of the intelligence reached the French. The first the French knew of the episode was when the Viet Minh regiment moved into action south of Hué. The French at once dropped paratroopers into the region, and the news account was that the Viet Minh suffered a severe setback. The truth of the matter is that the great majority of this regiment— well over two thousand—melted safely away in the jungles and the rice paddies to work their way to some rendezvous.

This type of operation is frequent and amazingly successful. As this account is being written in the winter of 1952 the news is full of these episodes. Unless one reads carefully, the impression is likely to be created that the French have had resounding successes in quelling the assaults of the Viet Minh. The truth is that the French positions are constantly infiltrated; the French "victories" are often engagements with Viet Minh forces far in the rear of the French lines. By military standards it is usually the Viet Minh that is strong. The Viet Minh keeps the French pretty much in fixed positions. Then it goes around the flanks, suddenly appears far in the rear, or turns up in the midst of a French stronghold. Its troops come and go with apparent ease, disappearing as mysteriously as they arrive, melting away in the rice paddies like a phantom army. The Viet Minh is, indeed, so mobile that it seems to be everywhere in the country.

The French would welcome an all-out engagement. But the Viet Minh is not accommodating. When the French take the initiative and move in force against the Viet Minh, the results are usually meager. The Viet Minh, though everywhere, seems to be nowhere.

In late August 1952 the French moved ten thousand troops into the heart of Viet Minh country in an all-out drive against a supposed stronghold. They used tanks, artillery, mortar, and planes. This movement, designed to operate as fast as lightning, struck with great force and speed. For twenty-four hours this powerful wedge drove deep into Viet Minh territory. The results—no Viet Minh captured, no Viet Minh troops engaged. One Vietnamese was killed by artillery fire, but whether he was a Viet Minh soldier no one knows. As one French officer said, "It's like trying to hit mosquitoes with a sledge hammer." The Viet Minh forces gave way before the assault, avoiding any engagement. They proved again that they are a phantom army. They showed the Vietnamese that the French cannot trap them or encircle them. They showed the peasants up and down the land that French troops, American armor, and all the skills of modern war are futile against them. When that happens, the Vietnamese—whether he is a Communist or not—smiles to himself and boasts to his wife. He is secretly proud of Ho Chi Minh, the underdog, who can make the French look silly. For it is the French that every Vietnamese hates or distrusts. The anti-French attitude is Ho Chi Minh's greatest asset. That strong feeling against the foreigner cuts deeper in Vietnam than even the misery and poverty of the peasant.

In the winter of 1952-53 the Viet Minh won an important military victory not wholly reflected in the news. It pushed west into the edge of Laos, skirting strong French positions. It now is in position to command the Mekong River that runs the length of the Associated States and pours into the China Sea south of Saigon. Once it controls the Mekong, its forces north and south can join hands; and all French positions in Vietnam will be outflanked. This maneuver may not be completed until the winter of 1953-54, or perhaps a year later. For the Viet Minh, Communist-style, precedes its military movements with political action. It is now indoctrinating the Mekong River valley with discontent and high promises. When it is adequately "softened," the Viet Minh army will move.

Meanwhile, the French forces hold fast at impregnable bastions. In Vietnam the Maginot Line psychology still dominates French military thinking. It is perhaps natural, since the French missed participation in the military strategy that won World War II. There is none of that experience in their background. But the impregnable bastions of the French in Vietnam are proving to be forts easily outflanked. The French have not learned the Viet Minh guerrilla tactics. And in spite of the great disaster they have experienced in Asia they still seem oblivious of the fact that political action is sometimes even more effective than military might.

A House Divided against Itself

Dong Khe is a small village of North Vietnam, sixty miles or so northeast of Hanoi in the rich and strategic Red River delta. The Red River delta is a rice-growing region. Wherever one looks there is wet paddy; and in August fields of rice, rippling in the hot wind, stretch to the horizon. In the north are low hills with lines soft and broken. Those are the hills held a year ago by the French and today by the Viet Minh.

The village of Dong Khe, not far from them, has changed hands several times since Ho Chi Minh unleashed his forces in the winter of 1946. In August 1952 I visited it with Pham Van Binh, then Governor of North Vietnam, and General de Brigade René Cogny of the French Army, the day after it had been freshly taken by the French. Vietnamese troops patrolled its muddy streets. They also walked the low dikes that extended far out into the rice fields surrounding the village, as if they expected the Viet Minh to rise suddenly from the paddies and make an assault. And one solitary Vietnamese soldier stood guard over a nearby swamp ablaze with the beautiful Japanese hyacinth.

A rehabilitation unit had arrived ahead of us and was busily engaged. This was one of the GAMO teams organized by the French to follow on the heels of the Army. I had heard of the work of the GAMO in Southeast Asia before I reached Vietnam. I had been told that its influence on the side of rehabilitation had done much to help heal the scars of civil war. In Saigon I had talked with the President of Vietnam about it. Nguyen Van Tam was appointed President by Emperor Bao Dai in June 1952. Tam, fifty-seven years old, is a slight man with great energy. He works quietly and unobtrusively. Yet he is bold and direct in his words and deeds, and is a good executive. Once head of the police, he is today a "strong" man feared by the people. He is feared because of his record. He obtained French naturalization and for years aided the French cause in helping arrest and repress nationalists and Communists alike. He is known best for his cruelty in torturing political prisoners.

I asked Tam about GAMO. He spoke feelingly of it. It was a poor system, he thought. He had opposed it and had tried to convince the French not to use it. His own system was much better, he insisted.

"What was your system?" I inquired.

"Stern justice for the Communists and their sympathizers," he replied.

Stern justice for the Communists and their sympathizers in the context of Vietnam meant only one thing—ruthless extermination of anyone who dared protest an injustice. I can only believe that GAMO, a creation of the French, also knows the technique of terror. One phase of its operations deals with ferreting out Communists from the conquered villages. I stood in a damp and dingy room while some suspects were being questioned. They had the flame of hatred in their eyes; they looked at me, not as hunted men and women who were finally cornered, but as militant crusaders who would never surrender their cause. Whether that cause was nationalism or Communism I could not discover. But I felt in the little village of Dong Khe the intensity of the feeling behind the revolution. And I believed from that moment the stories I had heard that GAMO was as insensitive to the distinction between a rebel who was a patriot and a rebel who was a Communist, as the French had always been.

GAMO is not, however, purely a police measure. At Dong Khe it had one unit organized for the dissemination of anti-Communist propaganda. There were banners and placards on display. There were booklets for distribution. There were comic strips showing Ho Chi Minh as a weak, ineffective, miserable creature supported by a big, bloody and rapacious villain called Red China.

There was one unit that had collected all the currency of the Viet Minh. The coins were in a half-bushel basket—dirty coins made of a lightweight metal and poorly stamped. There were bills printed on cheap paper and impressed with pictures of peasants. And the central figure on both the coins and the paper currency was the head of Ho Chi Minh. This GAMO unit was setting up a food-distribution center and arranging for the issuance of ration cards.

But before any villager could get a ration card he and his family had to be vaccinated for cholera. They stood in line—mostly women and children—their left arms bare. Vietnamese nurses sat in the open at tables loaded with medical supplies. Without looking up they wiped a spot clean on the arm in front of them and injected the vaccine. Dozens of people went through the line. Children cried, women who were new to the experience closed their eyes, others turned their heads and suffered the agony of anticipated pain. At other tables Vietnamese nurses dispensed salve for ugly sores on the children's heads. The heads were first clipped short and then the salve applied with daubers.

I had been witnessing for a half hour or so the operations of the GAMO when a young Vietnamese took me aside.

"It's all a fraud," he explained.

"What's a fraud?"

"The medical care the French are dispensing."

"What's fraudulent about it?"

"That's not real vaccine in the syringes."

"What is it?"

"Probably water."

"Why do you say that? Do you know for sure?"

"I do not know for sure. But I know the French; and the French cannot be trusted to do anything good for the country."

"You mean this GAMO operation is put on as a stunt for my benefit?"

"Exactly."

"The GAMO does nothing good?"

"Nothing—except of course to punish anyone who dares speak against the government."

I do not believe that broad indictment of GAMO. It has done good work in the rehabilitation of some villages. But I came to know that in this war-torn country of Vietnam there was one group more hated, more suspected, more reviled than any other; and that group was the French.

Dong Khe had changed hands so fast that there was a stunned and paralyzed look in the eyes of the inhabitants. Today it was the French and Vietnamese who were there. Yesterday it had been the Viet Minh. Who would be their masters tomorrow?

The village notables or elders—the administrative group that in Vietnam manages the commune—stood together in a small square to greet the Governor. This square was fifty feet across and lined by the low, one-story peaked huts with thatched roofs that distinguish the villages of this area. Most of the notables were dressed in white trousers, long black gowns, and black skullcaps. Their faces were so serious as to be sad. Their high cheekbones were emphasized by pinched cheeks and skimpy beards. It was a muggy, steaming day with not a breath of air. Black clouds that promised relief from the heat were on China's border to the north. But Dong Khe was suffocating. A young man dressed in white stood in the sun and gave an address of welcome, sweat streaming from his face. The then Governor, an energetic, idealistic man in his forties, stood in the shade and replied. And then the notables gathered around for a serious discussion.

The Communists had been there for months and had not treated the villagers harshly. But if the notables cooperated with the French, the Communists might kill them. Would the Governor leave the Army at Dong Khe for protection? Would the government defend Dong Khe in case it were attacked?

"You are here now. If we are here alone tomorrow, what will happen to us?"

That question runs through the minds of most people in Vietnam and expresses their feelings of insecurity. That one question is, indeed, symptomatic of the disintegrating influences that are loose in this ancient country.

These days, everyone is on a tentative basis in Vietnam, unsure of his status, uncertain of his future.

Vive la France

France has never offered Vietnam complete independence. She has never even offered Vietnam the degree of independence that a dominion such as India and Canada enjoys in the British Commonwealth, all the French propaganda to the contrary notwithstanding. France has offered Vietnam membership in the French Union. But membership in the French Union is compatible neither with independence, with federalism, nor with a dominion status. The bald truth is that the French Union is colonial in nature.

When the French broke with Ho Chi Minh in 1946, they turned to Bao Dai. Vietnamese nationalists, including Ngo Dinh Diem, met with Bao Dai in Hong Kong and asked him to call a National Convention of Vietnamese to set the terms and conditions on which Bao Dai should treat with the French. Neither Bao Dai nor the French would agree. Bao Dai went to Paris to negotiate with the French without any mandate or instructions from his people. Bao Dai was not willing to return to the throne without obtaining concessions. He obtained some. South Vietnam was united with Vietnam. Vietnam got a large degree of internal autonomy. She even got the right to diplomatic representation abroad and the right to an army. And she became a member of the French Union. But one who reads closely finds that even those rights are qualified ones, the French retaining a large measure of control. The French Union is represented in the Associated States by a High Commissioner; and the High Commissioner is represented in each of the states by a Commissioner of the Republic. These officers are free-wheeling French agents who maintain French influence and control in the three nations. French business and cultural interests are assured special prerogatives. Frenchmen are tried before mixed courts, and French law is to be applied to them. The French are preferred in appointment as foreign advisers and technicians. The French keep control of foreign relations and national defense.

The lack of independence of Vietnam in foreign affairs is apparent. "The heads of the foreign diplomatic mission to Vietnam will be accredited to the President of the French Union and to H.M. the Emperor of Vietnam." The diplomats from Vietnam will receive credentials "granted by the President of the French Union and initialed by H.M. the Emperor of Vietnam." And any agreements or treaties of Vietnam must be approved by the High Council of the French Union. As to military affairs, there is no agreement whatsoever governing the withdrawal of French troops.

Vietnam, to be sure, is represented in the French Union.

The organs of the French Union are the presidency, the High Council, and the Assembly. The President of France is the President of the French Union. The High Council—which is an administrative or executive arm of the presidency—is composed of delegates from France and from the associated states, of which Vietnam is one. The Assembly—which has consultative powers only—is composed of members representing the various countries in the Union. Of these, France has half and all the others the other half. Thus the delegates which Vietnam sends to the French Union have a forum but no real voice. All legislative power remains in the National Assembly of France.

Vietnam, Cambodia, and Laos (the three Associated States that have replaced pre-war Indo-China) are incorporated into an economic federation, and their currency is tied to the French franc. Each of the three is a member of the French Union. All three are under the ultimate authority of France when it comes to matters diplomatic and military. Vietnam, Cambodia, and Laos can become united as one nation in a federal system or otherwise only with the approval of the Parliament of France. Paris, not Saigon, remains the center of ultimate power of Vietnam. The web of French power has been rewoven, not removed. The curse of colonialism is still upon the land.

"Under the French Union," one prominent Vietnamese told me, "the French could strangle and starve into submission any Vietnamese government that showed itself less than docile."

The French have suffered tremendous losses since 1946. The cost in dollars has exceeded the French investment in all the Associated States. It has also exceeded the amount France received from us under the Marshall Plan. The annual cost of the military program is about $1,500,000,000, of which America pays indirectly about a third. The struggle of the French has reached heroic proportions, though French law prevents a Frenchman being drafted and sent to Vietnam. The war with Ho Chi Minh to date has cost the French (Colonials and

Legionnaires included) 160,000 casualties. Each year they are losing in officers almost the equivalent of the graduating class at St. Cyr.

These things, however, do not count with the Vietnamese. They remember the decades of grievances under French rule. They suspect every move of the French, every promise, every ingratiating act. French motives are suspect when the French say they will leave at the end of the war, when they say that the Vietnamese will have their independence. Even Vietnamese who can read may not be able to understand the verbiage by which Frenchmen rule the French Union. But those who cannot read, as well as those who can, know that Jean Letourneau, the French High Commissioner, not Bao Dai, occupies the Norodom Palace at Saigon, which to the people is what the White House is to us. Bao Dai negotiated for the Norodom Palace but did not obtain it. Rather than live in the second biggest palace in Saigon, he kept face by moving to Dalat. The people know that. They also know that the High Commissioner outranks Prime Minister Tam.

These simple things mean to the common people of Vietnam that the French are there to stay. That attitude more than anything else divides the country and gives Ho Chi Minh his strength. The presence of the French dilutes the patriotism of every citizen and promotes the forces of disunity. The ideal solution would be for the French to leave the country immediately, turning over all civil and military matters to the Vietnamese. But that move would be catastrophic. There is no Vietnamese army to take over the defense. The French in their long rule never allowed one. Not until 1951 did they start developing an army. There are, of course, Vietnamese soldiers fighting with the French. They number about 130,000. But there have been no officers to lead them. By the first of 1953 there were about eight hundred. And while a vigorous officer-training program is under way, it will take four or five years at the present rate to train enough officers to assume full responsibility for the defense of the country. Meanwhile the French must hang on. But the presence of the French gives Ho Chi Minh his most powerful platform. If the present trend continues, Vietnam will go the way of China.

The French are feeding the flames of Communism in Asia. They repeatedly proclaim, when seeking American aid, that Vietnam is as independent of France as Australia is of Britain, that they are fighting only to stem the tide of Communism in Asia. But when the Vietnamese suggest specific action to implement those pronouncements the French become indignant and threaten to withdraw their military forces. Thus the French implicitly admit that they remain in Vietnam to protect interests which they dare not confess at home or abroad.

Vietnam was saved from Communist conquest in the winter of 1950 by General de Lattre and by American military aid, as Governor Dewey shows in *Journey to the Far Pacific*. The General rallied the demoralized forces that France had in the field and America bolstered them with equipment. The fall of Vietnam today, as then, would imperil all of Southeast Asia. The prize is attractive, for Vietnam, Thailand, and Burma make up the famous rice bowl of Asia. Rice means power. China is hungry for rice. Japan imports 20 per cent of her food and is heavily dependent on rice. If the Communist forces had command of the food supplies of Asia, they would soon have the food-deficit countries at their mercy. Red China, like the China of old, seems to have imperialistic dreams. Red China in her present mood might turn to adventure in Southeast Asia, if the pressure in Korea were lifted.

At one time—perhaps even in 1946—Ho Chi Minh, though Moscow-trained, may have been more of a nationalist than a communist. Southeast Asia thinks that if his liberation movement had been recognized at the end of World War II, Vietnam would today be passionately nationalistic and aligned with Burma in the democratic-socialist group. The answer will never be known. The vast majority of the Viet Minh probably do not know enough about Marxist doctrine to make a choice. They are caught up in a patriotic liberation movement. But, as I have said, the high command is composed of dyed-in-the-wool Communists. And they have skillfully contributed to the disintegration of the nation.

Vietnam may yet be saved. The Vietnamese are strongly suspicious of the Chinese and their foreign policies; they want their independence from all outside powers, Asian as well as European. So the growing domination of the Viet Minh by Red China will not be popular with the people. Heroic political measures can still swing public opinion behind a Vietnam government. There is no reason why Vietnam cannot outdo the Viet Minh and take the popular following from Ho Chi Minh. But it will require a genuine democratic revolution to do it.

Some Vietnamese and Americans were discussing this question one afternoon at Hanoi. We sat in the lounge of the Hotel Metropole, where Ho Chi Minh used to have lunch, drinking black tea out of heavy white cups. A Vietnamese, wise in politics and close to the pulse of the nation, leaned over and said in a whisper, "If our people so desired, they could get rid of the Viet Minh in a week."

That is the tragedy of Vietnam. If Vietnam had the zeal of the Viet Minh, Vietnam would easily win. But it will take far more than guns and francs and dollars to produce that victory.

Sweeping reforms are needed, reforms that serve to rally the people against the threat from the north. The influence of the French has always been on the side of the landlords and the other vested interests. The influence of the present Vietnam government is on the same side. The weight of the government will always be on the side of the *status quo* so long as the French colonial attitude dominates the country.

There are those who say that the military victory must be won before solutions to the political, social, and economic problems are sought. But a strong Vietnamese army is essential to such a victory. And it will be impossible to put that army in the field if the political and associated problems are not solved first. Vietnamese soldiers are not willing to die for the perpetuation of French control. They must have the hope—the firm belief—that they are fighting for a peace which has no taint of the French influence.

Whichever way the situation is analyzed, the answer is the same. The cause of free Asia demands the complete liquidation of French political control. The French cannot withdraw their troops today. But if France announced today, in words admitting no ambiguities, that Vietnam would receive a dominion status, or if the United Nations assumed in Vietnam the role it served so well in Indonesia and undertook to guarantee Vietnam real and complete independence, the problems of Vietnam would begin to solve themselves. If France refuses to make that promise, no political measure, no military measure can arrest the processes of disintegration at work in the country.

Vietnam

When Arthur Goldberg resigned from the Court to head our United Nations delegation, Johnson wanted Abe Fortas, his old friend, confidant and legal adviser, to take Goldberg's place, and he asked me to talk with Abe. I did so and received a firm refusal, as Abe's personal affairs would not permit him to leave private law practice at that time.

Sometime later I heard over the radio a flash announcement that Abe was appointed. I got in my jeep and headed from Goose Prairie, Washington, our residence, to Yakima to reach a phone. En route I was flagged down by the Forest Service, through whom Lyndon had sent a message. When I got Lyndon on the phone he told me what had happened. At 11:45 A.M. he had Abe in his office doing final editing on a Vietnam announcement Johnson was to make. At 11:55 they finished and at 11:59 they walked to the door that opened on a press conference. Lyndon asked Abe to be present while he read the Vietnam statement, and Abe agreed.

With his hand on the doorknob, Lyndon turned to Abe and said, "Before announcing this statement, I am going to announce your appointment to the Court."

Abe was taken aback, saying they had been over that many times and his answer was still in the negative.

Turning full face to Abe, Lyndon said, "This Vietnam statement that you approved says fifty thousand more boys are going to Vietnam—perhaps to die. No one is ever going to shoot at you on the Court. Tell me, how can I send them to battle and not send you to the Court?"

Abe was silent a second and finally said, "Okay, you win."

When Lyndon told me the story over the phone, I said, "You bagged a good Justice, Mr. President."

What I have said so far puts LBJ in a poor light because he used people's frailties for petty or perhaps venal causes or employed them, as in Abe Fortas' case, to ambush a man. Yet as David S. Broder points out in his book *The Party's Over,* though Lyndon had powerful capabilities of persuasion on a person-to-person basis, he did not have them so much at the mass level. His technique was to use every representative of a group whose support he wanted as a convert. The persuasion was not across the room or at arm's length. It was nose to nose, with Lyndon putting on his hypnotic pressure. He was an amazing stunt man who personally went after every man or woman he needed in his political corner and worked him or her over to a fare-thee-well. Broder attributes this technique to LBJ's rise to power in the one-party state of Texas. Whatever the cause, it was person-to-person salvation administered by a most astute advocate. But his talents in this regard were limited. He could not sway the masses the same way. That is why, when those he had sold on the Vietnam war began to retreat, he was a lost soul. That is why he decided not to run again. Knowing the man and loving him for all his great points, I became physically ill to see his world collapse publicly on TV. He wanted to be loved by all, and when they left him on the war issue, it was a crushing, brutal, although inevitable and necessary, blow.

The Atomic Age drastically limits the use of force. It indeed calls for alternatives. The only known alternative is law. I thought perhaps I could get Lyndon to see that when I tried to induce him to speak at the opening of the *Pacem in Terris* convocation in New York City in February 1965. The theme was taken from Pope John's well-known encyclical; it was one in a series of conferences sponsored by the Parvin Foundation and arranged by the Center for the Study of Democratic Institutions of which Robert M. Hutchins was the head, I then being chairman of the board.

Lyndon at once panicked at the thought of making such a speech. I said that he could lead the nations of the world into a regime of law or at least call a working conference which would have that as an aim. He dodged, ducked and evaded the proposition, changing the subject and finally shunting me off to the staff that was instructed to sabotage me politely.

LBJ finally sent a letter: "I have no doubt that such a discussion, under private auspices, of the problems of peace will provide a major contribution to the greatest single problem of our time." But then came the typical abrasive tactics of LBJ; unofficial gatherings like this, he said, might be disruptive of official peacemaking efforts; this group was infringing on an area properly reserved for professional diplomats; it was attempting to exploit the President's prestige on behalf of a private group some of whose members were critical of his policies.

By the time of the 1965 conference the bombing of North Vietnam had started, and that bombing under the direction of LBJ provided an obbligato to all *Pacem in Terris* efforts. We decided, however, that since Vietnam overshadowed all *Pacem in Terris* conversations, North as well as South Vietnam representatives should be invited—that one should not be invited without the other. They both promptly accepted. Our group, working through the State Department, even managed to get permission to invite Ho Chi Minh himself—a man whom two of our group, Harry Ashmore and William Baggs, had met in Hanoi, where they interviewed him on the matter. LBJ's State Department cleared a letter of invitation, which he surely knew about. Ashmore signed the statement and mailed it. The condition included was Ho Chi Minh's— i.e., that while the conference continued, neither side would use the occasion to improve its military position.

Our hopes were high that at last conversations might start. We were soon disillusioned. LBJ had sent a secret message to Ho Chi Minh on February 2, 1965, which reached Ho Chi Minh before ours did. LBJ's letter set forth as a condition for cessation of bombing the most stringent demands yet made: advance assurance that Hanoi would halt all infiltration of troops to the South by land or by sea. There was, of course, no promise that the U.S. build-up in South Vietnam would also cease or that our troop movements to that country would stop. LBJ's letter stated further:

> *If you are able to accept this proposal, I see no reason why it could not take effect at the end of the New Year, or Tet, holidays. The proposal I have made would be greatly strengthened if your military authorities and those of South Vietnam could promptly negotiate an extension of the Tet truce.*

LBJ took note of public statements suggesting that

> *you would be prepared to enter into direct bilateral talks with representatives of the U.S. Government provided that*

we ceased "unconditionally" and permanently our bombing operations against your country and all military action against it. In the last day, serious and responsible parties have assured us indirectly that this is in fact your position.

Let me frankly state that I see two great difficulties with this proposal. In view of your public position, such action on our part would inevitably produce world-wide speculation that discussions were under way and would impair the privacy and secrecy of those discussions. Secondly, there would inevitably be grave concern on our part whether your Government would make use of such action to improve its military position.

With these problems in mind, I am prepared to move further toward an end in hostilities than your Government has proposed in either public statements or through private diplomatic channels. I am prepared to order a cessation of bombing against your country and the stopping of further augmentation of United States forces in South Vietnam as soon as I am assured that infiltration into South Vietnam by land and sea has stopped.

The key passages in our State Department-approved letter had read:

In our several discussions with senior officials of the State Department ... they emphasized that the U.S. remains prepared for secret discussions at any time, without conditions, and that such discussions might cover the whole range of topics relevant to a peaceful settlement. They reiterated that the Geneva Accords might be the framework for a peaceful solution.

They expressed particular interest in your suggestion to us that private talks could begin provided the U.S. stopped bombing your country, and ceased introducing additional U.S. troops into Vietnam. They expressed the opinion that some reciprocal restraint to indicate that neither side intended to use the occasion of the talks for military advantage would provide tangible evidence of the good faith of all parties in the prospects for negotiated settlement.

The State Department-approved letter was not published in the press at the time LBJ's statement was. This deliberate dissembling, whereby LBJ's right hand vetoed what LBJ's left hand was doing, was typical of the actions which created the enormous credibility gap.

A couple of years later we still hoped that Ho Chi Minh might attend the May 1967 Geneva conference, but on May 19 we received Hanoi's formal cancellation.

By April 1967 the South Vietnamese had been protesting Ho Chi Minh's presence in Geneva. Premier Nguyen Cao Ky himself announced in Saigon that he would demand a boycott of *Pacem in Terris II* on the ground that Ho Chi Minh had been invited and Ky had not. The State Department expressed its concern, and all parties were again assured that Saigon would be represented if Hanoi or the National Liberation Front (NLF) was, but would not be invited to participate alone. Invitations stipulating this condition were dispatched to two South Vietnamese whose names were supplied by the State Department: Ky's foreign minister, Tran Dan Do, and Dang Duc Khoi.

Soon we had evidence that LBJ and the State Department were using this contrived South Vietnamese issue to undermine the convocation. In Berne the U.S. ambassador, John S. Hayes, complained that in submitting the first invitation to Hanoi we had given Ho the option of blocking Saigon's participation by withholding his own; he did not seem to be interested in the explanation that this also worked in reverse, since Saigon could block Hanoi in the same fashion. And in Geneva we began to cross the trail of Roger Tubby, the U.S. ambassador to UN organizations, who was busily running down the convocation all around the diplomatic cocktail circuit.

The Saigon issue had its repercussions in Eastern Europe. Although the conditions for the Southeast Asian panel had first been discussed at the Geneva planning session and all developments had been covered with the Eastern-bloc foreign ministries, we began to receive sharp questions about the South Vietnamese role, particularly from the Soviets. They were assured repeatedly that unless both Vietnamese belligerents joined the panel, neither side would be permitted to address the convocation. This condition, incidentally, was rejected by NLF representatives in Prague and Moscow, who demanded that Saigon be barred as the price of NLF representation. Our refusal to do so terminated that negotiation.

Finagling over South Vietnamese representation continued during the convocation. As soon as we received Hanoi's cancellation we cabled the South Vietnamese foreign minister to inform him that we were withdrawing his invitation pursuant to our prior understanding. The response was that he had already departed for Geneva, even though this was a good week ahead of time. Tran Van Do and Dang Duc Khoi arrived in the company of the ranking public relations expert from Saigon's Washington embassy, politely forced us to reject his demand that he be allowed to address the convocation from the floor, and neatly created the kind of free-speech issue that is guaranteed to draw a glandular response from the American press.

LBJ's Administration was largely successful in implanting in the American media the notion that the *Pacem in Terris* convocation was deliberately and suspiciously loaded against the United States. The public, official position in Washington was initially benign, then neutral. It was not until May 23 that the State Department conceded to the Associated Press that the Administration had in fact decreed a "hands off" attitude for *Pacem in Terris II.*

After that, the wraps were off and the effort to discredit the convocation was carried openly into the halls at Geneva. A State Department "observer," Frank Siverts, took up a post in the press room where he could exploit such contrived items as the South Vietnamese protest and knock down any suggestion that anything of consequence was, or possibly could be, going on in the hall.

This public relations countertechnique is most effective with spot coverage. The ordinary reporter, trying to summarize hours of serious, complicated talk in a few hundred words or a few minutes of television exposure, is at a hopeless disadvantage even if he has an adequate background for the assignment, which he usually has not. Most of those charged with the daily file from Geneva proved to be vulnerable to a persuasive young State Department foreign policy expert standing by with handy interpretations as they were jammed against their deadline by the relentless flow of words.

In Geneva both Mrs. Douglas and I received, I first, pressures, and then, denunciation for not letting the South Vietnamese delegation be heard. But we all refused to turn the conference into a propaganda center for one group only. While we were still interested in dialogue, LBJ was interested only in a "consensus" that approved his project or plan.

There were important consequences following the crossing of LBJ's path by the Center. The Center was a foundation dependent on tax-deductible gifts for its support. LBJ turned the Internal Revenue Service loose on the Center in an effort to deprive it of this tax immunity. Though the tactic did not succeed, the obvious lesson was that anyone who dared cross LBJ's path was in danger of paying a heavy price.

The Vietnam "war," in the end the political undoing of LBJ, early became a real obsession with him. Our intrusion in that country's problems never had the solid backing of the American people, and at no time did Johnson ever dare go to Congress asking for a declaration of war. The whole martial regime which flourished in his Administration squeaked through crisis after crisis. Even the courts, unfortunately, refused to touch the issue because it was too "hot" politically, in the sense that to consider the matter would mean a head-on collision with the Chief Executive.

LBJ—like Nixon after him—always spoke of peace and emphasized how peaceful the intentions of Americans in Vietnam were. That of course, was fraudulent talk. Almost every day of the Johnson term brought an escalation of the war effort. Many nations, at his instigation, worked on the Vietnam peace problem, but little did they realize that he was making each of them a patsy, since he had no intention of settling the war or coming to terms with Hanoi.

One of the best potential intermediaries in this affair was Moscow, which had maintained a very close working relationship with Ho Chi Minh. Moreover, unlike the Chinese, the Russians were not suspect in the eyes of the Vietnam people. The Indian ambassador in Moscow generated many conversations with the Russian foreign office about the end of Vietnamese hostilities, and those messages would in time be transmitted to the Indian embassy in Washington. During many of the critical times in question, the top Indian official in charge in Washington was the minister, Dr. P. K. Banerjee, who was an old friend of mine, and one of the ablest and finest men I ever knew. He would quite often make a trip across town to see me and give me a report.

In December 1966 he came and relayed the message from the Russians that Ho Chi Minh was ready to sit down any day and talk with President Johnson, with a view to putting an end to the hostilities and resolving the differences between the two countries. Dr. Banerjee normally would have gone first to the State Department, but from his many contacts with Dean Rusk and his satellites, he knew that the message would probably never come to the attention of the President, or if it did, it would be presented in a sort of offhand, half-hearted manner.

This message was so urgent that Dr. Banerjee asked me if I would talk to the President about it at once. He would wait about twelve hours before officially sending the message through channels to the State Department. I said I would be very happy to do so, and that night I got the President on the telephone at the White House. I had not finished giving the entire message when he interrupted to say that this was a typical Russian trick, that messages like this had been coming through at a very rapid rate for a long time, that this was not a bona-fide effort, that there was a plan afoot to embarrass him, etc. He, therefore, did not want me to bother myself with the message. I reported this conversation to Banerjee, and, of course, nothing ever did happen.

Again, in February 1968, Banerjee came to see me saying he had an important message from Ho Chi Minh through the Indian foreign office. He thought it was of utmost urgency and that the President should know about it. Once again he felt that he could not trust the normal channels of the State Department to get it through, and he wanted me to try to communicate again with the President. I said I was doubtful I could accomplish much. I did, however, dictate a letter to Clark Clifford, which was delivered to him by hand. Fortunately, he was having dinner with the President that night, and Clifford handed the note to LBJ himself.

The message dealt with the main questions raised by Americans who did not trust Hanoi. It was indeed responsive to the President's statement at San Antonio, September 29, 1967, when he said, "The United States is willing to stop all aerial and naval bombardment of North Vietnam when this will lead promptly to productive discussions. We, of course, assume that while discussions proceed, North Vietnam would not take advantage of the bombing cessation or limitation."

The message that I delivered to Clark Clifford from Ho Chi Minh was as follows:

Q. *If the bombing ceases, when will talks start?*

A. *7 to 15 days.*

Q. *What will be the subject matter of the discussion?*

A. *Anything within the frame of reference of the Geneva Conference.*

Q. *Who will be parties to the talks?*

A. *North Vietnam and the United States. Either can bring in another party.*

Q. *Will any advantage of the United States be taken in case of cessation of the bombing?*

A. *Hanoi accepts Clark Clifford's statement of January 25, 1968.*

The position taken on that date by Clifford before the Senate Armed Services Committee was as follows:

SENATOR THURMOND: *When you spoke of negotiating, in which case you would be willing to have a cessation of bombing, I presume you would contemplate that they would stop their military activities, too, in return for a cessation of bombing.*

MR. CLIFFORD: *No, that is not what I said. I do not expect them to stop their military activities. I would expect to follow the language of the President when he said that [he would stop the bombing] if they would agree to start negotiations promptly and not take advantage of the pause in the bombing.*

SENATOR THURMOND: *What do you mean by taking advantage if they continue their military activities?*

MR. CLIFFORD: *Their military activity will continue in South Vietnam, I assume, until there is a cease-fire agreed upon. I assume that they will continue to transport the normal amount of goods, munitions, and men, to South Vietnam. I assume that we will continue to maintain our forces and support our forces during that period. So what I am suggesting, in the language of the President, is that he would insist that they not take advantage of the suspension of the bombing.*

In February 1968 Clark Clifford became Secretary of Defense and I was at the White House for the occasion of his swearing-in. Afterward, as I was going through the line, LBJ thanked me for the message from Hanoi and said, "I am going to do something about it." There was a great ring of sincerity in his voice, and I felt that he meant it. But there seldom was anything sincere about LBJ.

On March 31 he announced on television that he was willing to undertake peace talks with North Vietnam, and announced at the same time that he was not and would not be a candidate for re-election that fall. What all the implications were I did not know. LBJ doubtless saw in Hanoi's latest advance an opportunity to make political capital out of negotiating, and while the negotiations went on he might even use them to liquidate any other presidential candidate—Democrat or Republican—and if everything went all right, the decision not to run might be converted into the first presidential draft in American history.

One who takes the pains to dissect the public statements Lyndon Johnson made over the years about the Vietnam war and the terms for discussion which he would accept will find, when all those various statements are put together, that every subsequent statement qualified something which was in the previous statement. There never was any one statement that could be trusted as the complete, final, authentic, official, trustworthy statement of the President. He was constantly shifting and changing grounds and conditions, and in the meantime creating the greatest credibility gap in American politics up to Nixon's second term. As things turned out, LBJ never had the slightest intention of following up the Indian message concerning Ho Chi Minh's proposal.

Other events, however, were soon to engulf LBJ, and what happened subsequently is to the credit of Clark Clifford, not the President.

When Clark Clifford became Secretary of Defense he felt that his main contribution would be to bring the war in Vietnam to a conclusion. It was costing the country $2.5 billion a month; wasting the lives of thousands of American boys; tearing the people to pieces; and in terms of the settlement of world problems, it was achieving precisely nothing. So one of the first things Clifford did was to arrange a luncheon meeting in his office at the Pentagon to which he invited no one except the joint Chiefs of Staff. Clifford, who eats very sparingly, spent the entire hour telling of his plans to bring Hanoi and Washington together, to settle the war. He asked for the Chiefs' prayerful consideration of this and for their support. By the time lunch was over, no one else had said a word.

The joint Chiefs of Staff rose in unison, thanked him for the luncheon and walked out of the room, still silent.

Clifford realized he had a major problem on his hands. He knew that each member of the Joint Chiefs of Staff had a senator or two or a congressman who, at the signal, would sound the alarm and arouse public opinion behind some Pentagon proposal. Therefore Clifford knew that it was important to confer with the key senators and congressmen, briefing them and their assistants as to what the developments might possibly be vis-à-vis the Vietnam war. So Clifford spent the next two weeks on the Hill. He covered all the important bases. And then he had a second lunch with the joint Chiefs of Staff. He went over his original proposal, broadened and embellished it a bit, and then pressed for approval. Clifford told me that he did not get resounding approval, but he did get a vote of three to two that the Joint Chiefs of Staff would go along. It was enough for the next step, which was to try to line up LBJ. He went at once to the White House and talked to LBJ, told him of his discussion with the joint Chiefs of Staff, his proposals for a peace settlement, and the vote among the Joint Chiefs of Staff.

As Clifford related the story to me, the President was very displeased. In fact, LBJ was so unhappy at the news that not only would he not speak to Clifford, but for one week Clifford tried to get through to the President to talk with him or to see him, but to no avail. Clifford was certain that in a very short period he had exhausted his influence as Secretary of Defense and would shortly be returning to private life.

What happened in the inner workings of the President's mind no one knows. But this is the background of the speech he made on March 31, 1968, in which he said he would be happy to talk with Hanoi and that he would not be a candidate for re-election.

I think what actually happened was that following Clifford's reconnaissance of the situation, LBJ, too, sounded out opinion around the country and discovered that the public sentiment was overwhelmingly for the liquidation of the Vietnam situation. LBJ, who loved popularity more than anything else, was at as low an ebb as any man ever in the White House—prior to Nixon—as far as popularity went. Though this disapproval had been obvious to most people long before, it was not clear to LBJ, who was so insulated by his own stubbornness as well as by his firm conviction in the soundness of his political judgment.

The offer which LBJ had for an overall settlement of the Vietnam situation was outstanding. The 1954 Geneva Accords had contained the basic ingredients of a rule of law for settlement of the hostilities. Such a settlement could only be successful if it took into consideration the interests of all the Southeast Asian neighbors and if it marshaled world opinion behind the enforcement of any ultimate solution. The Geneva Accords were, in other words, the natural frame of reference for a discussion of the entire Vietnam situation.

LBJ chose a different method. He proposed direct talks between Hanoi and Washington; and in time Paris was agreed upon as the site. This method suited LBJ's political techniques because it was wholly freewheeling, and he could make the policy decisions as he went along. Unlike the Geneva Accords of 1954, Johnson's formula contained no basic principles. No other nations, except the United States and North Vietnam, were implicated, and there was no agreement to abide by any decisions. LBJ's way gave only a shadowy resemblance to a rule of law, though in theory it offered the possibility of a peaceful solution.

One day I was visiting with LBJ in the White House about a conservation matter. Since he knew I was opposed to his Vietnam policy, he waited patiently to see what side I was on concerning the matter at hand. When I had finished he crumpled the memo I had given him without reading it and put it in his pocket. I knew my cause was lost, as indeed it was. Then he asked me questions about Supreme Court vacancies and what replacement he should make of Tom Clark. He mentioned names and I commented on them. Regarding one, I said, "He will be very conservative on economic matters, and occasionally for liberty and justice on other matters."

"Liberty and justice," he said, "that's all you apparently think of. And when you pass over the last hill, I suppose you will be shouting 'Liberty and justice!' "

"You're goddamn, right, Mr. President," I replied as I left by one door and he by another.

LBJ and I had been through many crises together. Yet mostly he was a fair-weather friend. He wouldn't even speak to me in public when I issued the stay in the Rosenberg case. Once at Johnson City, while standing in a small group, I told him I was headed for Siberia and asked if he had any objections.

Before he could answer, an aide spoke up and said, "Tomorrow's press will carry a story that Justice Douglas is off to Siberia after clearing the trip with the President."

I watched LBJ's face freeze. He did not answer my question but changed the subject. He was so alarmed by the implications that when the announcement came from the summer White House about the social events of that weekend, I—the guest of honor—was not even mentioned as being present.

He was forever on the move and full of endless energy. Once in Johnson City we went out on Johnson Lake in a speedboat going sixty miles an hour while Secret Service men nervously rubbed suntan lotion on his exposed skin. He would direct the boat around one buoy and head for another, all the while screaming for more speed. Finally we slowed down and I left the speedster for the patrol boat, giving my place to one of his favorite blondes. As I rejoined Lady Bird I asked, "What is Lyndon doing when he's not going sixty miles an hour in a speedboat?"

"Going six hundred miles an hour in an airplane" was her answer.

In 1967, when LBJ made a lightning-fast round-the-world trip, he gave me a personal account. The reason for the trip was a memorial service for Prime Minister Harold E. Holt in Australia. He spent 59 hours on the ground and 53 hours in the air. He recounted every landing and every conversation. On the plane he slept a few hours every night, had a masseur relax him, worked on stacks of mail, signed dozens of laws just passed by Congress, and talked almost every hour with the White House on the phone. It was a needless, reckless journey. Some of us who knew him well were talking about the insane or meaningless nature of the trip; and we agreed that it was symbolic of a deep-seated urge in LBJ for self-destruction. He had to hurry, hurry, hurry. He went at lightning speed to court disaster.

Was he carrying the United States on the same suicide course? Many of us wondered.

He certainly developed a formula for the destruction of this country. Putting down the Vietnam "revolution" was draining the nation's coffers. How much more would be spent should Guatemala, Peru or the Philippines ask to be "saved"?

Modern wars are too costly to be fought. They rob domestic programs of necessary support. We are in a period of mounting disemployment due to technological "advances" that "save labor." Employment in the public sector is our only hope. Yet with the vast military expenditure, money for other purposes is hard to get from a conservative Congress. Without employment, the racial problem worsens, for the first to feel the bite of a layoff is the black; and the hard core of unemployed and disemployed is the black. So as we spun faster and faster in the Vietnam orbit, we spun faster and faster toward riots and chaos at home.

Another characteristic that had a corrosive influence on the country was Johnson's refusal to believe in the basic integrity of men. Gifted though LBJ was, he felt, I think, that every man has his price—and of course every country, too. He exercised shrewdness in trying to determine what the price was and what the vulnerable spot in the particular individual was. The result was tragic, for his tactics in time became transparent. A degenerative process set in; specific issues of war and peace were affected, a downgrading of values took place both at home and abroad. In the end, few trusted him. His lieutenants were trapped between loyalty to him, a commanding, dynamic person, and loyalty to the nation. Confidence was undermined, we became a nation whose power turned on manipulation, slickness and outwitting an opponent.

An insight into the growth of the "credibility gap" is seen in the following episode. In May 1968 after the Senate had passed the restrictive legislation concerning the wiretapping decisions of the Court, it sent the legislation to the House and to a conference committee. The chairman of the House conference committee was Emanuel Celler, an old friend whom I saw at a dinner in New York City in late May of that year. He arrived at the dinner late, with apologies.

He whispered to me that he had been detained, that LBJ had called him on the phone and laid out the following strategy: Our Court had held in the Berger case, in June 1967, that wiretapping was a search within the meaning of the Fourth Amendment, and that warrants had to be obtained before taps could be placed. But LBJ wanted sweeping exceptions. So he implored Celler, in fact he *directed* Celler, to get through the House broad, sweeping exceptions in favor of wiretapping by having such provisions attached to an appropriations bill. LBJ explained to Congressman Celler that in that way he would not be able to veto the provision. It would go sailing through and he, LBJ, would have the public excuse that to veto wiretapping he would have to veto the entire appropriations bill.

Years before, he had taken on Communism as the all-weather, foolproof political touchstone. The idea grew and grew in his mind as good opposing evil. He was the apostle of good, so even Vietnam became a holy affair. Thus a gifted man, propelled by a messianic cause which in turn was intertwined with a desire for self-destruction, became a dangerous world figure.

PART FIVE

Conservationist

My Wilderness, published in 1960, introduces eleven of Douglas's
favorite wild places; two are reprinted in this section. His feel for the
outdoors, his appreciation of the unique values represented by
wilderness, his understanding of the plants, animals, and geologic
history of the places shine through his writing. The sustenance that
he drew from being there is palpable. There is very little of explicit
campaigning for conservation and preservation values in these pages,
yet the stories he tells are probably his most compelling arguments
for protecting the ever-shrinking wilderness.

   The legal doctrine of "standing" determines who is considered to
have a sufficient stake in the outcome of a legal dispute to allow them
to be heard in court. In *Sierra Club v. Morton,* the majority of the
Court determined that the club's interest in conservation matters, by
itself, was not enough to give them standing to challenge an
administrative approval of a ski resort development in a national
forest. Douglas's dissent, excerpted here, picking up on a suggestion
from Professor Christopher Stone, argues that the inanimate objects
themselves should be held to have standing. Something close to
Douglas's position ultimately prevailed, as people who actually used
the wilderness were allowed to bring the challenge, but there is an
important difference between the voices of those who use the forests,
and the trees themselves—a difference that was close to Douglas's
heart.

Pacific Beach

The wildest, the most remote and, I think, the most picturesque beach area of our whole coast line lies under a pounding surf along the Pacific Ocean in the State of Washington. It is marked as Cape Alava on the north and the Quillayute River on the south. It is a place of haunting beauty, of deep solitude.

Whenever I hike it, I go in from Lake Ozette, a large freshwater lake, and take the trail west to Cape Alava. It's a good trail, about three and a half miles long, and passes through a thick forest. Giant Sitka spruce with their powerful upward sweep dominate the trail. This is the tree the lumbermen like for its strength, lightness, and uniform texture. It is choice for sounding boards in pianos.

Western hemlock, a hundred feet or more high, with thick, flat branches help shut out the sun. Their needles lie in a flat spray; their branches bend down at the tips, giving them a weeping effect. Their shade is dense; and being dense, the shade serves a high purpose. Young hemlocks thrive there; seedlings of other species are shaded out. This lovely tree was long despised by loggers. Now it is one of the chief sources of rayon in this country and the most common base of those plastics that are made from wood cellulose. Happily, it grows fast enough to keep ahead of the demands of those who harvest it.

Now and then a western red cedar with its stringy, grayish-brown bark, drooping limbs, and lacy branches also reaches high to claim a piece of the sky. This is the canoe cedar that the Indians used extensively, not only for canoes but for twine, hats, ropes, nets, baskets, and shawls. It is today unexcelled for resistance to decay. It makes our choice shingles, racing shells, and cruisers.

Closer to the ocean are the Oregon alder, whose grayish-white bark is adorned with blackish splotches—the tree whose leaves on the underside flash silver in the wind. Like the birch and aspen, this tree brightens the woods, as every fisherman knows. It loves creeks and bays and bogs. It furnished the firewood for the people who settled this area.

It is still the favorite. But it is a hardwood which lumbermen these days cut for an expanding furniture market.

These are the trees that unite to put a green canopy over this beach forest, a roof through which only occasional shafts of sunshine penetrate. Underneath is down timber so tangled and high that a horse can travel only with great difficulty. Logs ten feet or more in diameter are being reclaimed and turned to humus. This is an area of heavy precipitation—nearly twelve inches a month. Down logs are soon covered with thick moss and lichens.

In this wildwood are ferns shoulder high, salmonberries, nettles, blueberry elder (whose pithy stems make excellent flutes), and a shrub known as devil's club because of its sharp spines that tear the flesh and the big ball-like knot that grows at the base, where the roots spread out. The Indians valued this shrub for its medicinal and even magic qualities. They wore amulets of its wood, and they made an emetic from its bark which was administered with hot sea water.

Out of this almost impenetrable forest, Lars K. Ahlstrom early in the century made a clearing and built himself a home. He was a Swede who came in from the ocean after a shipwreck, saw the beach forest, and liked it. I met him on one trip and found him as refreshing as his accent. Now his ranch is in the Olympic Park. The buildings are drooping and will soon be reclaimed. Bracken and Oregon alder are taking hold in the fields where Ahlstrom once grew hay for his milk cows. The grass, blended with bright blue gentian, is knee-high. A black-tailed deer feeding in a pasture neatly cleared a fence on my approach. Only the memory of Ahlstrom's ranch would soon remain.

The trail drops off a dune of loose sand strewn with logs to a coarse-gravel beach, the site of an ancient Indian village. This is Cape Alava which was, until Alaska was added, the western-most point in the United States. Offshore about a mile is Ozette Island, and beyond it a reef so dangerous to ships that the Umatilla Lightship stays there permanently. One night August Slathar—woodsman and smoker of salmon *par excellence*—and I camped on the edge of this beach under an ancient spruce. A raging storm had driven a fleet of several dozen fishing boats to the lee of the island. The dim lights of their cabins bobbed like fireflies over the water. Beyond them a booming foghorn announced all through the bitter night that death and danger were present.

There is a creek that flows at Camp Alava, losing itself in the sands before it reaches the ocean. It is yellowish water, stained by hemlock and given that name by the local people. But hemlock water is usually sweet to the taste and healthful for man. One year, when Augie and I made the hike alone, this creek was running full. Another year, when seventy of us made the hike in protest to a plan to construct a road along the beach and despoil it, the creek was dry; even the spring from which it came was low. That year had been a very dry one. A region that averages 144 inches of rain a year had suffered a drought for three months. Usually this Olympic beach spouts a fresh-water stream every quarter mile or so. That year most of them had dried up. Usually the woods above the beaches are so moist that spruce and hemlock needles can be cleared away and fireplaces built almost anywhere. This year the forest was dry as a bone; the thick carpet of needles was like tinder; the fire hazard great. All fires had to be built on the beach.

This beach is one to walk at low tide. The coast line is a series of beaches, usually a quarter or a half mile long and guarded at each end by a headland, on a few of which the Coast Guard built lookouts during World War II. The points of these headlands cannot be passed at high tide. Then one must climb over them. They are only a few hundred feet high at most, but their pitch is steep; and some of them are thick with the salal bush, whose berries are dark purple and quite choice, the Indians making a drink out of them or drying the fruit for winter's use. But salal presents a thicket that is almost impassable.

On one of the first headlands south of Cape Alava is Wedding Rock, a dark-basalt cliff with broken rocks at its base. These rocks have served as a canvas for ancient artists. Here are lively petroglyphs carved on the rocks. Petroglyphs are common throughout America. Picture writing was not confined to any one tribe or group. It existed wherever there were cliffs for writing. Washington State, with its great basalt formations, is conspicuous for its petroglyphs. The ones at Wedding Rock are simple pictures of the killer whale, of Indian masks, and of men. Others seem to carry the mark of obscenity. Perhaps the Makahs to the north or the Quillayutes to the south carved them. No one seems to know.

Each headland presents a beach of distinction. Some have sand made from dark volcanic rock, and packed so hard that a deer leaves few tracks on it. Some beaches are filled with a whitish, loose sand that flows freely between the toes. Others have sand, too coarse for packing, that is streaked with pebbles. Some of this sand is so loose and heavy that half of every step is lost in a backward movement. A few are a millennium from hard-packed sand, being lined with boulders and ledges of rock that tides without number have yet to pulverize. Most beaches have logs strewn along them or piled high on their upper reaches. Some of them have fallen from the adjoining forest, worked loose by the angry tides that come with winter gales and bite ferociously into the land. Some logs have broken loose from booms pulled by tugs far out beyond the dangerous shoals. Logs that reach the beach in the winter have been rolled smooth by summer. Some giants have been piled so high by ferocious waves as to be dozens of feet beyond the reach of any high tide that comes in summer.

Pieces of ships, wrecked on hidden reefs, are often added to the pile. Once Augie and I came across a fishing vessel quite intact and sitting upright in the sand, as if in a drydock for repairs. And it is on these Olympic beaches that one can find the prized Japanese glass balls that have broken away from the fishing nets they help float and drifted thousands of miles across the Pacific. I have found so many I had no room to carry them.

The force of winds and tides is often so great as to change completely the character of some beaches from one year to the next. On my first hike Augie and I stopped for lunch on a beach of hard sand where a clear, cold stream came tumbling out of the forest onto the white beach. An Oregon alder with mottled bark leaned out over the beach. We stopped in its shade. A one-masted steamer far offshore headed north. Dry chips of driftwood made a quick fire, and we propped a stick against a rock to hold our teapot over the flames. The beach was almost as hard as concrete, and this smooth sand extended even beyond the limits of low tide. This day the ebb tide washed the shore softly and quietly. A spotted sandpiper, feeding near the shore, suddenly jumped into the air after an insect sailing by. The leaning alder, hard sand, the crackling fire, and gentle tide made an idyllic scene that I carried for years in my memory. My dream was to return to that spot, find an old spruce behind the beach for a camp site, and spend several days in the shade of the alder soaking up as much of the solitude as possible. Some years later the chance came. I hurriedly rounded the point marking the upper limits of my beach. What I saw made me disappointed. My leaning alder had disappeared. So had the hard-packed sand. The tree and the finely ground sand had gone out in some wild storm. Thousands upon thousands of tons of gravel had been deposited in their place. All that was left of the idyllic scene was my bright memory of it.

The storms that have pounded these shores have sent many ships and sailors to watery graves. Two disasters are memorialized. One is just above Cedar Creek, where I usually camp the first day out of Cape Alava. It is a difficult monument to find, for its site is heavily overgrown with ferns and salal bush. It was erected to commemorate a Swedish ship and eighteen crew members who perished in a storm on January 2, 1903. Their names were carved on this pointed granite shaft, and under them the names of the two survivors who erected the monument. The names are now indistinct, as wind, rain, and frost have slowly erased them. Below Cape Johnson—about midway to Lapush on the second day's hike—is the Chilean Memorial Monument, a copper plaque on a granite shaft commemorating a Chilean freighter lost in the treacherous waters off Cape Johnson. The monument was quite intact when I first saw it. But when seventy of us came through, the shaft was down and someone, who apparently came by boat, had made off with the copper plate.

When the winds are high and the days dark, the beach is forbidding. Every headland looms in ghostly fashion through the mist. The tops of the alder and spruce are lost to sight. The air is full of spray. The logs that cram the upper parts of the beach move with the waves that reach them. And when they move, the whole coast line seems animated. Great waves break on every headland, making passage treacherous. The beach at these times is no place for man. Then it's better to follow the elk inland and find shelter from the storm's fury in the thick woods.

On a summer's day this wilderness beach is a bit of paradise. The stars are bright at night; and if one has chosen his time wisely, he will find the moon shining over waters that gently touch the beaches. By morning, fog that is thick and low has swallowed the entire coast line. A person disappears from view at camp's edge or walks as a ghostly figure. Rocks and islands that lie offshore come and go in the swirling mist. The logs piled high along the shore assume strange and grotesque forms. Everything seems out of focus. As the ceiling moves upward, patches of fog still blur the vision, making offshore islands disappear and then come magically back into view. The place seems unreal—a part of some far-off place of mystery. The Hole in the Rock is at these times the most fascinating of all. It lies near the take-out point of the hike, above the Quillayute River near the northern edge of Rialto Beach. A huge granite cliff forms a shoulder that protrudes into the Pacific, blocking passage on foot. Wind and sand have worn a hole through it, a large arching cave that finally broke the barricade. Hard, glistening sand packs the beach. The cliffs rise high behind it. In the fog this opening in the rock is a keyhole to the supernal land where rolling mists form weird shapes and only the sound of surf is familiar to man.

The sun is always high when the fog has gone. Some days a fresh wind blows from the northwest. At other times there is no breath of air to make the alder leaves glisten. At these times I like to put my pack under a spruce and lie in the grass above the beach, watching the waves come in from Asia. When the wind is high there is always a booming sound from the nearby point. When the air is breathless, the waves are soft and gentle and faraway. Then the quiet of the bench above the beach is so deep I have heard the pods of the brome grass breaking—a faint, crackling sound that the ear can hear only when there is deep quiet. Time passes quickly in these idle hours of dreaming. I dream of far-off peoples who share the Pacific with us. I think of time and the universe and the unseen forces that have made the earth of which we are a part. I realize how small and minute man is in the cosmic scheme. Yet how bold and aggressive and dangerous he has become. Now he has unlocked the secrets and can destroy and sterilize for eons the good earth from which we all came. Earth, the hard sand below me, the waves that make it, the alder and spruce above me, the ferns and brome grass that envelop me—all this seems newly precious, almost sacred. We look to the heavens for help and uplift, but it is to the earth we are chained; it is from the earth that we must find our sustenance; it is on the earth that we must find solutions to the problems that promise to destroy all life here.

I like to lose myself in the solitude of this beach-the solitude that no automobile can puncture. It is then I think of a passage in Darwin's *Autobiography*:

> if I had to live my life again, I would have made a rule to
> read some poetry and listen to some music at least once every
> week; for perhaps the parts of my brain now atrophied would

thus have been kept active through use. The loss of these
tastes is a loss of happiness, and may possibly be injurious to
the intellect, and more probably to the moral character, by
enfeebling the emotional part of our nature.

I would add, that to be whole and harmonious, man must also know the music of the beaches and the woods. He must find the thing of which he is only an infinitesimal part and nurture it and love it, if he is to live.

These quiet hours of bright summer days are in a way the most rewarding that the beach has to offer. At low tide some of the flat lava ledges that extend a hundred yards or so to the sea show exciting produce. There is the seaweed known as sea sac or popweed, whose pods break with a crackling sound underfoot. Pompon kelp sends its tough streamers up from watery crevices. The split whip wrack floats its blades on the waves. Specimens of the sea girdle—the brown algae from which iodine is made—are scattered on the rocks. Pieces of the brown sieve, host to many seaweed tenants, are flat in placid pools. The fir-needle seaweed, used in Japan as a food, covers some of the rocks. And the red rock crust covers many of the rocks with a stony encrustation and, like other seaweeds, produces a variety of food for animals.

There are rivulets in these lava ledges where the waves have worn channels. Holes have also been worn there, some as big as a barrel. Gravel caught in a depression whirls and whirls under the force of the tides. Gradually the spinning gravel wears a deep hole in the black basalt. High tides fill these holes with water and with life.

This western shore of ours, thanks to abundant supplies of plankton in the water, is rich in marine life. The deep offshore waters and the wind play major roles in producing the plankton. The runoff waters from the land bring fertilizers which feed the plankton, once the sunlight starts. The growth is great until the fertilizers are used up. Then the plankton colonies die out, their constituent elements sinking to the dark, deep layers of the sea. Winds from the northwest push the coastal waters southward and outward. The reaction comes in the form of vertical currents from the depths. These upwellings bring up the fertilizers— phosphates, silicates, and nitrates. Then the colonies of plankton multiply fast. That is why the waters off this coast, unlike many others, have a high standard of fertility during the spring and summer.

That is the reason marine biologists love this area. We saw some of the marine fauna. One was the sand flea, which appeared in some coves by the thousands. They are one of the many scavengers that keep the edge of the sea clean. We usually saw them feasting on decaying seaweed. Many sand dollars, dark purple to black, were partly buried in the sand at low tide. They, too, scour the sand for bits of food.

The rocks were covered with acorn barnacles, small and grayish. Some rocks had colonies of them so thick the rock surface was completely covered. These small crustaceans open their hinged mouths in high tide and sweep the water with their appendages, searching for food. In the tide pools carved in the rocks there were many hermit crabs with bright red antennae, sometimes called clowns for the way they rush around. In one water-filled hollow were a large red starfish, several brown snails, some small red sponges, a few sea spiders, and big roundworms.

Sea urchins, whose name derives from a Latin word meaning hedgehog and who are related to the starfish, were also in these pools. They bristled with spines. These deep-sea denizens are one of our oldest forms of life. Fossil specimens going back 400 million years have been found. They were once used like oysters and clams for food—they can be found in some European and American markets to this day—and they are eagerly sought after by the crab and the sea otter. Once they were used by doctors to cure ulcers, tumors, scrofula, and kidney stones. The ones lying almost motionless before me were purplish in color. This purple urchin often uses its teeth and spines to grind away the rock to make the hole that catches the fresh tidewater.

In some of the tide pools I found greenish anemones—cylindrical shaped with long tentacles slowly waving. The green color is produced by symbiotic green algae which actually live in the tissues of the animal. This delicate flower of the sea can exist for long periods without food; then it seems to live on itself, shrinking in size as its fast continues. But even in the tidal pools its sensitive tentacles comb the water for food. These anemones seem to take all substances that the tides bring in, even inert matter. They are voracious feeders. They are scavengers and have been known to swallow a clam. They also swallow crabs, and have such a fast digestive process that they shortly spew out the shells.

Another active scavenger is the beach hopper, always present in great numbers. They seem aimless in their movements, going every which way. They perform an important function. Every tide brings in some carcass. But for these scavengers the shore line might reek. The busy, active beach hoppers help keep the edges of the sea clean, the sands as tidy as a swept hearth, the waters fresh. It not only digs out the meat from shellfish and picks all bones clean, it also reduces to fiber the great lacy weeds that the tides leave behind.

Overhead were the greatest scavengers of all, the seagulls that reported early every morning and followed us all day long.

On a warm, soft day the harbor seals (which some call hair seals) are present. This water, which is 51° in summertime, is ideal for them. The rocks and islands offshore have bizarre shapes. One is like a cake—such, indeed, is its name. Others are like partially submerged submarines. Some are pointed shafts, adorned at the top by a lone spruce or two. Others look like remnants of ancient blockhouses. They are all covered with seals on a warm day. There are many stories about these seals. One concerns Wesley Smith, who died in 1938. He was a big man—six feet two and weighing 220 pounds. He had sandy hair and blue eyes. He was a homesteader at Lapush and taught school there for twenty-two years. For five years he carried the mail from Neah Bay (which is north of Cape Alava) to Lapush. Part of the time he went by canoe. Usually he went on foot, making the forty-odd miles in two days of hiking, carrying the mailbag on his shoulder. He carried no pack with him, though he slept out. He never drank tea or coffee, and his food for one trip was one huge, thick pancake, fried in a large pan. So he traveled light. He always carried an ocarina, which he would play while hiking the beach. On calm, quiet days the seals would leave their rocks to follow him. They brought up the rear, staying about a hundred feet from shore. Once he had a chorus of thirty seals almost at his heels.

The harbor seals were active on my trips. The night seventy of us camped at Sand Point, which is about three miles below Cape Alava, the water was fairly alive with them as they came close to shore, apparently puzzled over our arrival.

I have seen marten swimming near the shore, and once a companion of mine caught a young sea pigeon too weak to fly, a bird whose true name is the black petrel.

Raccoon tracks are always numerous on the Olympic beach. These animals come down to find shellfish—clams and crabs—just as we do. I have also seen many bear tracks in the sand, but the bears have eluded me. Wesley Smith had a real encounter. A cub was near the water's edge and the mother was in the spruce. Wesley Smith was in between. The she-bear charged him. He dropped his mailbag and ran toward the open sea. The bear stopped momentarily to maul the bag and then went after Smith. He got as far out as he could without swimming when the heavy surf, pounding on his back, brought him back to the bear. Once more he retreated; once more the surf carried him in. And so it continued on and on, until the cub made for the woods. To this day the Indians at Lapush tell how one batch of letters from Smith's mailbag had teeth marks through them.

The elk are thick in the wilderness behind the beach. But they seldom come onto the sand. The deer are different. These are the black-tailed deer that seem to like seaweeds that the tides bring in. They mate in late fall, and the main concentration of fawn births is in June. In the month of June—the peak of the fawning period—deermeat makes up 50 per cent or more of the diet of the coyotes which frequent this area. Bear is the fawn's next worst enemy. For the first two weeks the fawn is hidden by its mother and suckled at night. Then the fawn follows its mother until it is weaned, in three to five months. Meanwhile doe and fawn travel together; when they are flushed, they break in different directions, the doe beating an obvious retreat to draw the predator away from her fawn.

The time to see these black-tailed deer is in early morning, when the fog is rising from the ocean.

I remember one such morning when Augie and I were alone. We broke camp shortly after five o'clock, and for the first half hour or so Augie, who took the lead, would disappear in billowing fog at a distance of a dozen paces. We picked our way carefully around the first headland. The rocks were slippery, the going treacherous, the pace slow. By the time we rounded this point the fog had risen above the treetops. Below us was a hard-sand beach shaped like a fishhook. We clambered down the tumbled pile of boulders and rested under a sheer cliff that bounds the north end of this beach. Sweet water trickled from a rock. A few alder leaned gracefully toward the ocean. But the fringe of trees bordering the beach was mostly spruce. It stood in thick groves along the edge of the forest. These spruce were shorter than the giants that grow inland. They were old—perhaps several hundred years old. They had lived in great adversity on the ocean's edge. They had felt through the decades the full force and power of the storms that break there. Unlike their brothers in the deep interior forests, they had trunks covered by numberless boughs, and their branches swept low to the ground. But what gave them grace and dignity was their wind-swept tops. Their crowns had been touched by every breeze that blew. The great blows from the south and west that come in the winter had shaped their crowns as the hands of a potter shape clay. Adversity had given them character and distinction. They had gained beauty and strength under the mighty forces that assaulted them.

Augie and I sat for perhaps a half hour lost in our thoughts; then I saw a movement in a stand of alders half way down the beach. In a second a doe stepped gingerly into view, her ears twitching. Sensing that all was well, she came down the bank onto the hard sand. Behind her came a spotted fawn not many weeks old. Mother and child stood as still as statues for a few moments and then headed toward the salt water's edge.

I had color film in my Contax, but to get a picture I had to move a dozen feet. That motion was enough to sound the alarm. The doe turned and faced me, her big ears up. The click of the camera frightened her; away she went, bounding toward the forest. She stopped at its edge to watch the fawn, who dropped flat on the beach and froze. I moved quickly into action. I took photos of it at fifty, thirty, twenty, ten feet. It did not move. It blended so perfectly with the sand, driftwood, and seaweed that I might well have passed it by. At ten feet I could see its heart beat. I moved to six feet, then to three. Still no movement of the fawn except for its heartbeat. Finally I reached out to caress it. Even when my hand touched the fawn the little one did not move. Its heart was pounding hard, but some instinct deeply ingrained and resting in influences that need no conscious act to command them held the fawn frozen to the ground. Only when I returned to the cliff where I had dropped my pack and waited silently several minutes did the fawn move. Then it trotted from the beach at some command of its mother.

When I first camped at Cedar Creek, the sloping beach that ran from majestic wind-swept spruce to the ocean was smooth and well packed.

Here we once found sea shell mounds which were part of the midden, or debris, of an ancient Indian village. It was probably a summer village. At some of these sites sea shell middens go down six feet. They mark camps where the Indians saw sunsets and sunrises without number during years when the ocean was washing the coast line far out where only islands stand today. Now the surf has carried most of the sea shell midden away. When the large group of us made the hike, I discovered that Cedar Creek had been transformed. Mighty tides and storms had piled coarse gravel twenty feet high midway on the beach. In front, the beach was just as smooth and charming as before. Behind the high gravel bar was a narrow belt of flatland. Then came Cedar Creek, at this point quite deep, and beyond it the forest. Since the wind was high, we decided to build our fire on the lee side. That arrangement was convenient for all our purposes. A great Sitka spruce had fallen years ago over Cedar Creek and now made an ideal footbridge.

So we built our fires and cooked on the ocean side of Cedar Creek, and put our bedrolls under the great spruce trees in the forest.

I never sleep better than when I am under a tree, and of all the trees I choose the Sitka spruce first.

It provides an ideal place for a sleeping bag. Its roots are mammoth, running close to the surface of the ground and extending far and wide. The height of these trees (200 feet is quite common) and their towering size (a diameter of 10 feet is customary) must create special problems for them, as they grow mostly in wet, soggy country. The roots seem to strike up and out, not down, in a heroic effort to grip the earth and hold their mighty master in place. The spots between these outcropped roots are made to order for bedding down. In the Olympic area of the Pacific Northwest the needles, which bristle on all sides of the twig at right angles, make a thick carpet on the ground. Eight inches of Sitka spruce needles is common, and they are as good as most air mattresses.

My spruce was right on the edge of Cedar Creek and close to the footbridge. Sig Olson was on the other side of the footbridge under another spruce. I went to bed early, Sandy, our Shetland sheep dog, by my side. Jupiter showed near a crescent moon. Then I was sung to sleep by the pounding of the incoming tide.

Sometime in the night skunks invaded our kitchen, across Cedar Creek from our bedroom. Sandy started barking. He was beside himself when the dishes were knocked off a log. It was all I could do to keep him from crossing the log to tackle the skunks. The skunks became agitated and gave up their foraging. They raced across the log, seeking to escape into the forest before Sandy descended on them. When they reached the other side and started to turn left, I counted them in the bright moonlight. They were four in all, and they seemed to be in a great hurry. Sig Olson's bed lay right across their path and Sig was in it. I had seen Sig move and knew he was awake. But now he was motionless. The four skunks walked right across his bedroll, stepping gingerly, so it seemed to me. Then they were swallowed up in the darkness of the brush.

In the morning Sig and I were laughing about the episode.

"What did you do?" I asked.

"What did I do?" he rejoined. "I didn't even breathe for a couple of minutes."

I always leave this primitive beach reluctantly. The music of the ocean front seems to establish a rhythm in man. For hours and even days afterward I can almost hear the booming of the tides on the headlands and the sound of the wind in the giant spruce.

On my last trip I turned inland at Rialto Beach to reach the road that leads to civilization. I had not gone far when I met a party carrying signs. They were protesting the preservation of this ocean strip as a primitive area and urging instead the construction of a highway that would turn it into another Atlantic City or Coney Island. That action was to me the desecration of a place of beauty and wonderment. I did not argue with the pickets. But I did ask them if all wilderness trails had to be paved, if all mountain peaks had to have chair lifts, if no sanctuaries could be left.

"Do roads have to go everywhere? Can't we save one per cent of the woods for those who love wildness?"

Middle Fork of the Salmon

The sixteen-foot rubber boat floated lazily in midstream. The water was so clear and calm I could see the reflection of a granite cliff that towered almost a mile above us. An otter swam noiselessly near shore. A kingfisher dived from an overhanging branch. Somewhere far up the canyon wall an eagle screeched. All else was quiet. Only by sighting a pine on the canyon wall could I tell we were drifting.

Ralph Smothers, my guide, and I drifted in silence. I was at the stern, sitting on the rounded edge of the rubber boat. I leaned against a three-foot stretch of canvas which Ralph had laced to upright aluminum tubing so as to protect passengers from spray. Ralph stood on the "deck" of the rubber boat—two wooden boxes, holding our groceries, that were placed midships. Ralph held a sweep in each hand—one fore and one aft. Each of these sweeps swung on a metal pivot, laced to the boat. They had three-foot blades that could be used to steer the boat or to propel it.

Soon a side current caught the boat and carried it at a brisk speed along the shore. Ralph, who is slight and wiry, moved the boat with deft side movements of the sweeps back to the center of the river, where we caught the main current. Now we drifted at about three miles an hour.

"Grouse Creek Rapids coming up," Ralph said. "We'll need the life jackets here."

We put them on as we rounded a corner of the canyon. Quickly a place that had been deep in solitude was filled with a roar. The rapids were immediately ahead of us.

Grouse Creek Rapids fall about eight feet in fifty yards. The river at this point passes over a ledge that is twelve feet wide and at one point is as sharp as a razor. Rubber boats have been cut to pieces here, when the pilot kept too far to the right. Ralph hit the slick of the falls near the center of the ledge and the boat slid over gracefully. Then it dived, the stern rising high in the air. The nose hit the bottom of the trough and the boat seemed almost to buckle, with its bow on one side of the trough, its stem on the other. Then it started up the big wave, called the rollback.

The boat climbed this wall of water in a flash, and for a split second hung over it in mid-air. Then we nose-dived a second time, and the stern flipped so high it showed blue sky between its bottom and the river. We crashed into the bottom of the trough with a thud that sent gallons of water into spray. Ralph turned to me with a grin as the boat leveled off and bobbed like a cork along the minor riffles at the tail of the rapids. With quick side motions of the sweeps he brought the boat to shore to pick up Bob Sandberg and Mercedes, who had been photographing the run from below.

The Middle Fork of the Salmon River in Central Idaho is a fast, white-water river for all of its 130 miles. During the first forty miles it drops sixty feet to the mile. The rest of the way it drops sixteen feet to the mile. It has eleven main rapids in its 130-mile length, not to mention the many pieces of white water that present no special navigation problem. Each of the eleven rapids has its own special risks. In some the danger is from concealed rocks. In others, the position of rocks often makes it necessary to change the course of the boat in the midst of the white water. In some, the main risk is the rollback wave at the bottom of the big drop-off. In every rapids there is the risk of the boat's turning sidewise and being crushed by the rollback.

Though some boatmen use oars or paddles, sweeps are by far the best guarantee of a safe journey. Yet even sweeps present problems. The blade of the sweep can take only a small "bite" of white water. If it dips too far into white water, no man can hold it. If he tries, he'll be yanked into the river. Ralph saw that happen once on Rubber Rapids, a falls so named for the bouncing one gets in a long series of big waves that stretch out a hundred yards or more. The boat behind Ralph entered Rubber Rapids properly and rode the first few waves easily. In a careless second the helmsman lowered the blade of the rear sweep too far into the rapids. The pull of the water was so strong and so sudden that the pilot, who had a fast hold on the sweep, was pulled out of the boat. That was not all. The sweep rebounded, knocking the passenger on the rear seat into the river too. Neither was drowned. But experiences like that make every Middle Fork guide cautious and careful.

The problem of each rapids is different at the various stages of summer. In July, the best month to run the river, many ledges and rocks are covered that in August are exposed or close to the surface. A change of a few inches in water level creates new navigation hazards. That is why careful guides usually tie up at the head of major rapids and walk

down the shore to study the depth of the slick, the size of the rollback, and the position of submerged rocks.

Greater risks come with high water. When the runoff of snow is at its peak, the Middle Fork rises seven feet or more. Then many ledges and sharp corners that present problems in July are rendered harmless. High water is dangerous. The torrent that pours through some of the funnels in the river at high water throws up rollbacks that no boat suitable for the Middle Fork can survive. These rollbacks flip a boat or swamp it. The history of the Middle Fork during the period of the runoffs is one of tragedy to boatmen. Prudent men do not run the Middle Fork when it is in flood.

Even in the low-water months of July and August there is one piece of white water that cannot be run. It is Sulphur Creek Rapids, sometimes known as Dagger Falls. It drops about twenty-five feet in fifty yards. In that drop it passes over two ledges. For small boats the risk of the sheer drop is forbidding. For larger boats the risk is not so much the drop as the ledges.

"I could clear the first ledge with my sweeps," Ralph says. "But one has to keep his sweeps in the white water to steer. If they ever hit that second ledge, I'd be finished."

Ralph lets his boat down Sulphur Creek Rapids on a 200-foot rope. Those who use smaller rubber boats or flat-bottomed wooden boats portage Sulphur Creek Rapids. Those who use the smaller boats do not attempt to run even Grouse Creek Rapids, but let their boats down on ropes instead. But Ralph runs them all except Sulphur Creek Rapids.

Each rapids has a foaming pool with different hydraulics. A few inches to the right or to the left makes the difference between success and tragedy. There is a thrill in doing it just right—and a satisfaction too.

Grouse Creek Rapids, which I described, was for me too breathless to enjoy. But as the days passed and I studied the river, I came to understand the engineering problems presented by each piece of white water. It was then a joy to see Ralph, a riverman in the best tradition, perform. He seemed to know exactly where the main thrust of the current was and where the boat need start its downward course in order to avoid the dangerous obstacles. I often watched him catch the main current inches from its center, and so avoid by a hair a dangerous ledge a dozen feet below. Often when we rode a rollback to the peak, it seemed that the boat would turn sideways. It was a thrill in that split second to feel Ralph catch a piece of spray with his rear sweep and straighten us out.

By the time we reached Granite Falls (sometimes called Dirty Drawers) my confidence in Ralph was unbounded. It was good that it was, for Granite Falls to me was the worst of them. Here the river drops eight feet. One enters the rapids over a wide ledge. The channel quickly narrows to a funnel that leads to a large rock on the right. There the water is deflected to the left for a few yards, where it pours onto another huge rock. The danger is in piling up on that second rock.

We dropped off the ledge with a sudden sucking sound and headed for the first rock. An easy touch of the rear sweeps fore and aft made us miss that rock by inches. Now we were in the main current, headed for the second rock. A touch of the rear sweep turned the nose to the right. The pitch of the stream raised the left side of the boat so that it tipped at a 45-degree angle. In that fashion we rode the roaring wall of water that poured off the right-hand side of the second rock. Not more than three or four seconds had passed since we entered the falls. But in that brief time Ralph had applied the precise pressure on the sweeps to avoid the two rocks and bring us into the clear.

In Porcupine Rapids we had climbed the main rollback and started down when Ralph was nearly thrown from the boat. "Got too big a bite of the white water with my rear sweep," he told me later. Both sweeps were knocked from his hands and Ralph went sprawling in the boat. He was up in a second and back on the deck. Yet in that second the boat had turned completely around in a trough and seemed doomed by an oncoming rollback.

Ralph Smothers was born to the river. His father, A. N. Smothers, has long been a riverman in Idaho. For years he ran the main Salmon River from Salmon City to Riggins. This river was the one that turned back Lewis and Clark, requiring them to take a tortuous overland route to the Snake River and the Columbia. It was on the main Salmon that Ralph, then ten years old, had his first experience with sweeps. He and his younger brother (killed in an airplane crash) were with their father on one of his runs down the main Salmon. The father fell and broke his ankle. They still had twenty miles of treacherous white water to run. Ten-year-old Ralph took the sweeps and under the guidance of his father, who sat at his feet, brought the boat through safely.

Ralph's first trip on the Middle Fork was also with his father. It was in the late thirties, when people in Idaho were still feeling the effects of the depression. There is some gold in the mountains of the Middle Fork—enough to keep a man in bread and beans. Ralph's father and another man went to look for it and took Ralph along. They searched much of the country to the west of the Middle Fork. They combed Big Creek, famous in history for skirmishes between the United States Army and the Sheepeater Indians, a branch of the Shoshones. Discouraged, they followed Big Creek to its junction with the Middle Fork, where they built a raft to run the thirty miles of the Middle Fork to the Salmon River. All the food they had left was coffee and rice. All went well until they hit Porcupine Rapids. There the raft was caught in a maelstrom of white water and broken in two. The passengers were thrown clear and managed to get to shore. They salvaged the pieces of the raft and the rice. Only the coffee was lost. In a few hours they had the raft repaired, and reached the main river in safety.

Ralph can make corn bread over a campfire that is as tasty as any in New Orleans. Though good-humored, he is a taciturn chap who seldom talks about himself. His wife, Rae, fills in the details. She seldom goes with Ralph on his trips, as she must stay with the children. When she goes she always gets wet. "You know," she said with a pleasant drawl, "I really think Ralph knows how to make a wave splash anyone in the boat."

Mercedes, remembering the times the waves had broken over us, looked at Ralph quizzically. Ralph grinned and said, "It would be no fun running the Middle Fork if you didn't get a little wet."

Changing the subject, he said, "You always got to figure that the boat will turn over."

"Did you figure that on our trip?" I asked.

"Sure I did," he answered. "Didn't you see my sleeping bag and air mattress wrapped up in the oilskin? I always keep a little air in my mattress, so the bed will float if we capsize."

One can reach the Middle Fork without too much trouble. There is a dirt road out of Stanley, Idaho, leading to Bear Valley Creek. Boats can be hauled to that point. Or one can shorten the trip by flying over

9,000-foot ridges and landing on one of the meadows in the upper stretches of the river, taking his rubber boat in the plane. That is what we did. It took three trips from Salmon City to Indian Creek in a Cessna plane, piloted by Mike Loening, to bring us and all our supplies to the Middle Fork. In four hours the job was finished. We could have packed in with horses. But that would have taken days. And time is precious on the Middle Fork in July, when the water is neither too low nor too high.

Once one reaches the Middle Fork he is in solitude that is profound. The canyon walls, studded with granite cliffs, rise a mile or more. Sometimes they rise sheer a thousand feet. The upper reaches are carved into great, spacious bowls. This region has an interesting geological history. Some forty million years ago it had been reduced by erosion to gentle contours. Then came the uplift, marked first by the intrusion of granite and later by basalt. During the glacial period the valleys had not yet been cut deep and narrow like a V. The grinding of the ice was felt only at what now are the higher altitudes—mostly above 6,500 feet. These glaciers gouged out deep amphitheatrical recesses that now stand out like big bowls above the narrow stream bed. After the ice receded, the narrow stream beds were cut by erosion. The land above the river, shaped into great basins and capped by granite crags, has only a few slopes that are heavily wooded. This is mostly open country with scatterings of trees and much sagebrush.

There are blue grouse and bobwhites on the slopes and, closer to the river, some ruffed grouse. High up on the ridges and in the bowls grow the white pine and, somewhat lower, the Engelmann's spruce. Down along the waterway are mostly the tenacious black pine, the dignified yellow pine, and the stately Douglas fir. Clumps of aspen often occupy a ravine. Here, too, is the brilliant fireweed. An occasional cottonwood grows near the water's edge, along with stands of willow. Streaks of mountain alder follow streams down the canyon slopes. Huckleberries grow here; so do the elderberry, snowberry, and the wild rose. There are scatterings of hawthorn along the Middle Fork, and here and there a hackberry, a chokeberry, and a cascara shrub. One can find Oregon grape and perhaps a Johnny-jump-up. Up and down the canyon are stands of mountain-mahogany that elk and deer like for browse. And in the lower reaches of the river the juniper known as Rocky Mountain Red Cedar grows.

Trails touch the river at some points. But not many people travel them these days. There are two dude ranches along the Middle Fork—

McCall's and the Flying B Ranch. Yet they are not greatly used. An occasional prospector's cabin still stands. But none is occupied; and the claims once worked have mostly been acquired by the Forest Service.

The result is a 130-mile stretch of white water in a canyon of a remote wilderness. The water is clear, pure, and cold. There are white sand bars without number, where one can make camp under a yellow pine or Douglas fir. In the lower reaches there are rattlesnakes on the ledges above the river. But the sand bars are clear of insects and snakes. These sand bars are filled with enough driftwood to satisfy generations of campers. And I remember some where mountain-mahogany, once pressed down by heavy snow, grows almost parallel with the ground and furnishes a convenient roof for sleeping bags. These sand bars have no sign of civilization on them—not even the tin cans and cardboard boxes which usually mark the impact of man on a wilderness. But their fringes are decorated with an occasional blue gentian or some lupine, or perhaps a larkspur. And miner's lettuce and a monkey flower may be found in, a shaded, moist place.

Up and down the Middle Fork there are mineral hot springs where deer and sheep come for salting. Here the Sheepeater Indians used to bathe. And today an ingenious traveler can find himself a hot shower bath.

The Middle Fork is one of the finest fishing streams in America. It has cutthroat trout that run up to three pounds and rainbow that run to two pounds. Occasionally a Dolly Varden is caught, and they have been known to run to five pounds. Steelhead and salmon also run the river, coming hundreds of miles from the Pacific to this remote Idaho stream to perform the ritual of spawning.

The prize of the summer fisherman is cutthroat or rainbow trout, both native to the stream. They are so abundant, a party could not possibly eat what its members catch. Our practice was to throw back everything we caught before four o'clock, even the one- or two-pounders. The fishing is so good that there is a drive on by conservationists to ban salmon eggs, spinners, and all bait from the river. The plan is to make the Middle Fork exclusively a fly-fishing stream. Even the fly brings more to the net than one can eat. We used the fly exclusively, concentrating on the bee and caddis patterns. I often fished the flies dry, quartering the river upstream and taking a long float. But I also caught many fish on the reprieve when the fly was wet. The truth is that these Middle Fork trout will strike almost anything that moves or floats. Their pools are rarely disturbed by man. They have not yet developed the wariness of trout that are hunted all summer long.

There are interesting caves along the Middle Fork. We saw one that was sixty feet long and twenty feet wide. Another lay under an overhang of a granite cliff. Both had petroglyphs on the rock walls. They were made years ago by the Sheepeaters. Those Indians were never more than two hundred strong. They were renegades who escaped to the safety of the Middle Fork and lived in its caves, eating mountain sheep and elk that they killed with bows and arrows and skinned with obsidian knives.

No Sheepeaters are left today. They were defeated by the United States Army in 1879 in one of the most difficult military campaigns we have conducted, and were shipped off to an Indian Reservation. Only the writings on the walls of the caves give any clue that man once lived here.

A few years ago Ralph Smothers spent three weeks in the Middle Fork with a man who was dying of cancer. A friend brought the sick man there. The three of them floated the Middle Fork leisurely, so that the dying man could know the full glory of this world before he passed on. There is, indeed, no finer sanctuary in America. The Middle Fork is substantially the wilderness it was a hundred years ago. Its forests have not been cut. The canyons are so remote and so treacherous there has been precious little grazing by cattle and sheep. The few planes that use its meadow have not altered its character. It abounds in game—deer, elk, bear, bobcat, cougar, coyote, mountain sheep, and mountain goat. There are even moose here; and there are also marten, muskrat, mink, and weasel. There are some fresh tracks on every sand bar.

Most of the game is high among the breaks in summer, coming down late in the fall. During the ten days we spent in the majestic canyon we saw none except mountain sheep. These sheep are very nervous to any movement above them. An appearance of man on heights that overlook them creates a panic. As long as man stays below them he can approach quite close. One afternoon we spotted ewes and rams on a bench overlooking the river. There were a couple dozen of them, mostly bedded down, only a few grazing. Ralph steered the raft so that we would pass below them. We skimmed the side of the cliff showing stands of a purple penstemon. The sheep were not more than fifteen feet above us. Yet not a one moved.

Back in Salmon City I talked with W.H. Shaw, Supervisor of the Salmon National Forest, about the Middle Fork. His eyes lighted up as he talked of the plans to make this a real wilderness area.

"It's so rugged that trails are not much use. We put all our fire fighters in by parachute these days," he said.

"How do you get them out?" I asked.

"We instruct them to return to the river, where a boat will pick them up," he answered.

The one who will pick them up will be Ralph Smothers, or one of a half-dozen other men who know its white water.

Back in Washington, D.C., I learned that there are engineering plans on file to put as many as nineteen separate dams along the Middle Fork in order to harness it for hydroelectric power. Those of us who have traveled the Middle Fork think this would be the greatest indignity ever inflicted on a sanctuary. The Middle Fork—one of our finest wilderness areas—must be preserved in perpetuity.

Man and his great dams have frequently done more harm than good. Margaret Hindes put the idea in beautiful verse:

> *Gone, desecrated for a dam—*
> *Pines, stream, and trails*
> *Burned and bared*
> *Down to dust.*
> *Now water fills the hollow,*
> *Water for power,*
> *But the bowl of wilderness*
> *Is broken, forever.*

I discussed this matter with Olaus J. Murie. "We pay farmers *not* to produce certain crops," I said. "Why not pay the Army Engineers *not* to build dams?"

Olaus laughed and said, "Good idea." And he went on to add that soon all dams for hydroelectric power will be obsolete.

We are, indeed, on the edge of new breakthroughs that will open up sources of power that will make it unnecessary, and indeed foolhardy, to build more dams across our rivers *to produce power.* Hydrogen fusion, with an energy potential that is astronomical, has not yet been mastered.

But it certainly will be. Solar energy, though not yet available by commercial standards, is in the offing. Nuclear fission already exists and promises enormous energy supplies. Science may yet save the sanctuary of the Middle Fork from destruction.

Standing for the Natural World

⤙

Sierra Club v. Morton   405 U.S. 727 (1972)

MR. JUSTICE DOUGLAS, DISSENTING.

I share the views of my Brother Blackmun and would reverse the judgement below.

The critical question of "standing" would be simplified and also put neatly in focus if we fashioned a federal rule that allowed environmental issues to be litigated before federal agencies or federal courts in the name of the inanimate object about to be despoiled, defaced, or invaded by roads and bulldozers and where injury is the subject of public outrage. Contemporary public concern for protecting nature's equilibrium should lead to the conferral of standing upon environmental objects to sue for their own preservation. This suit would therefore be more properly labeled as *Mineral King v. Morton.*

Inanimate objects are sometimes partied in litigation. A ship has a legal personality, a fiction found useful for maritime purposes. The corporation sole—a creature of ecclesiastical law—is an acceptable adversary and large fortunes ride on its cases. The ordinary corporation is a "person" for purposes of the adjudicatory processes, whether it represents proprietary, spiritual, aesthetic, or charitable causes.

So it should be as respects valleys, alpine meadows, rivers, lakes, estuaries, beaches, ridges, groves of trees, swampland, or even air that feels the destructive pressures of modern technology and modern life. The river, for example, is the living symbol of all the life it sustains or nourishes—fish, aquatic insects, water ouzels, otter, fisher, deer, elk, bear, and all other animals, including man, who are dependent on it or who enjoy it for its sight, its sound, or its life. The river as plaintiff speaks for the ecological unit of life that is part of it. Those people who have a meaningful relation to that body of water—whether it be a fisherman, a canoeist, a zoologist, or a logger—must be able to speak for the values which the river represents and which are threatened with destruction.

I do not know Mineral King. I have never seen it nor traveled it, though I have seen articles describing its proposed "development." The Sierra Club in its complaint alleges that "one of the principal purposes of the Sierra Club is to protect and conserve the national resources of the Sierra Nevada Mountains." The District Court held that this uncontested allegation made the Sierra Club "sufficiently aggrieved" to have "standing" to sue on behalf of Mineral King.

Mineral King is doubtless like other wonders of the Sierra Nevada such as Tuolumne Meadows and the John Muir Trail. Those who hike it, fish it, hunt it, camp in it, frequent it, or visit it merely to sit in solitude and wonderment are legitimate spokesmen for it, whether they may be few or many. Those who have that intimate relation with the inanimate object about to be injured, polluted, or otherwise despoiled are its legitimate spokesmen.

The Solicitor General takes a wholly different approach. He considers the problem in terms of "government by the Judiciary." With all respect, the problem is to make certain that the inanimate objects, which are the very core of America's beauty, have spokesmen before they are destroyed. It is, of course, true that most of them are under the control of a federal or state agency. The standards given those agencies are usually expressed in terms of the "public interest." Yet "public interest" has so many differing shades of meaning as to be quite meaningless on the environmental front. Congress accordingly has adopted ecological standards in the National Environmental Policy Act of 1969 and guidelines for agency action have been provided by the Council on Environmental Quality.

Yet the pressures on agencies for favorable action one way or the other are enormous. The suggestion that Congress can stop action which is undesirable is true in theory; yet even Congress is too remote to give meaningful direction and its machinery is too ponderous to use very often. The federal agencies of which I speak are not venal or corrupt. But they are notoriously under the control of powerful interests who manipulate them through advisory committees, or friendly working relations, or who have that natural affinity with the agency which in time develops between the regulator and the regulated. As early as 1894, Attorney General Olney predicted that regulatory agencies might

become "industry-minded," as illustrated by his forecast concerning the Interstate Commerce Commission:

> *The Commission is, or can be made, of great use to the*
> *railroads. It satisfies the popular clamor for a government*
> *supervision of railroads, at the same time that that*
> *supervision is almost entirely nominal. Further, the older*
> *such a commission gets to be, the more inclined it will be*
> *found to take the business and railroad view of things.*

Years later a court of appeals observed, "the recurring question which has plagued public regulation of industry [is] whether the regulatory agency is unduly oriented toward the interests of the industry it is designed to regulate, rather than the public interest it is designed to protect."

The Forest Service—one of the federal agencies behind the scheme to despoil Mineral King—has been notorious for its alignment with lumber companies, although its mandate from Congress directs it to consider the various aspects of multiple use in its supervision of the national forests.

The voice of the inanimate object, therefore, should not be stilled. That does not mean that the judiciary takes over the managerial functions from the federal agency. It merely means that before these priceless bits of Americana (such as a valley, an alpine meadow, a river, or a lake) are forever lost or are so transformed as to be reduced to the eventual rubble of our urban environment, the voice of the existing beneficiaries of these environmental wonders should be heard.

Perhaps they will not win. Perhaps the bulldozers of "progress" will plow under all the aesthetic wonders of this beautiful land. That is not the present question. The sole question is, who has standing to be heard?

Those who hike the Appalachian Trail into Sunfish Pond, New Jersey, and camp or sleep there, or run the Allagash in Maine, or climb the Guadalupes in West Texas, or who canoe and portage the Quetico Superior in Minnesota, certainly should have standing to defend those natural wonders before courts or agencies, though they live 3,000 miles away. Those who merely are caught up in environmental news or propaganda and flock to defend these waters or areas may be treated differently. That is why these environmental issues should be tendered by the inanimate object itself. Then there will be assurances that all of the forms of life which it represents will stand before the court—the pileated woodpecker as well as the coyote and bear, the lemmings as well as the trout in the streams. Those inarticulate members of the ecological group cannot speak. But those people who have so frequented the place as to know its values and wonders will be able to speak for the entire ecological community.

Ecology reflects the land ethic; and Aldo Leopold wrote in *A Sand County Almanac*, "The land ethic simply enlarges the boundaries of the community to include soils, waters, plants, and animals, or collectively: the land."

That, as I see it, is the issue of "standing" in the present case and controversy.

Selected Bibliography

Books by William O. Douglas

An Almanac of Liberty. Doubleday, 1954.

America Challenged. Princeton University Press, 1960.

The Anatomy of Liberty: The Rights of Man without Force. Trident Press, 1963.

Beyond the High Himalayas. Doubleday, 1952.

The Bible and the Schools. Little Brown, 1966.

The Court Years, 1939-1975: The Autobiography of William O. Douglas. Random House, 1980.

Democracy's Manifesto. Doubleday, 1962.

Exploring the Himalaya. Random House, 1958.

Farewell to Texas: A Vanishing Wilderness. McGraw-Hill, 1967.

From Marshall to Mukerjea: Studies in American and Indian Constitutional Law. Eastern Law House, 1956. Tagore Law Lectures, 1955.

Go East, Young Man: The Early Years: The Autobiography of William O. Douglas. Random House, 1974.

Holocaust or Hemispheric Co-op: Cross Currents in Latin America. Random House, 1971.

International Dissent: Six Steps Toward World Peace. Random House, 1971.

A Living Bill of Rights. Doubleday, 1961.

Mr. Lincoln & the Negroes: The Long Road to Equality. Atheneum, 1963.

Muir of the Mountains. Houghton Mifflin, 1961.

My Wilderness: East to Katahdin. Doubleday, 1961.

My Wilderness: The Pacific West. Doubleday, 1960.

North from Malaya: Adventure on Five Fronts. Doubleday, 1953.

Of Men and Mountains. Harper, 1950.

Points of Rebellion. Random House, 1970.

The Right of the People. Doubleday, 1958. The North Lectures delivered at Franklin and Marshall College, 1957.

The Rule of Law in World Affairs. Center for the Study of Democratic Institutions, 1961.

Russian Journey. Doubleday, 1956.

Strange Lands and Friendly People. Harper & Row, 1962.
The Supreme Court and the Bicentennial: Two Lectures. Fairleigh Dickinson University Press, 1978.
The Three Hundred Year War: A Chronicle of Ecological Disaster. Random House, 1972.
Towards a Global Federalism. New York University Press, 1968.
West of the Indus. Doubleday, 1958.
A Wilderness Bill of Rights. Little Brown, 1965.

Books about William O. Douglas

Ball, Howard, and Philip J. Cooper. *Of Power and Right: Hugo Black, William O. Douglas and America's Constitutional Revolution.* Oxford University Press, 1992.
Countryman, Vern, ed. *The Judicial Record of Justice William O. Douglas.* Harvard University Press, 1974.
Simon, James. *Independent Journey: The Life of William O. Douglas.* Harper & Row, 1980.
Wasby, Stephen, ed. *He Shall Not Pass This Way Again: The Legacy of Justice William O. Douglas.* University of Pittsburgh Press, 1990.

Index